RIDGEWOOD

IN THE COUNTRY CLUB DISTRICT

RIDGEWOOD

IN THE COUNTRY CLUB DISTRICT

A Historic Suburb in the "Best 60,000 City in America"—Springfield, Ohio

TAMARA K. DALLENBACH

ORANGE *frazer* PRESS
Wilmington, Ohio

ISBN 978-1933197-791

Published for The Turner Foundation by:
Orange Frazer Press
P.O. Box 214
Wilmington, OH 45177
Telephone 1.800.852.9332 for price and shipping information.
Website: *www.orangefrazer.com*

The Turner Foundation
4 West Main Street
Suite 800
Springfield, Ohio 45502
www.hmturnerfoundation.org
937.325.1300

Book and cover design: Chad DeBoard, Orange Frazer Press
Art direction: Jeff Fulwiler

Library of Congress Cataloging-in-Publication Data

Dallenbach, Tamara K., 1964-
Ridgewood in the country club district : a historic suburb in the best 60,000 city in America---Springfield, Ohio / Tamara K. Dallenbach.
p. cm.
ISBN 978-1-933197-79-1
1. Ridgewood (Springfield, Ohio)--History. 2. Springfield (Ohio)--History. 3. Neighborhoods--Ohio--Springfield--History--20th century. 4. Suburbs--Ohio--Springfield--History--20th century. 5. Home ownership--Ohio--Springfield--History--20th century. 6. Planned communities--Ohio--Springfield--History--20th century. 7. City planning--Ohio--Springfield--History--20th century. 8. Planned communities--United States--Case studies. 9. City planning--United States--Case studies. I. Title.
F499.S7D25 2011
977.1'49--dc22

2010041223

Printed in China

DEDICATION

In loving memory of my maternal grandmother, Lorene Jane Wade,
whose stories of "olden days" inspired my love of history.

TABLE OF CONTENTS

ACKNOWLEDGEMENTS

Throughout the process of researching and writing this book, I have been humbled by the generosity of the many people who helped me bring this project to completion.

First, I must thank my wonderful boss at The Turner Foundation, John Landess. It has been a joy to work for you, and with you, over the last six and a half years for the betterment of the community we both love. You are, quite simply, one of the finest men I have ever known.

I must also thank all of my co-workers at the foundation—Debbie McCool, Charlie McFarland, Kevin Rose, and Karen Wooten, as well as my former assistant—Jake Kallgren. Each has contributed in some meaningful way to this project and offered much moral support when my deadlines were looming.

I also want to express my gratitude to two very special women—Mary Lu Kissell Noonan and Sybil Burleigh Boehme—the daughters of the two principal figures of the Ridgewood story, Harry S. Kissell and Brown Burleigh. Each sat for hours of extensive interviews and provided much insight and a level of detail to this project that would have not otherwise been possible. One of the great delights of this project has been meeting many wonderful people along the way, and I count my time spent with these two gracious ladies among my most memorable experiences while working on this book.

I must also thank Mary Lu Noonan's children and their spouses—Peter and Margaret Noonan and Timothy and Eileen Noonan—for tremendous encouragement and support. They graciously shared their family photo albums and other treasures with me and offered much in the way of assistance. I am also grateful to Sybil Boehme's lovely daughter, Rachel Votaw. Rachel has given much time to locating, scanning, and identifying family photos and verifying information for me.

I am also grateful to Sue Bayley Drais, Carol Robertson Gray, John Harwood, Dorothy Anderson Huddleston, Dr. Sue Miller Jackson, Richard Link, and the late Peggy Kent Waln. Each of them sat for lengthy interviews and shared photos with me. Their memories and insights have contributed much to this book.

Many other people have offered assistance in some way and have my sincere thanks. They include Bob and Ruth Bayley, Cynthia Lamb Faust,

Richard Flickinger, Julie Garrigan, Aaron Hamilton, Joe and Rosemary Herron, Bob and Flossie Hulsizer, Tom Stafford, Sophia Vandiford and Virginia Warren.

A number of individuals at various archives, libraries, organizations and entities have provided congenial assistance with my numerous requests. They include Rick Yontz and DeeDee Rigney with Ridgewood School, Craig Taylor with the Springfield Country Club, Suzanne Smailes and Ken Irwin at the Wittenberg University Library, Virginia Weygandt, Kasey Eichensehr, and Natalie Fritz of the Clark County Historical Society, Connie Chappell and Heather Whitmore with the City of Springfield, Mary Oliver and Curt Dalton at Dayton History, Mackensie Wittmer at the Oakwood Historical Society, David Boutros at the University of Missouri-Kansas City, Nancy Horlacher at the Dayton Metro Library, Cynthia Requardt at Johns Hopkins University, Robin Stolfi at the Metropolitan Museum of Art, Annie Keville at the Cornell University Library, Michele Clark at the Frederick Law Olmsted National Historic Site, Vincenzo Rutigliano of the New York Public Library, Gino Pasi of the Wright State University Special Collections and Archives, and Frederik Heller at the National Association of Realtors.

Jean Moores McCulloch's contributions to this book actually started nearly a decade ago when I worked at the Clark County Historical Society. Being aware of my fascination with Ridgewood, she would, to my great delight, share her memories of growing up in the neighborhood. When the idea to turn the source of my fascination into a book was in its infancy, Jean provided me with many of my initial contacts. She has served as the go-to source for any questions about all things Ridgewood and often pointed me in new and exciting directions in my research. She painstakingly proofed the manuscript for accuracy. She has been a driving force behind this book from the beginning, and I will always be grateful to her.

Linda Moeller donated countless hours to help me ready the many images in this book. I am grateful for the way she devoted her skills to this project, and I have treasured working on it with her.

I must give a special thank you to my dear friend, Anne Benston. Anne sat side by side with me for months at the library as we painstakingly made our way, day by day, through thirty years of newspapers, mining for the smallest detail about Ridgewood. I'm not sure there is any way to adequately thank you, Anne, for the immense generosity of your time that you gave to this project. It was a momentous day when our paths first crossed a number of years ago—quite fittingly for two people who love this community's history—in the archives of the Clark County Historical Society. Your friendship is one of the joys of my life.

Anne and I are both grateful to Cathy Hackett, Kim Mackey and Romane Shaner of the Clark County Public Library for their assistance and especially their good humor, which made our arduous task bearable.

I also want to thank the fine people at Orange Frazer Press. They make beautiful books and I am lucky to have had them work on mine. My relationship with them has been a serendipitous one for I consider us kindred spirits and have gotten much joy out of working with them over the course of several projects.

My entire family has offered me tremendous encouragement and support throughout the course of this project, and I am deeply grateful to each of them. I must give special thanks to my husband, Nathan Dallenbach, and to my children, Rick and Jake Wait, who graciously endured many carry-out dinners and other deprivations while I worked on this project. And finally, I must single out my first teacher—my mother—Sharon Woolf, who taught me to love reading and learning before I ever started school. Whatever I have been able to accomplish in my academic and professional careers is due in large part to the solid foundation she laid for me so early in my life.

—*Tamara K. Dallenbach,* Springfield, Ohio
November, 2010

INTRODUCTION

A drive up North Fountain Boulevard in the autumn is one of the great pleasures of living in the mid-sized, Midwestern city of Springfield, Ohio. Towering trees, laden with leaves of varying shades of orange, yellow, and red, form a canopy over the roadway. That lovely waning light of autumn, which signals us each year that summer is fading, peeks through the trees and gently bathes the beautiful early twentieth-century homes that line the boulevard, giving them a storybook quality.

North Fountain Boulevard runs right through the heart of a neighborhood known as Ridgewood. Ridgewood shares the same characteristics—curving, tree-lined streets dotted with picturesque homes—of many pre-World War II suburbs across America. But Ridgewood is, in essence, a prototype of those neighborhoods. It has the distinction of being among the first fully planned, fully restricted subdivisions in the country. And Ridgewood's developer, Harry S. Kissell, was one of the most influential figures of the twentieth century in helping to propagate the "American Dream"—owning a single family home, built on a large lot in a pleasant neighborhood, far removed from the dirt and grime of the urban, industrial city.

In the popular imagination of the twenty first century, suburbia is most often equated with bland, post-WWII neighborhoods like Levittown, New York, which is populated with cookie cutter houses and devoid of virtually any real aesthetic beauty or charm. But suburbia was really born much earlier in the twentieth century when beauty—both natural and man-made—was still prized. Despite the upheaval of two wars and a catastrophic economic depression, it was also an era when a positive attitude still carried the day.

This book explores the story of a ground-breaking neighborhood that still influences the way Americans live in the twenty first century, as well as the story of its pioneering developer. It serves as a shining example of what one person with a can-do attitude can achieve. The story of Ridgewood and Harry Kissell also serves as a microcosm of American life in the first half of the twentieth century, a time before a certain world-weariness began to permeate our culture. It is the author's hope that the readers of this particular volume will take away not only a thorough history of a fascinating subject but that they are inspired by the go-ahead spirit of an earlier era and carry that spirit forward for the betterment of their own communities.

RIDGEWOOD

IN THE COUNTRY CLUB DISTRICT

1. Bird's eye view of the densely built industrial boomtown of Springfield, Ohio, circa 1890.

THE BEST 60,000

NO GREAT TOWN CAN LONG EXIST WITHOUT GREAT SUBURBS.
—FREDERICK LAW OLMSTED

Springfield, Ohio, in 1914 was a city brimming with confidence. It was a growing town with no end in sight to its expansion. Its prospects looked bright. And like many American towns in the early twentieth century, "progress" was its mantra. Springfield residents had reason to be optimistic about their city's future. The foundation for its success had been laid in the late nineteenth century when Springfield's manufacturing barons made their fortunes. And, in doing so, they transformed the city into an industrial boomtown.

Springfield was founded in 1801, and it grew slowly from a sleepy frontier town populated by a handful of white settlers to one of about 12,000 residents in 1870, when the boom times started in earnest. The 1870s marked the dawn of Springfield's heyday as one of the largest manufacturing centers of agricultural machinery in the world. The bustling factories created plenty of jobs and attracted the workers to fill them. Between 1870 and 1910, the city welcomed an average of about 8,500 new residents each decade and reached a population of 46,921 by 1910. But after 1910, the city's growing prosperity really gained steam, and the population started to surge. In only four years, from 1910 to 1914, the population swelled by 13,000 residents as newcomers poured in to take jobs in the city's booming business sector.

(fig's. 1 & 2)

CITY IN AMERICA

While the rest of the country was enduring an economic downturn in 1914, Springfield's factories were producing more goods than ever before, and the city reached a population of almost 60,000 residents. And thanks to the efforts of local businessman, Harry S. Kissell, Springfield was not just any old city with a population of 60,000. It was the "Best 60,000 City in America."

Harry S. Kissell was the quintessential early twentieth century businessman—and perhaps the greatest booster Springfield ever had. In the lingo of the day, he was a "go-ahead" fellow. He had "pep." He loved his hometown, but no one could deny that Harry Kissell was also a pragmatist. A booming Springfield meant a booming real estate business, and real estate was the family business. Kissell, a Springfield native, had graduated from the local liberal arts college, Wittenberg, in 1896. Afterward he explored a career in reading law, followed by a brief stint as a newspaper reporter, before finally following his father, Cyrus B. Kissell, into real estate. Cyrus Kissell had founded Springfield's first real estate business in 1884. By the time son Harry joined the company, they were billing themselves as "The Oldest Firm with the Newest Methods." *(fig. 3)*

3 (top). Harry S. Kissell, circa 1896.
2 (above). Early 20th century bird's eye view of downtown Springfield from High St. looking northeast. Note the comingling of commercial, residential, and industrial buildings.

Despite his initial reluctance, Harry Kissell thrived in the real estate profession. Cyrus B. Kissell died in 1903, at the age of fifty-four, leaving the business in the hands of his 27-seven-year-old son. Harry quickly rose to the occasion and filled his father's big shoes as *the* mover and shaker on the Springfield real estate scene. Harry first gained recognition in 1905 for putting together the complex real estate deal for a prime piece of downtown property. A parcel of land on the northwest corner of Main Street and Fountain Avenue, where Black's Opera House once stood before it burned to the ground in February 1903, was to be the site for the new Fairbanks Building—a thoroughly modern office building and theater—and at nine stories tall, Springfield's first skyscraper. *(fig. 4)*

The young man firmly established himself as a leader on the local real estate scene by successfully negotiating this deal, the largest real estate transaction in the history of Springfield up to that point. The towering Fairbanks Building, the equal of any of the finer new office buildings in major cities, would serve as the most obvious physical manifestation that Springfield was a city on its way up. When it was completed, the Kissell Real Estate Company took up offices on the seventh floor of the new building. It only seemed natural that the man with an unbounded faith in the progress of Springfield would locate his business in this monument to the city's future.

Harry Kissell was already considered a titan of Springfield business by the time he was canonized in the 1907 publication, "Springfield Men of Affairs," which featured a caricature that depicted him juggling his many real estate interests. In addition to the brokerage end of the business, the Kissell Real Estate Company

5 (top). Caricature of Harry S. Kissell from *Springfield Men of Affairs*, 1907.

4 (above). The Fairbanks Building, Springfield Ohio's first skyscraper.

managed rental properties throughout the city, including over 300 residential properties and apartments, and seventeen downtown office buildings, including the Fairbanks Building. *(fig. 5)*

Kissell's early career coincided with the transformation of the real estate business from a somewhat disreputable vocation in which swindlers and con artists ran amok to a highly organized and professionalized career field. In Cyrus Kissell's day, there were no exams to take or licenses required in the real estate business. Nor were there any official standards of conduct, making it ripe for unscrupulous practices like land fraud schemes. The respectable real estate agents of Harry's generation, however, were working to change that.

In 1908, the National Association of Real Estate Exchanges, later renamed the National Association of Real Estate Boards, was founded and helped set standards for real estate practices and professional conduct. The national association was followed by the formation of the Ohio board two years later, and, in 1911, along with a small group of local real estate men, Harry Kissell helped to found the Springfield Real Estate Board.

Harry Kissell's regular attendance at real estate conventions across the country made him an early powerhouse in the national real estate scene, and he always carried the rallying cry, "Boost Springfield," to every convention he attended. It was at the Sixth Annual Convention of the National Association of Real Estate Exchanges, held in 1913 in Winnipeg, Canada, where Kissell secured for his beloved city the esteemed title that would boost the confidence of Springfield's residents and provide the city's marketing slogan for the next decade.

Delegations of real estate agents representing eighty-five cities in the United States and Canada attended the conference, and on the sultry summer afternoon of July 28, the conventioneers gathered at the Industrial Bureau Building in downtown Winnipeg. Fifty-seven real estate men took part in a titanic verbal battle, each arguing that his city should be declared the best city of its size in America.

One by one, representatives of cities both great and small made their case for the coveted title. But it was Harry S. Kissell of Springfield, Ohio, who delivered a five-minute speech so convincing that the jubilant Springfield delegation returned home on the train with a silver loving cup in tow and the rights to the city's new title—"The Best 60,000 City in America." With a rightful sense of pride, Kissell came home buoyant from the victory and ready to tackle his biggest professional endeavor yet.

(fig. 6)

6. Trophy won by Harry Kissell for his "Best 60,000 City in America" speech, 1913.

A fashionable place to build

7. Map of Elmwood Place, Springfield's most fashionable neighborhood at the turn of the 20th Century.

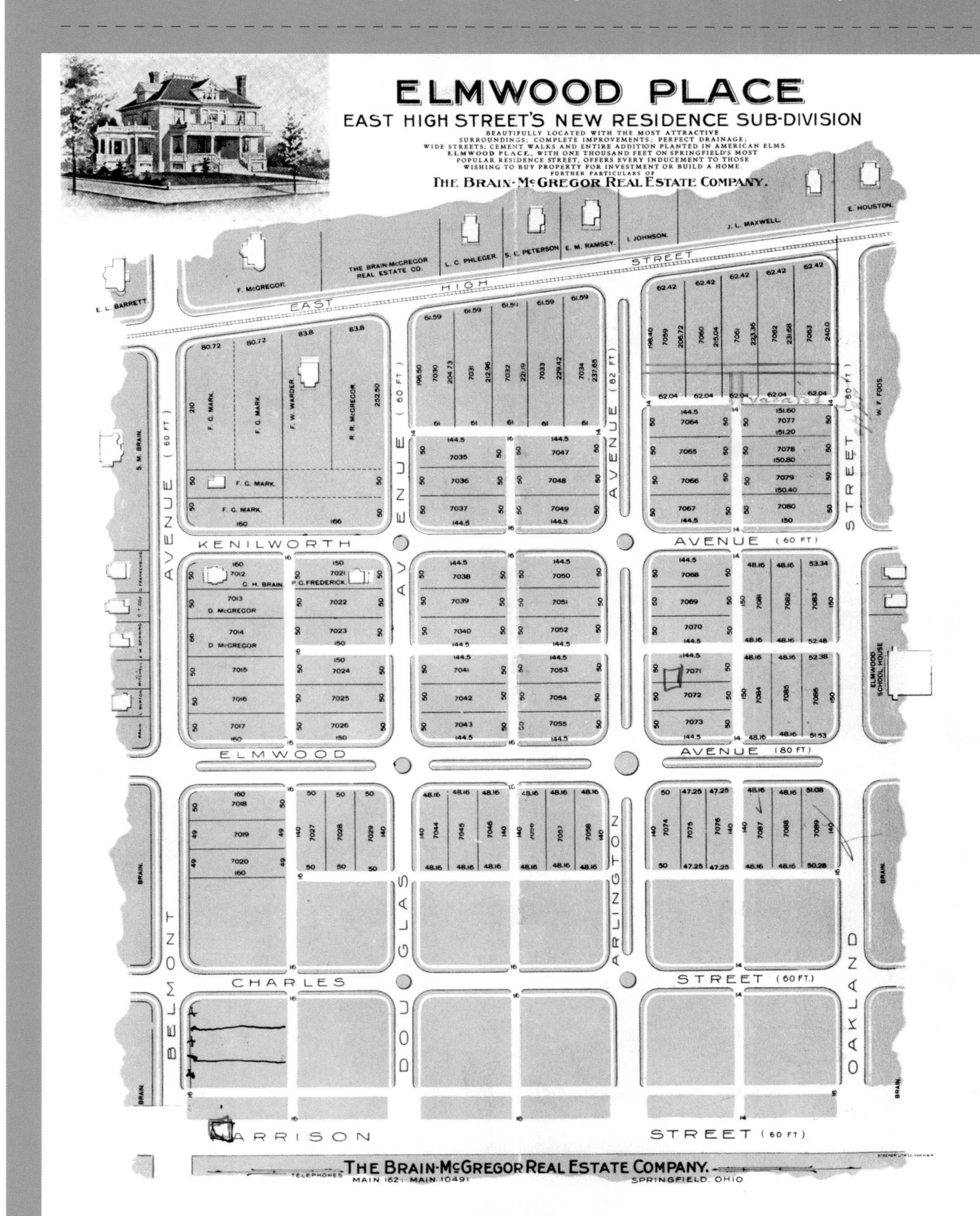

In 1913, the Best 60,000 City in America had a housing crisis. There simply were not enough homes to meet the demands of the rapidly growing city. Although builders and developers were frantically working to address this need, demand was outstripping the supply of housing stock. Much of the new development was taking place north of Buck Creek, and most of it was middle-class or working-class housing. The Kissell Building Company, a new offshoot of the Kissell Real Estate Company, had recently been created to address the housing need. In June 1913, Harry Kissell platted Pythian Heights, a residential development for moderate-priced homes along Pythian and North Lowry Avenues, north of McCreight Avenue. However, it was the "high-class" real estate market that really caught his fancy.

At the time, the fashionable upper-class residential districts in Springfield were South Fountain Avenue and East High Street. Since the middle of the nineteenth century, Springfield's wealthiest and most prominent citizens built their large homes and mansions along these two streets. East High Street began its reign as Springfield's most prestigious residential neighborhood in 1848 when Gustavus and William Foos purchased and platted lots on a stretch of land on the south side of East High Street, which ran approximately from present-day Penn Street to East Street.

8. Sketch of Phineas P. Mast's first home on W. High St., circa 1875.

East High Street would continue to be built out to the east over the next fifty years until the residential district stretched out past Belmont Avenue. In the early twentieth century, the East High Street corridor was still very much in vogue as a residential district. In 1902, the Elmwood addition was platted right off the south side of East High Street, between Belmont Avenue and Clairmont Avenue, and became the most fashionable place to build a new home for those of means. *(fig. 7)*

The history of South Fountain Avenue as a residential district mirrored that of East High Street to a great extent. Lots were platted on South Fountain Avenue as early as 1852, and over the next fifty years, the construction of new houses continued to march southward along the street in a chronological progression of ever-changing architectural styles.

Efforts to popularize other areas of the city for upscale residential districts never really got off the ground. In 1869, wealthy industrialist Phineas P. Mast had made an ill-fated attempt at promoting West High Street as an enclave for the affluent. In an effort to make the west end of Springfield more accessible, he ran tracks out West High Street for the mule-drawn streetcars of his Citizens Street Railway. Despite providing what was at the time a very modern means of transportation to the area and building three successive homes for himself there—culminating in 1882 with his grand stone mansion at 901 West High Street—Mast was resigned to live in lonely splendor in the west end. The area stayed a firmly working-class residential area. *(fig's. 8 & 9)*

Several other grand mansions were built outside of the East High and South Fountain corridors. Most notable were the now demolished, twenty-room, mansard-style house erected by Benjamin H.

10 (top). Sketch of the Benjamin H. Warder house, built on Lagonda Ave., 1876.
11(above). Edward Wren Mansion, built at 1115 N. Limestone St., 1889.

9. Phineas P. Mast's third home, built on the site of his original home at 901 W. High St.

MAST MANSION

Warder across from St. Bernard's Church on Lagonda Avenue in 1876, and the extant Edward Wren Mansion at 1115 North Limestone Street, erected in 1889. However, these two mansions were unusual exceptions to prevailing patterns of development. *(fig's. 10 & 11, page 9)*

Despite reigning as the supreme residential neighborhoods in Springfield throughout the nineteenth century, East High Street and South Fountain Avenue would eventually fall victim to changing ideas in residential development. It was booming industries in a rapidly growing city that generated the wealth that created these enclaves, but, ironically, those same factors would eventually lead to the demise of these two premier places to live in Springfield.

South Fountain Avenue and East High Street were very much a product of the time in which they were developed. In the nineteenth century, there was no real planning of residential districts. These two streets had developed in fits and starts like virtually every other residential neighborhood in the United States. Subdividers or independent builders would typically purchase a tract of land on the periphery of the city, carve it up into lots and build speculative houses or offer the empty lots for sale. Then the next enterprising person would follow suit. Developers worked autonomously with little or no regard for what anyone else was doing in the vicinity. Planning for the future, or a consideration of the common good, was nonexistent.

The result was haphazard growth in which homeowners had no control over what neighboring property owners might do, leaving them completely vulnerable to the impact of someone else's actions. In the era before zoning, which restricts areas of cities to certain uses, one could conceivably find a slaughterhouse, a livery stable, or some other offensive commercial enterprise suddenly popping up in what was once a purely residential area. Consequently, property values could be lowered overnight by the intrusion, and quality of life could be greatly curtailed. In affluent neighborhoods, the high prices commanded for vacant lots usually insulated wealthy residents from the worst kinds of these unwanted intrusions, but the same could not be said for the unlucky middle class and working class living in an industrial city like Springfield.

The dawn of the Industrial Revolution in the first half of the nineteenth century had radically altered the way that most of the American population had lived since the founding of the country. Until about 1860, most Americans lived in rural areas and farmed for a living. Founding father Thomas Jefferson had famously extolled the virtues of the agrarian life, one of self-sufficiency and independence.

Jefferson did not mince words when it came to his feelings about city life—"I view large cities as pestilential to the morals, the health, and the liberties of man." Throughout history, cities had been the home of the landless proletariat, and men of distinction like Jefferson regarded them with disdain. However, with the rise of the Industrial Revolution, the Jeffersonian ideal fell by the wayside as Americans abandoned the agrarian way of life and left the farms in droves looking for economic opportunity in the rapidly growing industrial cities and towns.

Before the advent of the electric streetcar, most of these new urban dwellers had to live in close proximity to the factories where they worked. Even the wealthy, who could afford horses and carriages, congregated at the periphery of the city. A horse and carriage or a mule-drawn streetcar averaged only about four miles per hour, making it impractical if not impossible for those who worked in the city to live much beyond its limits. As a result, cities quickly became over-crowded and unsanitary.

Jefferson's dire predictions were fast becoming a reality as conditions in growing American cities soon became insufferable. With the exception of the residences of some of the upper-middle class and the wealthy, urban houses were densely packed together on narrow lots with no front or side yards. Rear yards were smelly and dirty, a place that was home to outhouses, stables, chicken coops and, since garbage collection was a rarity before the Civil War, a place where refuse was routinely dumped. Moreover, in an era before the public parks movement gained momentum, green space in the city was at a premium.

In the larger cities, the housing situation was worse as poor urban dwellers were crammed into crowded tenement buildings. The squalor of the urban industrial city was most famously documented by social reformer and photographic journalist Jacob Riis in his 1890 book—*How the Other Half Lives*—in which he captured troubling images of life in the tenement slums of New York City. However, even in medium-sized cities like Springfield, Ohio, problems were rampant. Clean drinking water was a rarity and so was sunshine and fresh air, thanks to the continual belching of factory smoke. A nearly perpetual and choking smog settled over the city. Because of overcrowding, epidemic disease swept through Springfield fairly routinely. The use of horses and mules as the primary mode of urban transportation meant streets full of animal waste and its attendant odors. Add crime, prostitution, and poverty to all these other indignities, and the urban industrial city of the nineteenth century was a place rightfully reviled by the social critics of the time.

The brutal downsides of industrialization and urbanization soon inspired

12. Andrew Jackson Downing.

a growing movement for the agrarianism of old. The Jeffersonian ideal once again captured the popular imagination. The Romantic Movement in art and literature, which celebrated nature, was inspired in large part by the growing reaction to the Industrial Revolution. Popular nineteenth-century writers romanticized natural beauty, and social commentators called for a return to a simpler way of life.

This longing for a return to nature was evident almost from the dawn of the Industrial Revolution, and perhaps its biggest proponent was American landscape designer Andrew Jackson Downing. One of the most famous taste makers of his time, Downing was a proponent of public parks in urban areas and, whenever possible, a retreat to the countryside for those who could afford it. In his famous 1841 work—*A Treatise on the Theory and Practice of Landscape Gardening*—Downing idealized the notion of the English gentleman's estate. He urged upper-middle class and upper class families to buy a piece of land beyond the edge of the city to create their own "picturesque" country seat in the vein of the landed gentry of Europe. *(fig. 12)*

His works prescribed in exacting detail what the ideal picturesque retreat should look like. Downing was an advocate of emulating nature's beauty in landscape designs. He eschewed the rectilinear grid system by which land was divided in the United States. Moreover, he despised the crowded proximity of homes in the densely-built cities, even in wealthy neighborhoods. His landscape designs featured curvy drives; heavy, rambling plantings of trees, shrubs, and flowers; as well as picturesque cottages with irregular roof lines set on expansive lawns. *(fig. 13)*

13. Andrew Jackson Downing's ideal of a "picturesque countryseat."

Downing was wildly popular in his day and his works tapped into the yearning and nostalgia for a more pastoral way of life—one that rejected the man-made city and simulated a return to a connection with nature. While a mass retreat to farms was not practical or likely, Downing's ideas offered homeowners a compromise. One could escape the squalor of the industrial city, but could return for work or commerce as needed or desired. Downing also idealized the romantic European antecedents in residential architecture. In fact, he raised the rambling Italian or French farmhouse and the English country home to iconic status.

Downing's effort at finding a middle ground, literally, between rural life and city life, with a generous nod to the old country, ironically created a new, uniquely American concoction—the suburb. Downing also had a passion for the English "garden," what Americans refer to as a yard or lawn. Thanks in large part to his influence, Americans developed a penchant for the lone house isolated on a large piece of ground. This suburban ideal would be the object of much scorn and ridicule by scholars and social critics in the twentieth century, but in the newly industrialized world of the early nineteenth century, it made perfect sense. What would be derided as sprawl in the late twentieth century seemed the perfect solution on the heels of the Industrial Revolution—the perfect compromise between city and country life.

Downing's work inspired the first of what today would be referred to as a suburb—the "picturesque enclave." The first of these was Llewellyn Park,

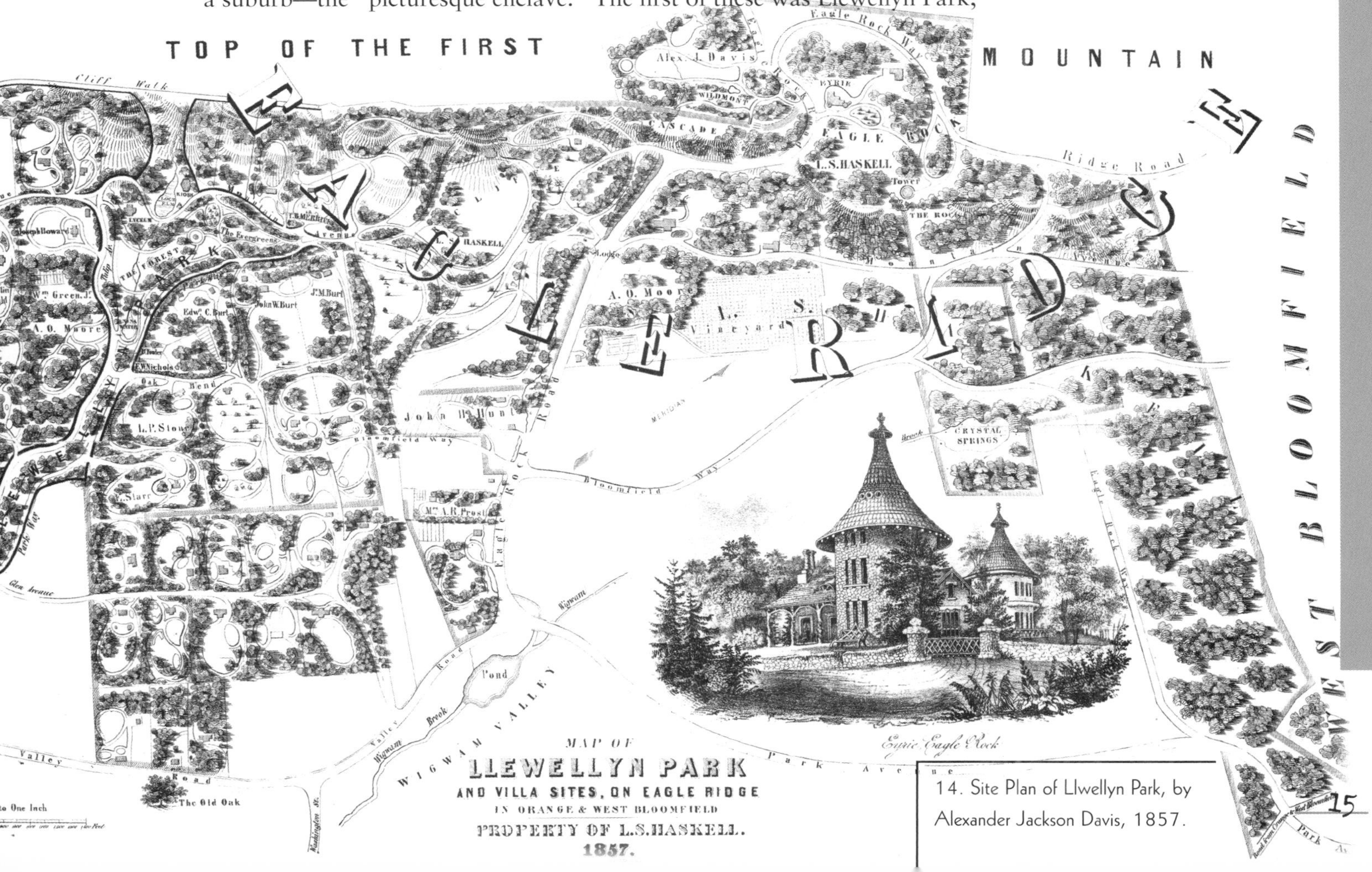

14. Site Plan of Llwellyn Park, by Alexander Jackson Davis, 1857.

Welcome to Riverside

15. Plan for Riverside, by Frederick Law Olmsted & Calvert Vaux, 1869.

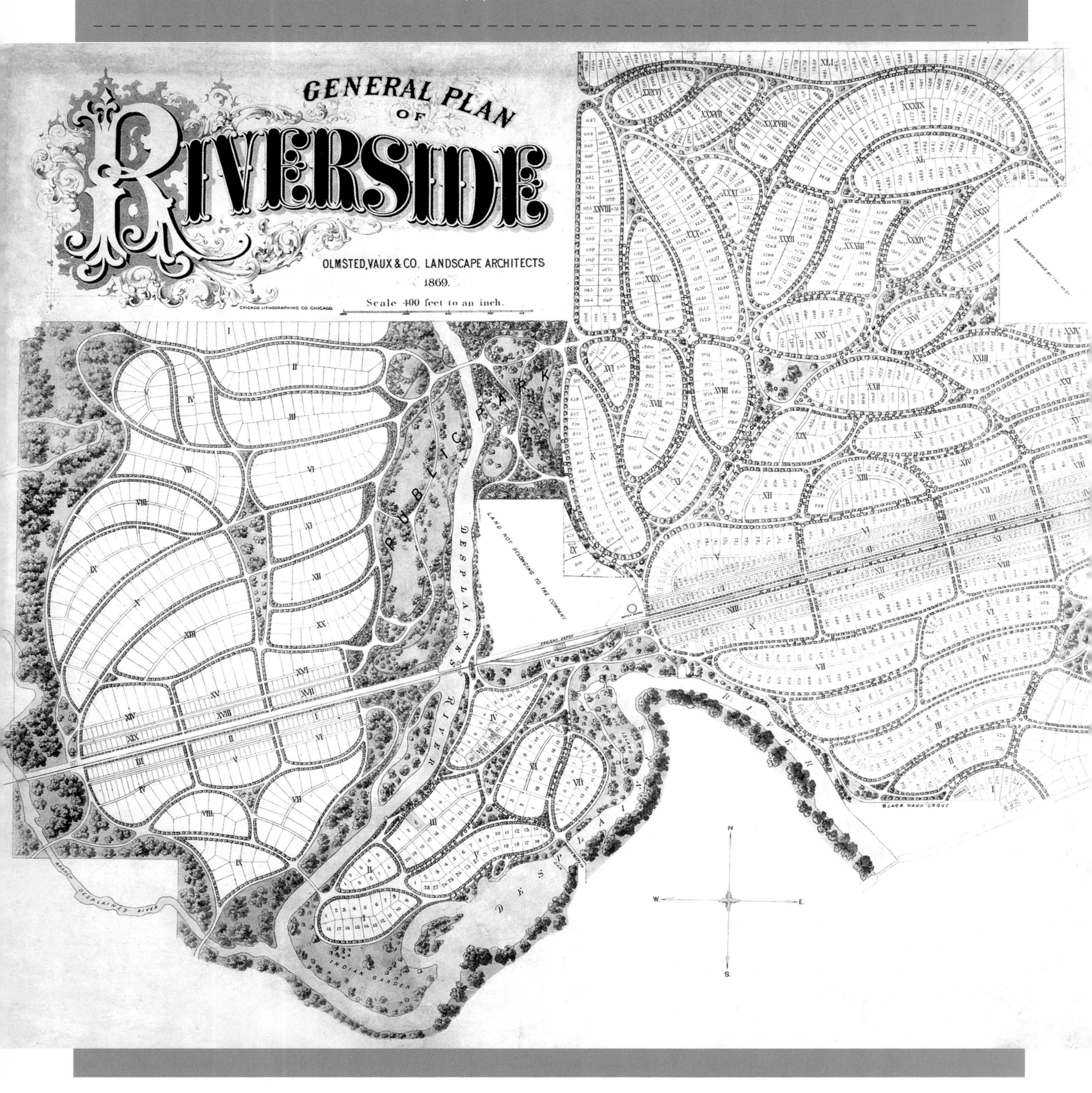

which was developed in 1857 in West Orange, New Jersey, by pharmaceuticals magnate Llewellyn Haskell. Llewellyn Park took its inspiration from the emerging trends of landscape architecture and city planning, both a reaction to the conditions in the industrial city. Haskell hired the most celebrated landscape architect of the period, Alexander Jackson Davis, to transform his land, located twelve miles outside of New York City, into a picturesque enclave for the wealthy. Davis worked with the mountainous terrain, careful to preserve its natural beauty that featured waterfalls, ponds, and cliffs. Ten miles of pleasure drives wound their way through forests and meadows. Thousands of shrubs and trees were planted, and charming rustic bridges were erected. *(fig. 14)*

Llewellyn Park was a stark departure from the way residential land had been divided in American cities. The popular grid system used by surveyors simplified the division of land in cities and created cookie cutter lots that were twenty-five feet wide and 100 feet deep. In Llewellyn Park, the minimum lot size available for purchase was one acre, but larger estates were common. One of the biggest innovations in this early suburb was that the roads followed the topography of the land. Early landscape architects regarded the curving road as more picturesque and likely to inspire bucolic thoughts. It also served as a deterrent to both traffic and the future conversion of residential districts into commercial ones. The curvilinear road thus became the hallmark of the picturesque suburb. Llewellyn Park also introduced an early form of the neighborhood association, as well as the concept of restrictive covenants, and community events to inspire community spirit and neighborhood identity.

It was America's most renowned landscape architect, Frederick Law Olmsted, who would truly popularize the picturesque enclave. Llewellyn Park had been the exclusive province of the wealthy, but the second major picturesque enclave catered to the upper-middle class. In 1869, Frederick Law Olmsted and his partner, Calvert Vaux, who had made a name for themselves in the 1850s by designing Central Park in New York City, received the commission for Riverside, a 1,600-acre tract nine miles outside of Chicago. Olmsted and Vaux took the nondescript land that was essentially prairie and sculpted and planted it into a suburban oasis. *(fig. 15)*

Olmsted's design, utilizing curving roads and thousands of trees and shrubs, made for a haven rich with pastoral charm. Land was set aside for public parks, and smaller "green space" areas were beautified with plantings. Because Olmsted lacked confidence in the tastes of individual owners, he instituted a covenant that required houses to be set thirty feet back from the road and required that owners must plant at least one tree in the planting strip

16. An affluent section of Roland Park, Baltimore, Maryland, 1912. Note the curvilinear roads.

along the road. Riverside provided the archetype for the planned suburb, but two later evolutions of the suburb would have a more enduring influence.

Roland Park, located five miles outside of Baltimore, was conceived in 1891 by a group of American speculators and backed by an English syndicate interested in investing in growing American cities. Together they formed The Roland Park Company for the purpose of developing an upscale suburban neighborhood. One of the parties active in the formation of the company, Edward H. Bouton, served as its general manager. As a result of his work in Roland Park, Bouton would become iconic in the twentieth century real estate development scene.

George Kessler, an engineer who had designed the boulevard and park system for Kansas City and had worked under Olmsted on Central Park, was hired to lay out the development. Although preservation of trees was a priority to the point of rerouting sidewalks, the first stage of Roland Park was not laid out with curvilinear streets. This would change when new lots were platted after the turn of the twentieth century. Initially, though, in order to maximize profits, investors wanted more regular lots with fifty-foot frontages and depths of 150 feet.

The Roland Park Company expended a considerable sum, more than $100,000, to put in sanitary and storm sewers, graded streets, sidewalks and gutters, and utilities. This was an unheard-of expense on the part of developers at the time. A maintenance fund was also established, and lot owners were charged a small annual fee to take care of garbage, ash and rubbish removal and the expense of operating streetlights.

One of the major innovations that Bouton pioneered in Roland Park was the most comprehensive set of deed restrictions ever utilized by a real estate developer. While there was much trepidation that restrictions might deter some buyers reluctant to have their rights as property owners compromised, he banned all commercial development, noxious elements such as privies and the raising of hogs, and required houses to have setbacks of thirty to forty feet from the road. He also set a minimum value for homes to be built in the subdivision.

By the time the second section of Roland Park was platted in 1901, Bouton was stipulating in the sales contract that buyers must submit their architectural plans for review and approval in order to maintain architectural consistency in the development. Restrictions were initially in perpetuity, but that was later amended to renewal every twenty-five years with a majority vote from property owners. While these types of improvements and covenants are considered standard in the twenty-first century, they were ground-breaking at the time.

At the time Roland Park was being developed, the planning of most subdivisions was limited to simply laying out streets and lots. Roland Park, however, represented a comprehensive, planned approach to suburban residential living. Not only did it offer the antidote to the ills of the city by providing ample space, fresh air, sanitary conditions, and plenty of trees and flowers, it offered a neighborhood with a permanently preserved residential character. *(fig's. 16 & 17)*

While Bouton believed wholeheartedly in the necessity of restrictions to preserve the character of a residential neighborhood, there was no denying that they could be controversial. One of the most questionable practices involved the use of racial and ethnic restrictions in deeds. In addition to restrictions on setbacks, commercial activity, etc., many developers of affluent, early twentieth century suburbs employed occupancy restrictions based on racial and ethnic backgrounds. This was a marked departure from earlier residential patterns in which African Americans, ethnic minorities, and poor whites often lived in close proximity to affluent whites. With the advent of the restricted subdivision, affluent whites could, for the first time, segregate themselves in practice from poor whites and officially from African Americans.

The pitiful truth, however, was that the racial restrictions written into deeds were pure pretense. Racial inequalities in economic opportunities at the time precluded many African Americans from locating in these types of suburbs, and even affluent blacks were unlikely to make an effort to do so given the tenor of the times. African Americans were the group most frequently precluded by deed restrictions, followed by Jews. Exceptions were usually made for African American live-in servants, however.

18. The junction of 57th St. Terrace & Ward Pkwy. in the Country Club District, Kansas City. This wedge-shaped lot inspired the one at the junction of Harding and Hawthorne Roads in Ridgewood, where the original Ridgewood School was built.

17. Middle-class section of Roland Park, 1912. Note the heavily planted "parklet" in front of the house to the right.

Ironically, in this strictly segregated society of the early twentieth century, many of these black live-in servants became beloved members of the household and were regarded with the kind of esteem and affection usually reserved for family members. These affectionate personal relationships were often amplified by the fact that servants would frequently be with a particular family for years, even decades. In a time of unbending racial segregation, the servant-employer relationship was one of the few opportunities for whites and blacks to interact on a regular basis, actually get to know each other, and move beyond perceptions based on racial stereotypes. The unfortunate reality, though, was that, despite the insight these relationships may have provided, strict racial segregation would persist for decades.

Another early twentieth century developer, Jesse Clyde Nichols, known popularly as J.C., was greatly influenced by Edward Bouton and Roland Park. J.C. Nichols began developing his "Country Club District" in Kansas City in 1906. What Bouton would originate in Roland Park, Nichols would perfect and expand upon in his own grand scale development. The enormous plat, beginning with 1,000 restricted acres, remains the largest contiguous residential development planned by one individual in the United States.

Nichols was completely enamored of the idea of "planning for permanence," and his acquisition of large tracts was a deliberate measure to prevent unwanted intrusions in his neighborhoods and to ensure their long-term stability. Nichols located his suburb next to the Kansas City Country Club, which enhanced the social cachet of his upscale development—an idea that several of his contemporaries, including Harry Kissell, would duplicate with great success. Nichols pioneered a number of other ideas that would be widely copied in suburbs throughout the balance of the twentieth century. He was the first developer to transfer the responsibility for enforcing deed restrictions to the neighborhood homeowners association, thus taking the onus off the developer. In 1923, he developed the world's first automobile-oriented shopping center, the Country Club Plaza, which adjoined his residential district. The shopping center offered conveniently located shopping and ample parking, limiting the need to make taxing expeditions to the downtown area. Nichols Country Club Plaza inspired the post-World War II suburban strip mall trend that hastened the demise of many downtowns. *(fig. 18, page 21)*

Edward H. Bouton and J.C. Nichols were part of a small, elite group of real estate men who shared a vested interest in land use policy. All were passionate advocates for the emerging profession of city planning and the use of zoning to protect the value of real estate investments. And these titans of early twentieth century suburban development counted among their numbers one Harry S. Kissell of Springfield, Ohio.

Kissell was certain that this new type of development that Bouton and Nichols were pioneering was right for his city. He was confident in the continued prosperity of the Best 60,000 City in America, confident that a growing class of successful businessmen and professionals would demand the best in a new kind of neighborhood—one away from the grime, smog, and noise of the city but still within a reasonable daily commute for the breadwinner of the household. Modern businessmen would require a modern neighborhood with all the up-to-date amenities like sanitary and storm sewers, good pavement for their automobiles, and plenty of green space for their children to romp and play—all the things that the older affluent neighborhoods lacked.

Kissell himself was a resident of South Fountain Avenue. He lived with his parents Cyrus B. and Lucretia Kissell at 1103 South Fountain until his marriage in 1901 to Olive Troupe, a fellow South Fountain Avenue resident and the daughter of successful local druggist and banker Theodore Troupe. Harry and Olive were married on October 17, 1901, in the parlor of the Troupes' home at 724 South Fountain Avenue. The newlyweds took up housekeeping next door, in a double house owned by the bride's father, at 728-730 South Fountain Avenue. Almost exactly one year later, Harry and Olive Kissell welcomed their first child, a son named Roger, on October 12, 1902. Much to their great sadness, their beloved boy was born with cerebral palsy and would, to the heartache of his adoring parents, struggle with the physical effects of his condition throughout his life. *(fig's. 19, 20 & 21)*

In 1913, when Kissell succeeded in having Springfield proclaimed the Best 60,000 City, South Fountain Avenue was still a highly-regarded, affluent neighborhood and would remain so for several decades. It was filled with many of Springfield's leading citizens and their fine homes, many of which were stunning examples of high-style architecture. However, South Fountain Avenue was very much a product of the Victorian era. With few exceptions, houses were built fairly close together with small front yards and virtually nonexistent side yards. While most South Fountain residents had indoor plumbing, backyards were still largely considered service areas where odorous carriage houses and, in a few cases, privies still existed. Thanks to the lasting

influence of Andrew Jackson Downing and the growing suburban movement, however, the preferences for how homes were sited on lots, and the way various parts of the lots were used, were gradually changing. Increasingly, homeowners wanted larger lots with expansive front and side lawns that provided not only space but also plenty of opportunities for beautification. In the early twentieth century, community beautification was an emerging trend and popular magazines of the times promoted it as an antidote to the dirty industrial city, bringing landscaping one's home into vogue even among those of moderate incomes. *(fig. 22)*

20. Olive Kissell and the infant Roger Troupe Kissell, 1902.

Advents in technology and transportation were also influencing the ideal of a perfect home site. With the introduction of the incinerator and icebox, smelly rubbish boxes disappeared from the rear yard. Indoor plumbing also helped reduce the need to segregate the rear yard as a service area. Closely built Victorian homes had helped prevent glimpses of utilitarian rear yards that typically could only be reached by rear alleys. The front porch, where many a pleasant evening was spent in mild weather, had been an important aspect of these Gilded Age homes. In the early twentieth century, however, the new, noisy automobile had ruined that.

The automobile also required that carriage houses be re-purposed as garages. This was problematic because one had to reach them through the narrow alleys at the back of lots. The fragile rubber tires of early automobiles did not fare well in the muddy ruts or gravel of back alleyways. Moreover, the hidden carriage house,

19. The Theodore Troupe home at 724 S. Fountain Ave. A portion of 728-730 S. Fountain Ave. is visible to the right.

once relegated to the back of the lot for good reason, did not allow proud automobile owners to adequately display their new status symbols. Long, narrow lots just no longer fit the bill for the way people wanted to live. East High Street managed to stay in vogue longer than South Fountain Avenue because most of the homes were built on larger, estate-style lots with ample front and side yards. Nevertheless, other trends would lead to East High Street homes being regarded as dated as well. *(fig's. 23, 24 & 25)*

At the beginning of the twentieth century, tastes in homes and how they were outfitted were changing, making some of Springfield's finest homes start to look old-fashioned. While some East High Street and South Fountain homes had been among the first in the city to have electricity when they were built, many of them were still dependent on gas and had to be retrofitted for electricity, leaving unsightly conduit visible. Retrofitting houses had become big business for The Springfield Light, Heat, and Power Company. One could get an eight-room home wired and outfitted with new brass fixtures for $41.60, and there was even a monthly payment plan. But a new home, with electrical wiring concealed in the walls and plenty of convenient outlets to plug in all the latest electrical appliances, was quickly becoming a status symbol. The unsightly conduits used to cover the wires in a retrofitted house were considered an eyesore and looked down upon by the fashionable set.

East High Street and South Fountain Avenue houses had another problem—"the servant problem." These large, rambling houses, typically over 4,000 square feet of living space, required live-in servants to run them. Victorian housewives constantly lamented the problem of trying to find good help, and popular periodicals of the day offered tips on overcoming this dilemma. Nevertheless, the problem would grow exceedingly worse after the turn of twentieth century for several reasons.

Servants often found that they had more personal freedom by getting out from under the watchful eye of their employer and taking factory jobs. This trend would increase during World War I when many domestic workers left service to take wartime jobs in factories. Rising nativist sentiment and anti-immigration

21. Roger Kissell on S. Fountain Ave., circa 1910.

movements in the early twentieth century, culminating in severe immigration restrictions in the 1920s, helped seal the fate of the ornate, enormous Victorian house. Not only had the supply of cheap, old-world craftsmanship been cut off, but the supply of people to clean these domestic masterpieces was gone as well. Simpler homes that were easier to maintain were now in demand, and the panoply of newfangled electrical appliances to ease the housewife's burden also helped fuel this trend. The servantless household became more widespread as more laborsaving devices became available.

Tastes in architecture and interior decoration were also changing. The highly ornate Victorian house of South Fountain or East High Street had started to look dated. As part of the reaction to the industrial revolution and a yearning for simpler times, Colonial American and European revival styles were coming into vogue. The modern housewife yearned for a quaint Dutch Colonial, or an English

22. View of the east side of S. Fountain Ave., taken from Perrin Ave. Note the closely built houses.

24. The John Foos house, 810 East High Street.

Tudor. It would be another seventy years before the homes of East High Street and South Fountain Avenue would be rightfully regarded as architectural masterworks again.

As a major player on not only the local real estate scene, but the national one as well, Harry Kissell was monitoring this myriad of growing trends that would impact his profession. He had planned a new home for himself and his family in the 1800 block of East High Street. Construction materials were on the ground on his building lot, but the changes that were afoot in domesticity weighed heavily on him. Kissell could see the writing on the wall for neighborhoods like South Fountain Avenue and East High Street, and he knew an emerging opportunity when

23 (left). The Asa. S. Bushnell house, 838 E. High St.
26 (middle). N. Fountain Ave., looking southwest. Cassilly St. intersects to the right.
25 (above). The Ross Mitchell house, 302 E. High St.

27 (above). The future site of Crescent Dr. This strand of mature trees, a rarity in Phase I of Ridgewood, was referred to as "The Orchard."
28 (below). Grube (Harding) Road before Ridgewood was developed. On the south side of the road "Pythian Woods" is visible.

he saw one. So, in 1913, he took stock of the situation, called off construction of his East High Street house, and decided to seize the moment. He would give Springfield its first thoroughly modern suburban development.

He had his eye on the perfect place—a piece of ground lying north of McCreight Avenue, the northern limit of the city at the time, and bounded to the east by North Limestone Street and to the north by Home Road. Kissell predicted that the future growth of the city would be to the north. There was plenty of open land there and much of the new residential construction was already taking place north of Buck Creek these days. The north side of Springfield had never been marred by much business or trade, and the area north of Buck Creek had another major advantage—there were no dangerous sections of railroad tracks to cross. The local newspaper routinely covered stories of pedestrians or automobiles being struck by trains, a troubling frequent occurrence at the time. At their worst, trains were a safety hazard, and at their most benign they were a perpetual source of noise and an annoying cause of delay for motorists and pedestrians trying to make their way across town.

Kissell also saw his alma mater, Wittenberg College, as an asset to the north side. Wittenberg had been there for three quarters of a century and had drawn people of culture and refinement to the neighborhood. Wittenberg's beautiful campus, the nearby Cliff and Snyder Parks, Ferncliff Cemetery, and many wooded sections in the area offered opportunities for lovers of nature. In addition, and perhaps most important, The Springfield Country Club offered much in the way of recreational and social activities.

Over the previous two decades, a number of fine homes had been built along North Fountain Avenue, north of Buck Creek and adjacent to Wittenberg College, making the street a splendid approach to the new neighborhood Kissell was imagining. He envisioned extending North Fountain Avenue beyond McCreight Avenue with a grand boulevard running all the way to the increasingly popular Springfield Country Club. The city's once fashionable urban club for gentlemen, the Lagonda Club, was falling on hard times as the city's elites were transferring their allegiance to the Springfield Country Club, located a mile north of the city limits. Fresh air and outdoor recreation, especially the new, growing passion for the game of golf, was beating out the dark, smoke-filled retreat in the dirty city, making it fast a relic

of another era. The trendier country club would serve as the perfect anchor for a new type of neighborhood. *(fig. 26, page 29)*

The land Kissell coveted was mostly rural. Farm fields, animals grazing in pastures, orchards, and a few strands of towering forest trees occupied most of this land. If one stood on the knoll where the Springfield Country Club clubhouse was located, and looked to the south and the west, they could see for miles out over undulating hills, beautiful valleys, and scenic wooded ridges. The Ohio Pythian Home had chosen one of these ridges, just north of McCreight Avenue, to build its state orphanage. Its location, where Mercy Hospital would be built in 1950, was purported to be the highest point in Springfield outside of the soldiers' mound at Ferncliff Cemetery. Two greenhouses represented the only commercial activity in the area at the time. *(fig's. 27, 28, 29 & 30)*

In 1813, early Springfield pioneer Maddox Fisher had been the first white settler to acquire this particular tract of land. Fisher was a successful local businessman and would be a driving force behind the creation of Clark County and the selection of Springfield as its county seat in 1818. After his death in 1836, the land was divided into various tracts, which then changed hands many times over the years. In the second half of nineteenth century, Adam Grube operated a brick plant there on a broad swath of land that encompassed the area where North and South Broadmoor Boulevard and North and South Kensington Place would later be platted. For decades, future homeowners on

29. View of the countryside from the Springfield Country Club clubhouse.

this site would discover bricks every time they turned over a spade of dirt.

The brickyard was long gone by the time Kissell was contemplating the area, however, and with the exception of the two greenhouses, which seemed benign to him—compared to the noxious factories in the city—it remained largely unspoiled by commercial intrusions. It was everything the dirty, crowded, smoggy city was not. It still bore the imprint of the Native Americans who once made the area their home. Their trails could still be found in the woods that bordered the country club. This was the antidote to modern urban life that Kissell was looking for. He could envision this bucolic area as the perfect setting for a community of fine homes in the latest artistic styles with all the modern conveniences. He would build the best there was to offer in residential developments—clean, healthy, spacious, but most of all modern. He would call it Ridgewood and it would be the finest residential district that Springfield had ever seen. Baltimore and Kansas City would have nothing on his beloved Springfield. Now he only needed to acquire the land.

30. The Ohio Pythian Home orphanage, located on the northwest corner of McCreight Ave. & Fountain Blvd. It was later demolished and Mercy Hospital was constructed on the site.

High-class residential living

34. The ornamental brick entrances at the northwest and northeast corners of McCreight Ave. and Fountain Blvd. The Eakins house is visible in the center, the original Jefferson School is to the right.

2 A MAMMOTH UN

BUYING THE LAND FOR HIS NEW, "HIGH-CLASS" RESIDENTIAL DEVELOPMENT WOULD PROVE TO BE NO SMALL FEAT FOR HARRY KISSELL.

Thirty-eight separate owners had to be persuaded to part with all or some of their land. If any one owner said no, all might be lost. The first order of business, however, was to establish the entity that would actually acquire the land—The Kissell Improvement Company. On February 25, 1914, Kissell and his trusted associate, Brown Burleigh, incorporated The Kissell Improvement Company with capital stock of $100,000. Brown Burleigh was a young, up-and-coming Springfield resident who had earned his stripes and Kissell's admiration over the last five years while serving as secretary and sales manager of the Kissell Real Estate Company. *(fig. 31)*

Once the new improvement company was established, Burleigh and Kissell went to work on purchasing 120 acres of land that had not been for sale. With a combination of persistence, tact, patience, and diplomacy, the two were able to make the near impossible a reality. In the short span between March and May of 1914, Kissell and Burleigh arranged deals for all the tracts of land they needed and most of what they really wanted, save one. One large tract of land, where North and South Broadmoor Boulevard and North and South Kensington Place were later platted, was in question.

This was the strip of land where Adam Grube

ERTAKING

had once operated his brickyard, and it was now in the hands of his heirs. Ultimately, the Grubes agreed to part with the eastern portion of the tract, allowing Kissell to run his boulevard through this section and plat North Kensington Place and South Kensington Place. The remaining portion of the Grube land to the west, though, where North Broadmoor Boulevard and South Broadmoor Boulevard were later platted, was not for sale. The location of that particular piece of ground kept it from being a deal-breaker. Kissell could still acquire enough land to ensure a large, stable neighborhood, relatively free from future commercial intrusions. But he always hoped to buy that land if it became available, and when he platted the lots along North Fountain Boulevard that bordered it, he left an entrance to provide accessibility for the Grubes, and, hopefully, one day himself. *(fig. 32)*

Another potential snafu involved land owned by John Doyle. Doyle owned a smaller tract just north of the Grube land. It laid along Home Road between St. Bernard's Cemetery to the west and Limestone Street to the east. Doyle lived and operated a greenhouse on the western section of this tract. He, too, was willing to part with enough land to allow Kissell to extend Fountain Boulevard all the way to Home Road, but that was it. The new boulevard would divide Doyle's land roughly in half. His home and greenhouse would now be on the west side of Fountain Boulevard, and a section of undeveloped land would be on the east side of the boulevard, where Trenton Place and Shawnee Boulevard were later platted.

When it came to the land acquisition, one of the most important pieces of the puzzle was a tract owned by John A. Blount. Blount was a member of one of Clark County's earliest settling families. His father, J.R. Blount, had been in business with the Kissell family back in the 1870s when they had formed Kissell, Blount and Company to manufacture agricultural machinery. John A. Blount's mother was a member of the McCreight family, whose lands had extended over much of the northern half of the city at one time. As one of the McCreight heirs, John A. Blount was in possession of an empty piece of ground in an area that is now bounded by the contemporary roads of Harding Road (then known as Grube Road) and McCreight Avenue to the north and south, and North Limestone Street and Fountain Boulevard to the east and west.

John A. Blount had his eye on developing the city to the north as well when, in 1912, he proposed an extension and widening of North Fountain Avenue all the way north to Grube Road. In December 1912, he had submitted a layout for "Blount's Plat." In addition to extending Fountain Avenue from McCreight Avenue to Grube Road, he platted streets to the east, where present-day First, Second, Third, Roosevelt, and Fifth Streets are (Roosevelt was originally named Fourth street until construction of Roosevelt Junior High was completed on North Limestone Street in 1923). He intended to use these same numerical designations for the first four streets, but at the time he christened what is now Fifth Street as Blount Street. Unfortunately, Blount's declining health prevented the extension and widening of Fountain Avenue and the development of this land. *(fig. 33)*

Acquisition of part of this tract of land was essential not only for the new grand boulevard, but also for the proper entrance to Ridgewood that Harry Kissell envisioned. Kissell was planning to erect a pair of brick entrances, which would bear the Ridgewood name, on either side of the street leading into his new development—something that would set it off from the rest of the city and give it an air of exclusivity, a forerunner of the gated community of the future. Ridgewood would be at once separate but still part of the larger community. By utilizing the brick entrances to quietly announce that one was now entering Ridgewood, Kissell reinforced a sense of neighborhood identity. Creating a unique neighborhood identity establishing Ridgewood as a brand was a tactic that would be repeated over and over again in the marketing of the development. *(fig. 34, page 34)*

In one of the more bittersweet happenings surrounding the development of Ridgewood, John A. Blount realized that because of his failing health his own plans were not to be, and out of fond regard for the Kissell family, he parted with a portion of the land, enough for Kissell to construct his boulevard. In doing so, he handed off his dream of the city's northern expansion to the ambitious, young Harry Kissell.

Miraculously, by late May of 1914, after only three months' effort, Kissell and Brown Burleigh had managed to acquire all the land necessary to make Ridgewood a reality. Although Kissell filed the original plat for Ridgewood, Ridgewood Phase I, in July 1914, out of deference for Blount's feelings, he held off on platting his portion of the Blount land until after Blount's death in January of 1915. As a result, this section, even though it was the entrance to Ridgewood and constructed at the same time as Phase I, would thereafter be known as Ridgewood Phase II.

While Kissell and Burleigh were busy acquiring land for Ridgewood, the Kissell Company was already making headlines with its "Electric Cottage." To drum up publicity for its new Pythian Heights subdivision, the real estate

31. Brown Burleigh.

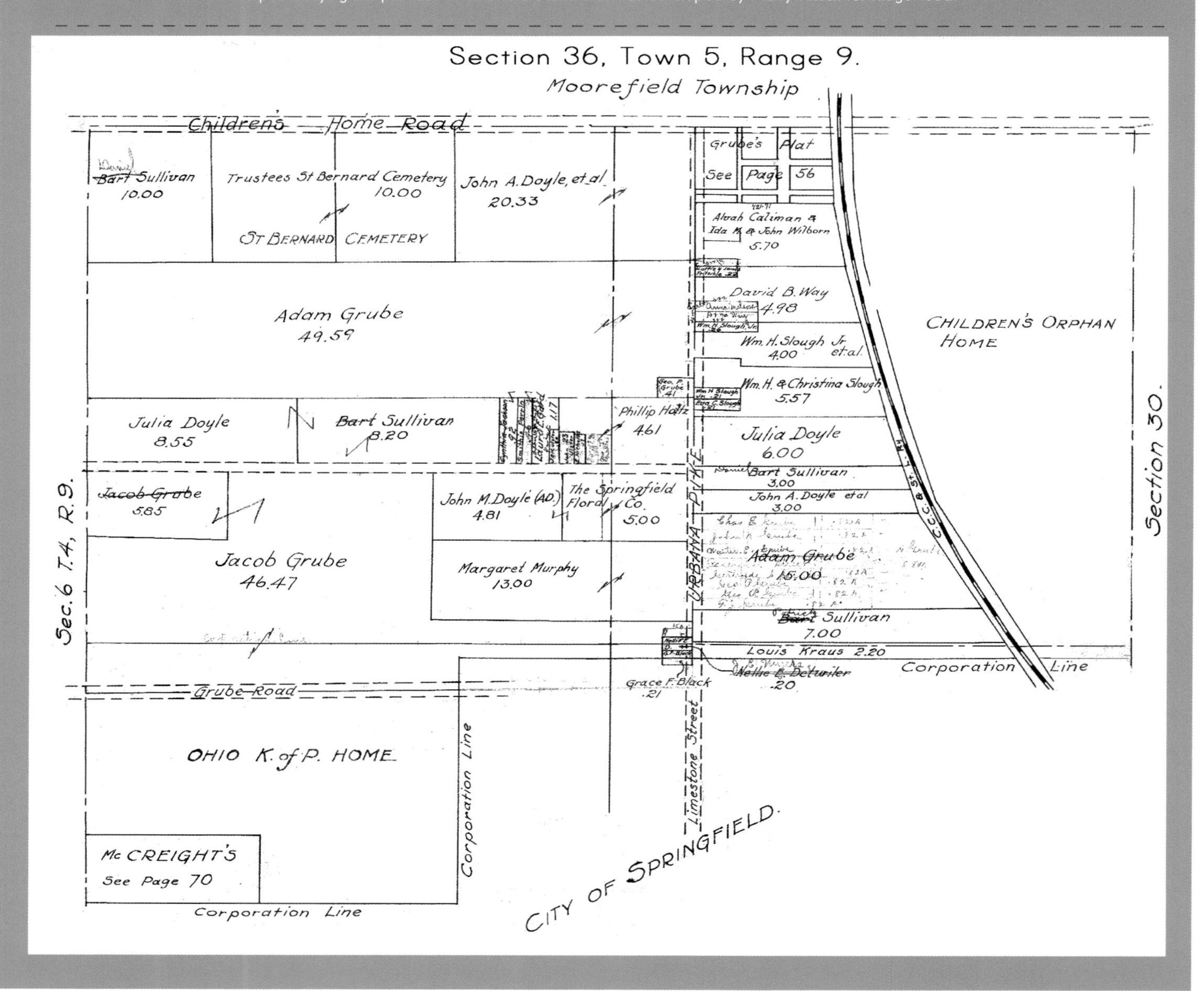

32. Map identifying the previous owners of the land that was developed by Harry Kissell for Ridgewood.

company became partners with The Springfield Light, Heat & Power Company and Springfield's leading interior decorators, Fitler and Hill, to fully outfit a bungalow at 1211 North Lowry Avenue with every newfangled electrical contrivance and the latest home furnishings. The Electric Cottage was heavily advertised and was open to the public each afternoon and evening for a week in late May 1914. Springfield's first model home was a huge success, drawing crowds of curious people and plenty of attention to Kissell's first major foray into suburban developments. *(fig. 35, page 42)*

At the same time that the Electric Cottage was enjoying great publicity, plans were taking shape for the recently acquired land nearby. Kissell had

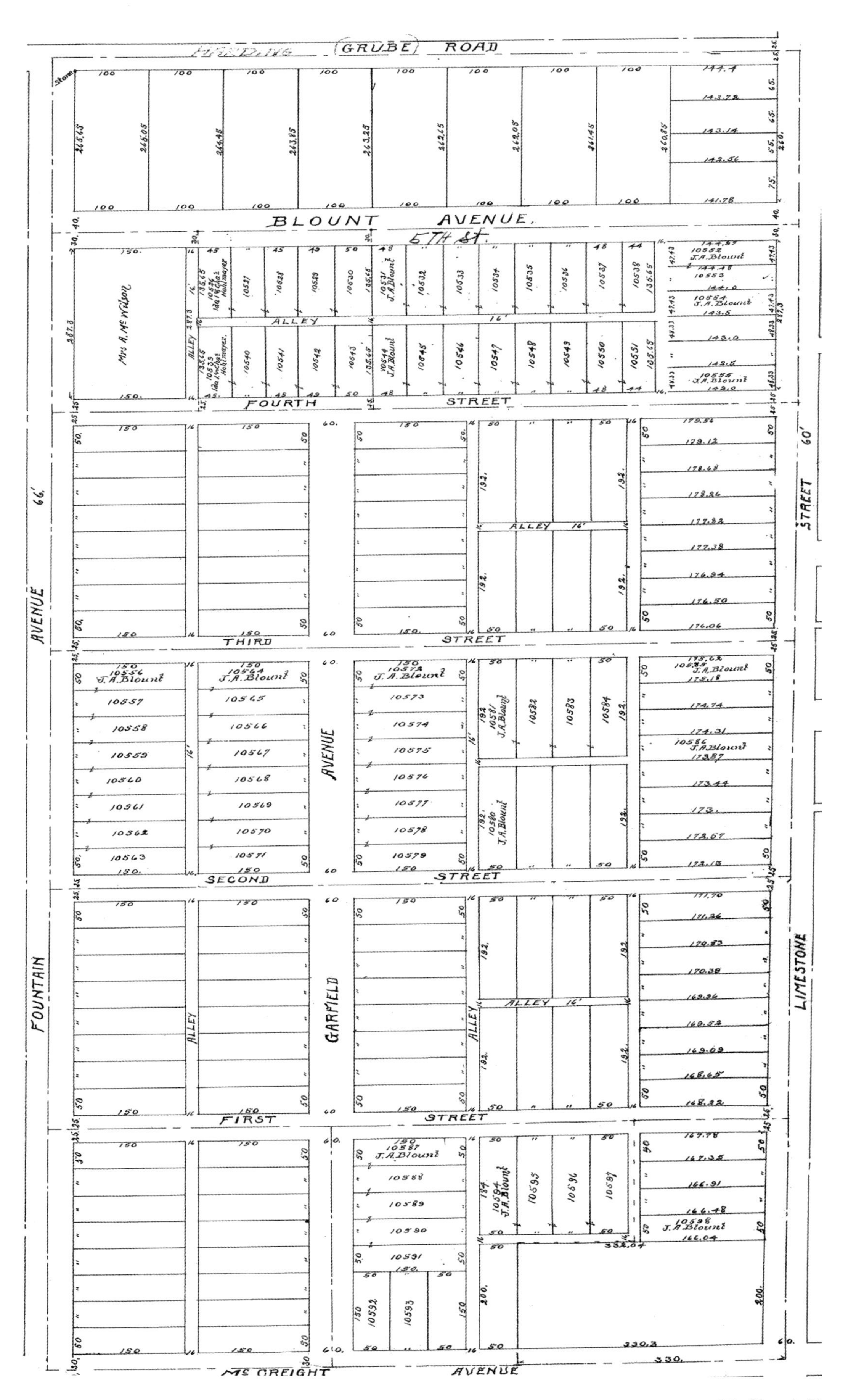

33. Blount's Plat.

I.O.O.F.
ENGLEWOOD RD
HAMPTON PL
STRATFORD PL
FLORAL AVE
KENSINGTON PL SOUTH
KENSINGTON PL NORTH
HOME RD
SPRINGFIELD
COUNTRY CLUB

36. Bird's eye view sketch of the site plan for Ridgewood, 1914.

spared no expense in the planning of Ridgewood. He hired Elmer B. Wight, a noted Cleveland landscape architect, who had laid out a considerable part of Cleveland's park system. His background was fitting because Kissell was determined that Ridgewood would be the "beauty spot" of Springfield, a park-like setting that would offer all the things that the older residential sections of town lacked. *(fig. 36 on previous page)*

Using, as a starting point, Kissell's desire for a grand boulevard down the center of the development, Wight worked out the details of streets, park spaces, streetcar waiting stations, and lot arrangements. Fountain Boulevard would be 100 feet wide with a beautiful parkway in the center. State of the art asphalt roadways would flank either side of the center parkway. The

THE ELECTRIC COTTAGE

WALL PAPER

Interior Decorations

Window Shades

Cretonnes

Be Sure and Visit the Electric Cottage

After careful consideration on the part of the General Electric Co. and Kissell Bldg. Co., **Fitler and Hill** were chosen to install the decorations in the new Electric Cottage, thereby again attesting to the superior ideas and workmanship of **Springfield's Leading Decorators.** With our extremely large corps of expert workmen, we are in the best possible position to render prompt service.

We guarantee absolutely all our work.

FITLER AND HILL

SPRINGFIELD'S LEADING DECORATIVE PARLORS

Bell 802. 32 and 34 N. Fountain Avenue. **Home 1323-A**

35. May 24, 1914 advertisement for the Electric Cottage.

37. Detail of the streetcar tracks in the center parkway of Fountain Boulevard, 1917.

roadways would be bordered by ten-foot wide grass planting strips and wide cement sidewalks giving way to the expansive front lawns of the new homes. Houses would be required to be set back fifty feet from the lot line, making the distance from a house on one side of the street, across the boulevard, to the house on the opposite side of the street an amazing 200 feet. This meant an incredible sacrifice in profit for the sake of carrying out the ideals of suburban living—space and beauty. *(fig. 37)*

While envisioning Ridgewood, Harry Kissell and Brown Burleigh had visited Edward Bouton's Roland Park in Baltimore and J.C. Nichols' Country Club District in Kansas City, and they were well-versed in the advantages of the curvilinear street. While Kissell chose not to simply divide up the entire

38. 1917 image of the Eakins home, 1220 N. Fountain Blvd. Note the central parkway in the boulevard, the elm trees in the planting strip, and the unsightly telephone poles located to the rear of the lot.

EAKINS HOME

plat of Ridgewood into straight lines and narrow streets in order to produce the greatest number of lots, he was a practical businessman. His intent was to target the largest range of customers possible who fell under the "high grade" real estate market label, from the solidly middle class to the very affluent. Everyone from Springfield's wealthiest business owners, down to entry-level managers, fell into this category. Sections of the suburb, which featured straight streets and smaller lots, were included in order to provide a number of price options to potential buyers, and the plat was laid out in a manner so that the less expensive homes would not detract from the higher priced ones.

Ridgewood Phase I and II would include most of Fountain Boulevard, Crescent Drive, North and South Kensington Place, Hampton Place, Stratford Place, twelve lots on Grube Road, and part of Englewood Road. (About half of the land on the south side of Englewood Road was owned by someone else and was known as Wilbert's Plat.) Very small portions of both Dover Road and

39. Streetcar waiting station on the triangular parklet at the intersection of Fountain Blvd. and Ardmore Rd.

Ardmore Road were constructed at the time as well. Fountain Boulevard was mostly straight by necessity, with the exception of a small bend in the road just north of the entrance to present day Broadmoor Boulevard, to accommodate the preexisting John A. Doyle house (now 2215 North Fountain Boulevard). The gentle curve in the road also aligned its terminus perfectly with the gates of the Springfield Country Club.

As the largest and most prestigious allotment in the development, Fountain Boulevard lots would command the highest prices. Crescent Drive and North and South Kensington Place would each follow the curvilinear form and be the second and third highest priced lots, respectively. The straight Englewood Road, Hampton Place, and Stratford Place would offer more economical home sites for young, up-and-coming businessmen and professionals of more moderate means. A section of land to the west of Fountain Boulevard and Crescent Drive that was to be developed later, was envisioned at the time as following the rectilinear grid pattern.

Elmer Wight honored Kissell's desire to make Ridgewood a park-like setting and designed a landscape lush with greenery and plantings. Over 1,500 American elms were eventually set out in the planting strips. Over 1,000 shrubs would be planted in the central parkway in the boulevard and in the triangular park spaces at street intersections. A splendid ornamental street lighting system was also planned. And in keeping with the emerging trend in early, planned subdivisions, restrictions were instituted that established minimum setbacks for houses, minimum spaces between houses, and banned fences, one-story houses, billboards, all commercial enterprises, and, interestingly, the making or selling of intoxicating liquors. The restrictions also set minimum prices for houses that could be built on each particular street. *(fig's. 38 & 39)*

Ridgewood would have every modern improvement available at the time. It would have the distinction of being the first development in the city to have both storm and sanitary sewers. All of the telephone and electric poles would be located at the rear of the lots to conceal infrastructure that was essential but considered unsightly. At the time, not one but two sets of telephone lines were required because Springfield had two competing phone companies—the Springfield-Xenia Telephone Company and the Central Union Telephone Company of Springfield, known popularly as the "Home" and "Bell" telephone companies, respectively. Customers of the Home Company could only dial other Home customers, and the same was true of the Bell system. Businesses and homes that could afford it had both services and two separate phone numbers with double the bills. As absurd and inefficient as it sounds, it was not unusual in the early twentieth century to have multiple providers for public utilities and services, each of which required their own equipment and infrastructure. Common sense eventually won out and the competing telephone companies were consolidated and placed under the jurisdiction of the Public Utilities Commission of Ohio in 1920.

In planning a new residential neighborhood far removed from the center city, transportation to and from Ridgewood became a central issue and was given great consideration. In the era when the automobile was still a luxury item, inexpensive, reliable public transportation was essential for the success of a new suburban residential development. Even subdivisions like Ridgewood, which were marketed to the business and professional class, needed public transportation. Harry Kissell rightly assumed that most of the families who bought lots in his upscale subdivision would own an automobile. Early automobiles, however, could be temperamental and unreliable. The entrance to Ridgewood was exactly one mile—a twelve-block walk from the heart of the downtown business and commercial district, which was considered the practical limit for foot travel at the time. While this was a reasonable walk in mild weather, the thought of making such a trek in bad weather might have been a deterrent for some potential residents. In addition, most families who owned automobiles, even affluent families, owned only one. In the early twentieth century, automobiles were primarily used by men. Early automobiles required considerable labor to start because they were hand cranked, and they broke down frequently, making them impractical for what was then regarded as the genteel and weaker sex. In an era when virtually no woman of means worked outside of the home, the automobile was the province of the man of the house and served as his primary source of transportation to and from work.

That meant reliable transportation was necessary for his wife and children left behind in the suburbs. While some affluent Springfield couples employed a chauffeur who could deliver the husband to work and then return to ferry the wife around on errands and such, it was a luxury exclusive to only the wealthier families. In most middle- and upper-class households, not only did the wife need her own source of transportation, but the children did as well. While the Jefferson School for elementary students was located on McCreight Avenue, right at the entrance of Ridgewood, consideration had to be given on how to get older students clear over to the Central Junior High School on the southwest corner of High Street and Wittenberg Avenue, or to Springfield High School on South Limestone Street. Regular streetcar accessibility, conveniently located, would address all these issues.

Another concern for the affluent residents of a suburban development was the ability for domestic help to be able to commute daily to their place of employment. In the old neighborhoods of South Fountain Avenue and East High Street, if servants did not live in the house with the family they served, they usually lived nearby. On East High Street, many of the "daily help" servants lived on the side streets off East High Street. In some cases, domestic servants lived in small enclaves that were virtually in the backyards of the homes where they worked. The Weimers Section, located just behind some of the grand homes of the wealthy in the 800 block of East High Street, was home to a number of African American domestic servants well into the middle of the twentieth century.

To some extent, the same pattern was also true for South Fountain Avenue. Daily help sometimes lived in modest homes on nearby streets, and an African American neighborhood was tucked in immediately behind the fine homes on the west side of South Fountain Avenue. Winter Street (now known as Piqua Place), was an unpaved street, dotted with modest cottages and sandwiched between South Fountain Avenue and South Center Street to the east and west and Mulberry Street and Liberty Street to the north and south. Like the Weimers Section on East High Street, Winter Street was the home to a number of daily domestic servants serving the South Fountain Avenue neighborhood.

Many of Springfield's servant class in the nineteenth century were Irish immigrants, or their descendents, who lived in a neighborhood surrounding St. Joseph's Catholic Church on Kenton Street, an area known popularly as Irish Hill. In the 1870s, Irish immigrants had flocked to the neighborhood to take jobs in the nearby factories where the Champion Reaper was being manufactured. While the fathers of these Irish families worked at Champion, the vast majority of their young adult, unmarried daughters worked as domestic servants in the homes of Springfield's wealthy and middle-class residents. Because of Irish Hill's proximity to both East High Street and South Fountain Avenue, servants who did not live-in with their employers were able to commute on foot to work.

The new suburban developments of the twentieth century, however, were creating a radical change in the way people lived. Advances in transportation made it feasible for people to live farther from where they worked. The electric streetcar could travel up to twenty miles per hour and the automobile could reach top speeds of forty miles per hour, allowing the affluent to now live, for the first time, outside of the crowded city with all its ills, and import their household help daily via streetcar. The mixed neighborhoods of the nineteenth century, where servants had lived in close proximity to their employers, on side streets and in back alleyways, was becoming a thing of the past. *(fig's. 40 & 41)*

Good streetcar service was simply a necessity for Ridgewood to flourish, and Harry Kissell was determined to offer the best service possible to his new development. Springfield residents had two options for car service to the north end. They could take the Ohio Electric Railway car, which was the interurban line that ran north through the city to Urbana, or they could take the Springfield Street Railway line, which provided local streetcar service to various destinations throughout the city. The Ohio Electric line ran out North Fountain Avenue, then veered right on McCreight Avenue, and finally left on North Limestone Street before heading on to Urbana (North Limestone Street, north of Buck Creek, was generally referred to as the Urbana Pike at the time). Passengers could disembark from the interurban on North Limestone Street. Alternatively, they could ride the Springfield Street Railway Company's K of P car. The K of P car ran out North Limestone Street, veered left on McCreight Avenue, and let passengers off just past the Knights of Pythias orphanage. Either option delivered riders within a reasonable walking distance to the entrance of Ridgewood. However, residents who lived in the far north end of the development, closer to the Country Club, would have a considerable walk to and from the streetcar.

40. Mule-drawn streetcars, introduced to Springfield in the 1860s by Phineas P. Mast, could travel up to four miles per hour.

Kissell had something better in mind. He dreamed of offering streetcar service through Ridgewood, right down Fountain Boulevard all the way to the country club entrance. Kissell was familiar with the statistic that 90 percent of all the homes in cities were built within four blocks of the streetcar line. If he could get the streetcar to run down the boulevard, even the remotest parts of Ridgewood, once all of the land was developed, would be within four blocks walking distance to catch a car. As soon as he and Brown Burleigh had finished their feverish acquisition of land, Kissell launched an ambitious campaign to procure streetcar service that would deliver Ridgewood residents virtually to their own front doors.

Kissell approached the Springfield Street Railway Company about the possibility. In 1913, Street Railway officials had applied for and received a franchise from the city to extend streetcar service on North Limestone from McCreight Avenue to Home Road. (Home Road was originally known as Children's Home Road, so named for the Clark County Children's Home, built in 1878. By the turn of the twentieth century, it was referred to simply as Home Road.) Taking stock of the emerging northward trend for new development in the city, the Street Railway Company predicted continued population growth in the North Limestone Street area. The city planned to extend pavement on North Limestone Street from McCreight Avenue out to

41. Electric streetcar in front of the Fairbanks Building. Electric streetcars revolutionized transportation when they arrived on the scene in the 1890s.

42. Vacant lot on the southwest corner of N. Kensington Pl. and Limestone St. Limestone St., before it was a busy commercial strip, is visible to the left. Image circa 1925.

43. Postcard image of N. Limestone St., circa 1915. Note the double set of interurban tracks in the street.

the Home Road that summer. However, once Kissell tendered a proposition to Street Railway officials for them to operate a line through Ridgewood, they changed their mind about the Limestone Street franchise.

Before the Ridgewood proposition came to life, Street Railway officials regarded North Limestone as the major thoroughfare in the north end of the city. North Fountain Avenue was simply a nice residential street that dead-ended into McCreight Avenue. In the minds of Street Railway officials, however, the Ridgewood proposition was a game-changer. It amounted to a virtual guarantee of hundreds of new customers in the immediate future instead of a gradual population increase over time on Limestone Street, north of McCreight Avenue. A line servicing Springfield's newest and most desirable neighborhood was a more attractive offer, but it would require getting out of its existing franchise contract. *(fig. 42)*

A lot of finagling, plotting, and politicking behind the scenes ensued, but finally a plan emerged. On Saturday June 6, 1914, Springfield Street Railway officials filed an application to begin streetcar service on North Limestone Street between McCreight Avenue and Home Road, but with the codicil that, per their franchise agreement, they could lay a double set of tracks, instead of the single set of tracks that everyone had anticipated.

This application was a distinct red herring. The Ohio Electric Railway already had a double set of tracks on North Limestone, which accommodated its interurban cars to and from Urbana, and Street Railway knew another set of double tracks would leave no safe room for an automobile to stop. Sharing the interurban's existing tracks was not an option either because the two systems used rails spaced at different widths, a uniquely Springfield oddity.

When electric streetcars were first introduced in the city in 1891, the decision was made to continue utilizing the four-foot gauge rails that the old mule-drawn streetcar system had operated on instead of widening them to the standard four by eight-and-a-half-inch gauge set of tracks that most streetcars, and later the interurban, used. This was purely a money saving measure. Once the interurban arrived on the scene at the turn of the twentieth century, new wider-gauge tracks had to be laid for it, resulting in some instances where in the same street there was a set of tracks for the interurban and a different one for the streetcar. *(fig. 43)*

This worked fine as long as each had a single set of tracks. A double set of tracks, however, which allowed multiple streetcar or interurban cars to operate in two different directions at the same time, consumed a considerable amount of most residential streets. This became more problematic as the automobile came into widespread use. In cases where a double track was impractical due to space limitations, a single track with sidings—where one car could wait as another passed in the opposition direction—was usually the answer.

Controversy erupted as word spread about Springfield Street Railway's obvious maneuver to get out of its previous franchise. North Limestone Street residents, intent on getting the streetcar service on their street, were ready to call the Street Railway's bluff and retained their own council. James P. Goodwin represented the North Limestone Street residents at a city commission meeting held on Monday, June 22, 1914, and stated that his clients wanted the extension to go out Limestone Street, even if it meant four tracks instead of three in the street. Goodwin plainly accused the Street Railway Company of not wanting to live up to its franchise agreement because it had another plan afoot in North Fountain Boulevard. "The street belongs to the people," said Goodwin, "and they have the right to demand the services promised within the franchise agreement."

Attorney Paul C. Martin, on behalf of the Street Railway Company, countered that extending the service on Fountain Boulevard instead of North Limestone meant that those who lived on Limestone Street would have to walk no farther than those on North Fountain Avenue did to get a car. He described in great detail Kissell's plan for a 100-foot wide, one-mile boulevard extending north from McCreight Avenue to the Springfield Country Club. Streetcar tracks would run down a center parkway with roadways on both sides. The central parkway was to be surrounded by cement curbing to segregate the streetcar tracks from the roadway to help prevent accidents. There would be no battle between motorists and the streetcar on North Fountain Boulevard because each would have its own space. *(See fig. 37)*

After listening to attorney Martin's description of the proposal, the commission invited Kissell to speak. He painted what the newspapers would describe the following day as "a beautiful word picture" of the exciting and novel new development, describing the boulevard and the triangular park spaces positioned where the side streets intersected Fountain Boulevard. At various intervals along the boulevard these triangular parklets would be occupied by attractive and convenient Spanish Mission-style streetcar waiting stations to shelter riders from inclement weather. The opposing attorney, Goodwin, dismissively stated that Kissell's "magnificent picture of paradise" was irrelevant and that this case was a cold proposition of law, and the Street Railway Company was bound to honor its original agreement.

Lobbying on both sides of the issue continued, and behind-the-scenes discussions attempted some sort of compromise. After three weeks of wrangling, City Commissioner Burton J. Westcott announced that a resolution had been found that should prove satisfactory to both parties. The Ohio Electric Railway would provide a car on a twenty-minute schedule to service North Limestone Street between McCreight Avenue and Home Road, freeing the Springfield Street Railway to proceed with the Fountain Boulevard project. The compromise addressed the needs of the North Limestone Street residents while being mindful of the fact that the considerable investment Harry Kissell was making in the Ridgewood project would improve all property values on the north end and, perhaps more important to the city commissioners, raise tax revenue for the city. At 5:30 a.m. the following morning, the new car service began out North Limestone Street.

Five days later, on July 20, 1914, Harry Kissell and Brown Burleigh were before the city commission to officially present the plat for Ridgewood. The *Springfield Daily News* hailed the addition as a complete departure from the way previous additions in the city had been laid out, and stated that it served as evidence that Springfield was assuming many of the progressive ideas found in much larger cities. The Ridgewood addition marked the first time that a Springfield residential development had been planned as a whole, instead of the haphazard and piecemeal manner in which previous residential areas had developed. Ridgewood was to be a place of natural beauty, but with all the modern amenities—the perfect compromise between city and country. It was Springfield's first fully modern, fully restricted, fully planned, picturesque suburb. With much praise for the attractive and progressive way the development was laid out, the city commissioners accepted the plat without reservations.

Work began immediately. A mammoth steam shovel was placed at McCreight Avenue to cut through the land where the big hill of the Knights of Pythias land met the flatter land of the old Blount plat to the east. Construction of the grand boulevard was officially under way. One hundred fifty men were set to work in grading operations and in starting the large trunk sewer line, which would be laid through the addition. On Saturday, July 25, 1914, a *Springfield Daily News* reporter quoted an ambitious Kissell as saying that they hoped to have Fountain Boulevard finished, the streetcars running, and some lots ready for sale by fall, an optimistic assessment given the enormity of the undertaking. *(fig. 44)*

An engineering corps was stationed on the ground to continually oversee the work of the entire development. Chief Engineer George Haller, who, for the previous thirteen years, had been connected with the Big Four Railroad engineering department in Springfield, headed the group. The corps also included four other experienced, full-time engineers. In addition, there was a team of inspectors to check sewers, water lines, gas lines, and all cement work. The contract for the laying of storm and sanitary sewers and water pipes in the development had been let to Smith and Wetzel, a Dayton company. A big ditching machine arrived on July 25, 1914, and excavation proceeded through August. At the same time, foreman William McDaniels had about a hundred of his men at work grading and laying cement curbs and gutters.

Water mains were to be installed under the direction of the City Waterworks Department with an agreement that The Kissell Improvement Company would pay for the entire cost, including the pipes, valves, fire hydrants, labor, and the contractor's profit. The city would then take over the improvement and repay The Kissell Improvement Company, without interest, at such time when revenues from those utilizing the line reached 6 percent of the cost. The water installation alone represented an outlay by The Kissell Improvement Company of over $11,000, a significant up-front investment of capital that paid no dividends. Ultimately, it would take ten years before there were enough houses built in the development so that revenue would reach 6 percent and the company could recoup the money.

The massive Ridgewood project quickly became the talk of the town and

44. Looking north from the intersection of N. Fountain Ave. and McCreight Ave., before construction of Fountain Blvd. began, June 3, 1914.

would be the subject of much speculation and gossip, even when it came to something as seemingly insignificant as the water installation. At the end of August, a rumor was swirling that Harry Kissell and the city were at odds over his desire to locate fire hydrants at the rear of lots, just as he had done with the electric and telephone poles. While the claim was entirely without merit, it took disclaimers in the newspaper from both Kissell and City Manager Charles E. Ashburner to finally put the bogus charge to rest.

Meanwhile, the Ridgewood storm sewer, which would also prove to be a source of controversy in the future, was being connected to the existing city sewer at the intersection of North Fountain Avenue and McCreight Avenue.

The existing sewer would quickly prove insufficient to handle all the new development in the north end of Springfield. In the spring of 1916, one year after the Ridgewood development first opened, torrential rains caused water to back up because the inadequate city storm sewer could not carry it away. Water got into the basements of the handful of new homes that had been built in Ridgewood, and the story went all over the city that the subdivision was wet, and its sewer system was defective.

Wet cellars, then as now, were an anathema, especially in a brand new residential development that already represented an enormous gamble on the part of its developer. Wet cellars were considered a nuisance at best and a health hazard at worst. Eventually, the city was forced to enlarge the section of the storm sewer that ran south from McCreight Avenue to College Avenue to afford necessary relief to the entire area. But the sewer issue would continue to haunt Kissell, forcing him to spend considerable energy to combat misleading perceptions, until it was finally resolved some years later.

While the city had been somewhat cooperative with the water improvement in Ridgewood, it was less so when it came to the sanitary sewer lines. The entrance to Ridgewood was approximately four blocks from the nearest sanitary sewer outlet at the intersection of Grube Road (Harding) and Plum Street. Even though Grube Road was an existing road that pre-dated Ridgewood and was now within city limits, the Kissell Company had to pay for sanitary sewer pipe to be laid down Grube, from Fountain Boulevard to the intersection of Plum Street, in order to hook up to the city sanitary sewer. The tab came to $5,095 and, to add insult to injury, anyone living in the vicinity had the privilege of tapping the new sewer without compensating Kissell.

Despite numerous obstacles, substantial progress on the mammoth undertaking of constructing the new subdivision was evident by mid-October. On October 18, 1914, Brown Burleigh reported to the newspaper that over a thousand shrubs had just arrived to be set out in the triangular parklets and the center parkway of the boulevard, as soon as these sections were finished. The Springfield Street Railway had completed the necessary preliminary work of laying tracks in the intersection of North Fountain Avenue and McCreight Avenue and was now pushing the construction of its tracks north out the new boulevard. By November 8, the Street Railway Company was nearing the halfway point of the boulevard and beginning the excavation north of Grube Road.

Paving of the roadways on either side of the center parkway in the boulevard, as well as on the side streets, was also set to begin that first week of November. Good pavement would be a hallmark of Ridgewood and essential to its success in the new era of the automobile. Few things in the early twentieth century captured the public imagination like the automobile. An automobile meant personal freedom. No longer was one bound by the schedules or routes of public transportation. No longer did one have to deal with the stench and labor associated with the increasingly old-fashioned mode of transportation—the horse. While still largely the toy and status symbol of the wealthy and upper-middle class in 1914, the number of automobiles on the road multiplied exponentially each year in the first two decades of the twentieth century. In 1905, there were only 8,000 registered autos in the United States. However, by 1915, there were 2,332,426 and counting. In 1905, only one in every 1,078 Americans had an automobile. By 1920, that ratio would be one in thirteen.

Automobile mania was sweeping the country, and Springfield was not immune. An "Auto Notes" section in the local newspaper kept readers up to date on the latest models and any automobile- related issues, and automobiles accounted for a considerable proportion of the advertisements in the newspaper. Springfield residents had founded an Automobile Club in 1905. By the time Ridgewood was completed in 1915, the club would boast 300 members, including Harry Kissell, and was celebrating its tenth anniversary with a banquet at the Arcade Hotel. The Springfield Automobile Club worked in conjunction with the National Automobile Association in lobbying against taxes on gasoline and autos. The club also erected "safety first" signs near schools and crossings to protect children and pedestrians in a period when traffic control had not quite caught up with the need for it. The club also offered rewards for information leading to the conviction of persons who stole articles from, tampered with, or stole autos belonging to members.

As automobile usage increased, so did the demand for good roads. Given the growing popularity of "machines," as the men of the era referred to them, developers like Harry Kissell were quick to use improved roads as a sales tool. Kissell expected the residents of his upscale development to be motorized and knew that good roads would be an enticement for potential buyers. Unlike the durable steel rims of wagons and buggies, early automobiles had fragile rubber tires. Even with increasing automobile usage, though, good pavement remained a novelty, not only locally but nationally as well. Astonishingly, as late as 1920, there were virtually no paved roads between American cities. Trains and the interurban were still the primary source of inter-city transportation, and people had a hard time believing that autos and trucks would ever replace them. Paving was also very limited even within city limits. Much of Springfield's roads would remain unpaved as late as 1935. In 1914, when Ridgewood was being developed, bricks were still the predominant road surface on the main thoroughfares of the city. However, bricks made for a harrowing, bumpy ride in an auto and were rapidly falling out of favor. *(fig's. 45 & 46)*

45. Late 19th century view of the unpaved street at the northwest corner of Fountain Ave. and North St.

The Clark County Good Roads Council, a division of the Springfield Chamber of Commerce, worked actively to improve the quality of local roads and provide for their upkeep. Good roads that could accommodate increasing automobile usage were considered a necessity to a progressive, modern city's success in the early twentieth century. They were fast becoming an important economic development tool. The Good Roads Council, just like the Automobile Club, was also active in promoting safety. The council worked to identify unsafe crossings and visual obstructions to try to curb the fatal car crashes that became a disturbingly frequent occurrence as automobile usage increased.

Ridgewood would be Springfield's first true automobile suburb. Although the streetcar was still essential, the needs of the motorist were given special consideration in this upscale subdivision.

46. Early 20th century view of W. High St. Note the brick paving.

Even the triangular parklets, placed at street intersections in the subdivision, served a dual purpose. They functioned as both a beautifying element, and they prevented traffic back-ups at intersections by dividing the traffic and funneling motorists to the left or the right, depending on which direction they were turning. Because Ridgewood was to be an automobile suburb, no malodorous carriage houses were necessary, and unsightly rear alleys could be eliminated. The new trend of wider suburban lots afforded the exalted automobile the reverence it deserved. Instead of a back alley that was intentionally hidden from view, the newfangled "driveway," visible for all to see, offered the opportunity to conspicuously parade one's prized possession with each coming and going. The new status symbol even got a little home of its very own—the "garage."

For most of the nineteenth century, an improved road had meant a macadamized road. Macadamizing was an early method of road improvement invented by Scotsman John Loudon McAdam in 1820. His method involved spreading consecutive layers of increasingly smaller stone on the roadbed, culminating in a surprisingly smooth and dustless surface that was resistant to erosion. Macadamized roads served the traveling public well in the days of slow-moving, horse-drawn transportation, but with the advent of the automobile, they quickly became problematic. Fast moving automobiles kicked up awful dust clouds and quickly destroyed the road surface.

In the early twentieth century, as automobile usage became more widespread, tar started to be used in road construction. Tar was often incorporated into gravel as a binding agent. This helped to prevent erosion and eliminate dust. All of the side streets in Ridgewood would be paved with this type of mixture—Tarvia macadam. Tarvia was a popular brand name of a high-grade refined tar that dominated the market in that period. Tarvia macadam represented a significant improvement over most roads in Springfield at the time. However, the grand boulevard through Ridgewood would be of the most state of the art method for road paving at the time—asphaltic concrete. Asphalt was a by product of petroleum production that made roads waterproof, relatively noiseless, and dustless. Asphalt gained popularity at the beginning of the twentieth century as petroleum refinement was increasing. Asphalt roads were actually two-course roads. First a layer of concrete would be laid on the road bed, then the asphalt layer would be rolled out on top, making for the most durable type of road, impervious to water, wear, and erosion. *(See fig. 37, page 43 & fig. 68, page 100)*

The Cleveland Trinidad Paving Company, the oldest and most reputable paving company in the country at the time, which had a number of plants across the nation, received the contract for constructing the roads in Ridgewood. In early November, 1914, the race was on to try and finish the boulevard before winter set in. Special permission had to be sought from the city so that paving work could proceed on Sundays. The asphalt layer could be put down in cold weather, but the concrete base layer had to be finished before extreme cold set in.

47. Image of a Tarvia macadam road being sprayed with tar.

Work was also proceeding on the Tarvia macadam roadways on the side streets. The Tarvia used in Ridgewood, Tarvia X, the highest grade the company offered, came from the company's Cleveland plant. To ensure the quality of tar arriving for Ridgewood, The Kissell Improvement Company stationed a special inspector at the plant in Cleveland. The Tarvia was then shipped by rail to Springfield in 10,000-gallon tank cars. Upon arrival, the tank cars would remain on the tracks of the D.T. & I. Railroad. From these cars, 500-gallon tank wagons were filled with tar and driven to Ridgewood by four-horse teams. In order to keep the tar warm, a fire was kept burning under the tanks as they made their way to the development. Another inspector assessed the tar when it arrived at its final destination in Ridgewood. The tanks were then connected to a steamroller and the Tarvia was pressure sprayed onto a top course of the macadam, binding it into a solid mass. A final layer of fine sand was spread on top and then thoroughly rolled with a ten-ton road roller. *(fig. 47)*

The novelty of this undertaking would turn it into quite the public spectacle, much to the delight of Harry Kissell and Sales Manager Burleigh. Intent on capitalizing on the curiosity of Springfield residents, The Kissell Improvement Company ran an advertisement on December 3, 1914, in the *Springfield Daily News* inviting prospective buyers and the general public to come out to Ridgewood and inspect the quality of the work being done. The ad advised them to take any streetcar marked "Ridgewood" from the transfer station downtown and get off right where the work was being done. This would mark the beginning of Ridgewood as a popular destination for sightseers. For years to come, riding the streetcar through Ridgewood to monitor the neighborhood's progress would be a popular pastime among Springfield residents.

By mid-December, workers were sloping the terraces at the entrance of North Fountain Boulevard on the Pythian Home side, and excavating and grading was underway in Crescent Drive and North and South Kensington Place. Much of the work slowed or ground to a complete halt in the depth of winter, but the buzz surrounding the project did not. Old real estate men shook their heads, discussed the folly of investing so much up front, and doubted the gamble would pay off. Rumors continued to swirl among cynics, and optimists followed the progress with great anticipation.

The year 1914 had been a whirlwind one for both principals of The Kissell Improvement Company. In addition to his business undertakings, Harry Kissell was always actively involved in civic affairs. At the beginning of the year, he had suggested and helped organize the Springfield Rotary Club. It would remain, along with Ridgewood, one of his most lasting legacies to the city. And in nine short months, Harry Kissell and Brown Burleigh had acquired the land for the biggest, most exciting, most talked about real estate gamble ever undertaken in Springfield and had pushed the project well under way. The company had made headlines with its novel Electric Cottage, drawing hundreds of interested visitors. And 1914 was a great year personally as well for Burleigh and Kissell. On September 22, 1914, Harry and Olive Kissell welcomed a baby daughter into their family, Mary Lucretia Kissell, Mary Lu for short, who would quickly become the apple of her father's eye. And, on November 14, 1914, Brown Burleigh married the lovely Miss May S. Fait of Baltimore, Maryland. *(fig's. 48 & 49)*

The year 1914 had been a good year for Springfield as a whole, too. Despite the economic downturn nationally, the year came to a close with much optimism among residents. The year before, Harry Kissell had been one of a group of local men who drafted the charter adopting the City Commission–City Manager form of government. The goal was to professionalize the affairs of the city and run it like a business, to take it out of the red, and improve the quality of services and infrastructure. In 1914, the city had secured as its city manager no less than the man who had invented the form of government—Charles E. Ashburner of Staunton, Virginia. Ashburner, together with a city commission composed of five successful local businessmen, were putting the city on sound financial footing and making long overdue improvements. City departments were systematized and over $1 million was spent on improvements, which included

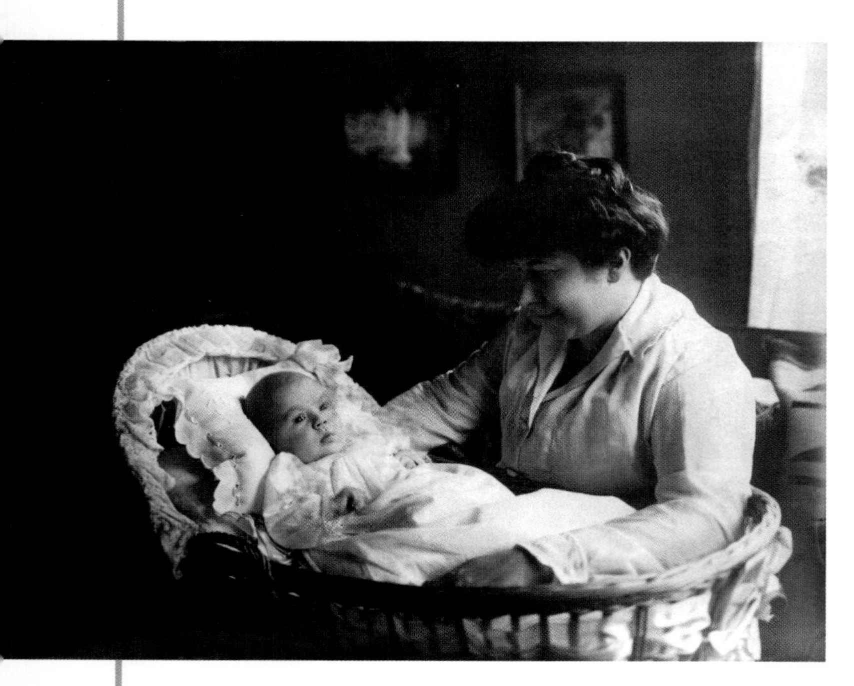

48. Olive Kissell and the infant Mary Lucretia Kissell, 1914.

upgrading parks, and extending sewers, streetcar lines, and road pavement.

In the private sector, over $2 million in new buildings were erected in downtown Springfield in 1914, and $400,000 was expended on new private residences. Not only had the building and home improvement industry provided plenty of jobs, but the manufacturing sector did as well. Springfield factories seemed immune to the recession and continued to churn out goods. The year closed on a hopeful note. The December 20, 1914, edition of the *Springfield Daily News* contained an entire section devoted to ways citizens could "Make Springfield Grow and Prosper in 1915." Suggestions ranged from community beautification measures like banning outdoor market stalls on Fountain Square (which was likened to the residents of East High Street hanging their laundry outdoors), to buying Springfield-made products whenever possible, to the construction of a new hotel to accommodate all the conventioneers expected once the construction of the new Clark County Memorial Hall was completed. Vaudeville impresario Gus Sun even penned an article encouraging Springfield residents to carry the infectious spirit with them when they traveled and boost Springfield by signing, "Springfield, Ohio, the Best Sixty Thousand City in America," after their names on hotel guest books. Yes, progress was Springfield's mantra and Harry Kissell was determined that Ridgewood would be a big piece of the equation.

49. May S. Fait, the bride of Brown Burleigh, November 14, 1914.

50. The Lagonda Club Building, at the northwest corner of High & Spring Streets.

IN THE COUNTRY

IN THE EARLY MONTHS OF 1915, HARRY KISSELL AND SALES MANAGER BROWN BURLEIGH WORKED OUT THEIR SALES TACTICS AND ADVERTISING STRATEGY IN ANTICIPATION OF A JUNE DEBUT FOR LOT SALES.

Early on, Kissell had made the decision to adopt the successful strategy pioneered by J.C. Nichols in Kansas City. Springfield's newest development would be branded "Ridgewood in the County Club District." At the time, only a select few developers in the country were utilizing the strategy. Ben and King Thompson of Columbus, Ohio, also had a large residential "country club district" development under construction in 1914, which would later be incorporated as Upper Arlington. Developer Hugh Prather had done likewise with Highland Park, a prestigious Dallas suburb. This small, elite club of high-grade real estate developers recognized the advantages of locating their new additions in close proximity to a country club. The country club conveyed social status on a development, raised its property values, served as a bulwark against objectionable uses of adjacent land, provided green space, and offered social and recreational opportunities for residents far removed from the life of the city.

A country club movement was sweeping the nation in the early twentieth century. Country clubs came into existence and became popular during this period for much the same reason suburbs developed and became fashionable. Both were made possible by developments

CLUB DISTRICT

in transportation. And the desire to escape the grime and congestion of the city and retreat to a more healthful atmosphere made country clubs and suburbs a natural fit. A penchant for outdoor pursuits, especially the growing popularity of golf, also helped fuel the rise of the country club movement.

In the 1880s and 1890s, city clubs had been popular social institutions for wealthy gentlemen. In an era before home entertainments such as radio and television, retreating to one's club in the evening was a popular diversion for men of that era. The clubs provided a refuge in the city to relax, smoke, dine, take exercise, and discuss the current events of the day. In 1893, a group of wealthy Springfield businessmen had incorporated the Lagonda Club for just that purpose. The members then purchased land on the northwest corner of High and Spring Streets and erected a beautiful Italian Renaissance Revival-style building at a cost of $25,000. The Lagonda Club officially opened in November of 1895. It was predominately social, offering members assembly and banquet facilities, reading rooms, a dining room, and rooms for indoor sports. Temporary lodging was also available to members. Wives of members enjoyed social privileges for special events, but it was primarily the bastion of men. *(fig. 50)*

But as the flight from the dirty, crowded city began in earnest in the early twentieth century, and Springfield's most affluent residents began moving to the periphery of the city, the Lagonda Club floundered. The club continued to limp on for some years, but by 1922 the Springfield Country Club was reigning as the premier social and recreational club in Springfield, and the members of the Lagonda Club were forced to sell their building. It then became the new home of the chamber of commerce.

Back in better days, the Lagonda Club's chief competitor had been Springfield's first country-type club, north of the city. Founded in 1898, the original country club was located one mile north of the center of town on the site of what is now the northwest corner of McCreight Avenue and North Limestone Street. The land had originally been part of the vast Alexander McCreight estate. Alexander McCreight's early nineteenth-century Federal-style house was still standing on the property and was pressed into service as the country club's clubhouse. Pasture land was converted into a nine-hole golf course. Springfield's first golf course was not an especially scenic or challenging course, being mostly level ground with no traps or bunkers and, interestingly, its greens were sand. Space was limited on this site and the club eventually outgrew it. Members wanted to expand activities in the future and were hoping to one day have a "sporty" 18-hole course with grass greens. More land was necessary in order to make that a reality.

The current Springfield Country Club got its start in 1906 when one of Springfield's most prosperous residents, Robert H. Foos, began contemplating the need for a larger place for outdoor recreation and sports for himself and his wealthy friends. Foos was aware that country clubs were becoming popular in cities across the United States and felt that the time was ripe for a growing community like Springfield to have a better club. He called together a group of friends to mull over the idea, and a search for land began at once. Fellow organizer Robert Rodgers located a farm north of the city that had once been part of the estate of William S. Thompson, a Springfield financier who bred Shetland ponies in his spare time. The farm lay north of Home Road and neighbored an area to the north and east that, at the time, remained in the hands of the Thompson family and was known as Signal Hill, so named due to a local legend that Native Americans had once built fires there and sent smoke signals that could be seen for miles.

In 1906, the portion of the old Thompson estate that country club organizers were interested in was owned by John A. Doyle. Doyle operated a greenhouse and lived on the south side of Home Road across from the farm in question and the neighboring Signal Hill land. Eight years later, Doyle would sell Harry Kissell a portion of his land on the south side of Home Road so that Kissell could complete Fountain Boulevard. But well before Ridgewood was ever platted, or the Springfield Country Club was located there, a number of Irish had lived in this rural area. St. Bernard's Catholic Church had established a cemetery in the area in 1879, and at the end of the nineteenth century Doyle located his greenhouse just east of the cemetery. The Doyle greenhouse grew only roses. At the time, Springfield grew more roses under glass than any other city in the world and was fast becoming known as the "Rose City." (In fact, there was a second greenhouse in the area, The Springfield Floral and Fern Company, located on the southwest corner of North Limestone Street and Floral Avenue, where St. Teresa's Catholic Church would be built in 1931.) *(See fig. 32, page 38 & fig. 36, page 40)*

Later residents protested against the Doyle greenhouse because it smacked of commercialism and they didn't want it there. It wasn't the greenhouse itself that posed a problem but the attendant piles of dirt, fertilizer, and an abundance of packing and shipping crates that were considered unsightly. And Doyle burnt bituminous coal to heat his greenhouse, a soft coal that burns dirtier than the harder anthracite coal. When winter set in, and he had to fire heavily to maintain adequate temperatures, the smoke really became

53. The original Springfield Country Club clubhouse.

objectionable. While future Ridgewood residents would complain about the greenhouse, it did not seem to deter the organizers of the Springfield Country Club in 1906. They found the grounds to be "admirably adapted for the purpose of a country club," and they purchased sixty and a half acres from Doyle and erected stone pillars on Home Road to mark the entrance to the new club. *(fig. 51)*

The entrance gave way to a curving drive that led to the soon-to-be completed clubhouse. An 1826 Federal-style house dubbed the "Manor House" came with the property, but the intent was to remodel an enormous barn that sat just southwest of the original homestead, for use as the clubhouse. The Manor House would serve as a temporary clubhouse until the remodeling of the barn could be completed. The huge barn sat on a ridge with a commanding view of the Mad River Valley, one of the most beautiful spots in the area and one that afforded cool, sweeping breezes on hot summer days. Local architect Robert C. Gotwald was hired to handle the remodeling at a cost not to exceed $4,000. The clubhouse would feature an enormous cement porch that wrapped around three sides of the building. During the summer months, the porch could be enclosed with screen, and in the winter with glass, to provide dining space with magnificent views of the surrounding countryside. The main entrance into the building would open into a large, open living room space with heavily beamed ceilings. *(fig's. 52 & 53)*

Comfort, not pretentiousness, was the aim for the décor of this room. It would be furnished with simple Mission-style furniture, card tables for the ladies, and easy chairs where they could pass the time with embroidering or reading while the gentlemen faced off on the golf course. Formal and informal events, including card parties, tea parties, luncheons, receptions, and dinners,

51. The original stone pillars at the entrance to the Springfield Country Club.

could be held on the large porch, in the interior dining room, and in the living room. The women's locker room would provide numbered wire lockers for each female member, as well as a lounge furnished in feminine white wicker and white enamel dressing tables.

The kitchen, where the club's chef held court, would be located in the basement, along with the men's locker room. A ballroom was planned for the top floor of the clubhouse where dances, a favorite activity of club members, could take place. The ballroom would be finished with white walls accented by woodwork in a delicate shade of green and French doors that opened out onto the porches. Numerous windows would provide abundant light and spectacular views for miles. Once the clubhouse was finished, the Manor House would be retained for various purposes. During the summer months, club members could lodge in the Manor House if they wished and enjoy the fact that it came fully equipped with live-in servants.

Perhaps most important to club organizers, six acres of the club grounds were to be set aside for a nine-hole golf course. After completion, it would quickly become one of the most popular spots in the area among wealthy men. The dream of an eighteen-hole course was still in the offing, but the Springfield Country Club immediately became Springfield's most exclusive club, with new members requiring approval of the club's board of governors. By the time Harry Kissell was platting Ridgewood, the club had a membership of nearly 400, with a considerable waiting list. Membership was de rigueur for the city's most prominent residents.

The Springfield Country Club was the ideal complement to

52. 1920s era image of the Manor House.

54. Fountain Blvd., where it intersects with Ardmore Rd. and Crescent Dr., circa 1925. Note the ornamental streetcar pole. A team of horses is visible to the right.

Ridgewood and the perfect draw for the type of people Kissell was hoping would become Ridgewood residents. The promise of fresh air, wide-open spaces, outdoor sports, and unparalleled prestige were an unbeatable combination. The Country Club clubhouse could function as the social center of the Ridgewood community, a plus especially for those who might be reluctant to leave behind the social opportunities of the city.

As winter receded and gave way to spring of 1915, work began again in earnest on Ridgewood. By late May, all the gas, water, and sewer lines were in. All the telephone and electric poles had been erected. While there was still much work to complete in the rest of the development, Fountain Boulevard was done. Work necessary for the streetcar had been completed before the first snowflake had flown the previous winter. The Springfield Street Railway Company had finished the streetcar tracks and installed the ornamental poles that carried its overhead lines. A new type of 1,000-watt nitrogen lamps were hung on the ornamental brackets on the streetcar poles to provide ample illumination at night. *(fig. 54 & 55)*

The roadway in the boulevard was paved, and the unique combination curb and gutter system was finished. The curb and gutter system had been the suggestion of Brown Burleigh, and would thereafter be referred to locally as

55. Looking north from the intersection of N. Fountain Ave. and McCreight Ave., February 14, 1915, at the newly completed N. Fountain Blvd. Compare to fig. 44, page 57.

the "Ridgewood gutter." Unlike the old gutters that were common throughout the city, the gently sloping Ridgewood gutter eased the sharp demarcation between the street and yard, and faded gracefully into the grass planting strip. In the other streets in Ridgewood, grading, paving, and the installation of curbs and gutters was proceeding. And the charming Mission-style streetcar waiting stations were being erected. *(See fig. 39, page 46)*

One of the new development's most distinctive features, its ornamental lighting system, was also being installed. On a trip to Chicago, Kissell had admired the granite lamp posts used in Lincoln and Washington Parks and thought they would be perfect for Ridgewood. They had a fresh look compared to the old-fashioned lampposts used elsewhere in Springfield. They were modern, but not ostentatious or flashy. They had an understated elegance that suited his vision for the neighborhood. The lampposts were being placed at street corners, as well as near the streetcar waiting stations, and at regular intervals along all the streets in the development. At intersections, the lamp globes were imprinted with street names, serving double duty as both street signs and sources of illumination. A good deal of the shrubbery had been placed in the triangular park spaces during the previous fall, and a number of new plantings were being set out this spring, including hundreds of American elms. Finally, and most symbolically, the ornamental brick entrance bearing the Ridgewood name was being erected at the threshold of the development at Fountain Boulevard and McCreight Avenue.

As opening day for lot sales loomed, activity in Ridgewood went into overdrive. Workmen hurried to complete the lighting system. Chief engineer George Haller drove the grading and paving operations toward completion. A temporary sales office was erected on a lot on the east side of Fountain Boulevard, across from Dover Road where the Guy and Jane Bayley House, at 1926 North Fountain Boulevard, would eventually be built. And the

Unrestricted Springfield

56. A photographic depiction of unrestricted sections of Springfield, from a 1915 Ridgewood promotional booklet.

Ridgewood streetcar, which would be occupied mostly by potential buyers and sightseers for many months to come, was running regularly between the development and the downtown transfer station.

As construction was moving towards completion, Harry Kissell and Brown Burleigh hashed out the final marketing strategy. As sales manager, much of the burden of whether Ridgewood would be a success or not fell squarely on Burleigh's shoulders. Kissell admired Burleigh's sharp head for business and urbane sophistication and felt that he was the perfect man to turn the vision of the Ridgewood proposition into a reality. Like Kissell, Burleigh was a Springfield native, born in 1883 to a prominent local family. He was also a Wittenberg graduate. He had various jobs before joining the Kissell organization as secretary and sales manager in 1908.

Harry Kissell conveyed his opinion on the importance of the role of a sales manager in not only selling lots but in shaping the development into a desirable neighborhood when he told a group of fellow realtors that he believed that the most effective sales managers needed to have considerable knowledge of architecture and interior decorating. He felt that these qualities were essential in order for them to guide prospective lot buyers in the types of homes they would build. While he didn't go as far as Edward Bouton and reserve the right to approve all architectural plans, Kissell was intent that Ridgewood not be "a conglomerate mass of houses" but that "it be well worked out together."

Kissell wanted Ridgewood to be architecturally harmonious, but most of all he wanted it to be a neighborhood—a community. The last thing he wanted was a bunch of empty lots. He wanted building activity, and so the focus would stay on the end product when courting prospective customers. While they would never turn away anyone wanting to buy a lot on speculation as an investment, they would concentrate on finding buyers who wanted to build a home. Encouraging early building was essential to the success of any new suburb. Potential customers needed to see homes going up in order for them to have faith that Ridgewood would really develop into a neighborhood and not suffer the fate of many early suburbs that ended up as vast wastelands on which only a few houses were ever built.

In late May, Burleigh was also busy readying his sales team, making sure each of his men was familiar with every square inch of the property, could speak with ease and fluency of the amenities Ridgewood had to offer, and had mastered the details of the restrictive covenants. Salesmen began working prospect lists and making preliminary calls to let potential buyers know that lots would soon go on sale.

A high-quality promotional booklet had been prepared to explain the ideas behind the development of Ridgewood and the many amenities that it would offer. The booklet was to be mailed directly to a select list of prospective customers right before sales began. A map with a bird's- eye view of the new development was included, but one of the most interesting aspects of the booklet was a photographic depiction of the unrestricted sections of Springfield. The images showed billboards on empty lots next to a fine house on East High Street (whose owner would later move to Ridgewood), unsightly fences and telephone poles in other areas, and examples of stables and other unwanted commercial development intruding into otherwise nice residential districts. It provided a vivid and effective display of what had happened locally in areas without restrictions and offered Ridgewood as the remedy to such problems. *(fig. 56)*

Because the idea of a "restricted" subdivision was such a novelty in 1915, Kissell penned an article that appeared that spring in the *Springfield Daily News* to explain the philosophy behind such a development. His task was to sell the new idea and turn a perceived negative into a positive. The goal was to get potential buyers to see that a few judicious restrictions of one's property rights would result in considerable protection of their property values. Once this was accomplished, the restrictions could be utilized as an effective sales tool. Later ads would declare, "The restrictions are worth the price of the lot," but changing the perceptions of people would take time.

Besides the novelty of the restricted suburb, Kissell and Burleigh had other obstacles to overcome. They were asking Springfield's finest citizens, many of whom were already comfortably ensconced in nice, established neighborhoods, to leave behind neighbors and friends for what was essentially empty land out in the countryside with a few saplings and some very nice roads. The big question was—Would they be willing to take the leap of faith?

Community interest in Ridgewood was mounting as opening day loomed, and the newspaper followed the progress with great detail. On Sunday, June 6, 1915, the newspaper announced that the entrance "arches" had just been completed and the lights had been turned on along the boulevard for the first time. The newspaper also reported, "During the last few days hundreds of people have driven through the boulevard in automobiles and other vehicles and admired the improvements completed. The waiting stations are finished and ready for use." The paper also noted that home construction was already under way—"The Kissell Building Company has broken ground for two handsome homes to be erected in this addition by Harry S. Kissell and Brown Burleigh.

Others are to be started within a short time from present indications." Sunday, June 6, 1915, was also the day that the very first advertisement for Ridgewood appeared in the newspaper. The ad proudly announced that after a year of frenetic development work, lots in "Ridgewood—In the Country Club District" would go on sale Thursday, June 17, 1915.

Later that week, The Kissell Improvement Company held a banquet for members of the Springfield Real Estate Board at the Arcade Hotel. Local realtors were provided with advanced promotional materials and price lists, and then transported out to the plat to see the improvements firsthand. Brown Burleigh and his sales team explained the pricing system of the various areas of the development. Some big developers of high-grade neighborhoods in other cities would deride Kissell for allowing other realtors to make sales in his development, but Kissell understood the reality of his own situation.

There was, at the time, virtually no competition for the high-grade real estate market in Springfield. Although this would change in the near future, the market would never be glutted with high-class residential property. Kissell was not competing for affluent buyers with his fellow board members at the time. He essentially had the market cornered, but he also knew that other realtors had loyal customers who would go to them first when seeking to upgrade, and Kissell wanted them to bring those buyers to Ridgewood. It was business he could not afford to turn down. In fact, he offered the same commission to outside realtors that he paid his own salesmen, 4 to 7 percent, on the sale of each lot.

Kissell was confident that this wouldn't demoralize his sales team because these were customers that his men would never have gotten a chance at anyway. It proved to be a smart move because in the first year, Kissell's competitors sold about $40,000 worth of Ridgewood lots for him. And there was a feeling of honor among the real estate agents in Springfield. No one would attempt to steal away a Kissell salesman's prospect. They played square with each other. The real estate profession in Springfield was a particularly well-knit community. Although they were ardent competitors, they were first and foremost honorable gentlemen, an antidote to the shysters and con men that had run amok in the real estate business in the previous century.

Following the initial newspaper advertisement on June 6, 1915, large Ridgewood ads continued to run each day in anticipation of the opening day of sales on June 17. Earlier that spring, Kissell and Burleigh had worked out the advertisements that would run almost daily throughout June and July. Ads would focus on offering Ridgewood as the answer to the potential buyer's desire for space, light, fresh air and sunshine, and freedom from dirt, noises,

and bad smells—a healthful haven that was the antidote to city life. Ridgewood would also be promoted as a place of both architectural and natural beauty, one of social advantages with its proximity to the country club, and, due to the restrictions, a safe investment for homeowners. The sprawling yards, ready for landscaping and beautification, were also the focus of several advertisements.

One major selling point was that, unlike other residential sections of the city, the developer had paid for all the improvements in Ridgewood. In the early twentieth century, the cost of extending public services and improvements such as sewer, water, and pavements were shouldered by the property owners along a particular street in the form of assessments. Property owners had to petition the city for improvements and pay for them in annual installments of five to ten years. However, in Ridgewood, the price of the lot included all improvements. A number of early "developments" in or near Springfield did not have any improvements at all. Often a plat was filed and lots were simply staked off, and that was the sole contribution of the developer. Other times, developers would promise improvements that never materialized. This happened with such frequency that finally the city started insisting on a minimum level of improvements in a new development.

Subsequent ads for Ridgewood would drive home the message that it was in close proximity to the city but offered freedom from the smoke, noise, smell, and congestion of the city. "Out of the Noise Zone into the Ozone," the first Ridgewood slogan, reflected this idea. Other amenities—convenient streetcar service, ample streetlights, large lots in a park-like setting, the quality and proximity of the Jefferson School (one of the newest public schools at the time)—were also featured. Another ad bid people to come and see the effects of the granite lamps that were being placed every 150 feet along the streets of Ridgewood. "Have you been through Ridgewood at night? It's a revelation," the ad stated.

Another feature touted in ads for years to come was that the elevation of Ridgewood was fifty feet higher than that of Fountain Square in downtown Springfield. One of the most desirable qualities of Ridgewood was that it was sited on a large ridge that ran along the city's northern edge between two river valleys, which meant sweeping southwest breezes that supposedly kept the temperature many degrees cooler than in the rest of Springfield. This was a huge selling point in the days before air conditioning. The elevation was also plugged as a plus for health reasons because sewage flows downstream. Back in the days when all sewers, both storm and sanitary, emptied into Buck Creek, this claim was probably given great weight by prospective buyers and most certainly fueled the "northward trend" of new residential development.

One early Kissell advertisement drew comparisons between Ridgewood and other prime residential streets like North Fountain Avenue. Although there were a number of fine homes on North Fountain Avenue between Buck Creek and McCreight Avenue, the street was only sixty-six feet wide as opposed to the 100-foot-wide Fountain Boulevard. The pavement on North Fountain Avenue was fourteen years old and ready for replacement, a cost that property owners would have to bear. Furthermore, there were no restrictions to protect homeowners. The interurban line ran right up the center of the street, instead of having its own safe, segregated space like the streetcar in Ridgewood, and it provided no direct service to the avenue. North Fountain Avenue residents had to disembark from the interurban on North Limestone Street, then walk several blocks west to the avenue. Or they could ride the streetcar into Ridgewood and backtrack south to their homes. In addition, setbacks of houses on North Fountain Avenue were much smaller than the fifty-five-foot setback line on lots on North Fountain Boulevard. *(See fig. 26, page 29)*

Even though North Fountain Avenue lots lacked many of the amenities of Ridgewood, some had sold recently for $50 to $60 a front foot, whereas a Ridgewood lot on the boulevard could be had for the same price and included all the improvements. Comparing Ridgewood lot prices to those in older upscale neighborhoods was an effective sales tactic that would be used over and over because the highest-priced lots in Ridgewood were still often lower than the lowest-priced lots in established residential areas such as East High Street and Elmwood Place, which had fewer amenities and no restrictions.

Two days before lots officially went on sale, an ad announced that Ridgewood homesites would be available on a convenient payment plan—10 percent of the price of the lot in cash was required, and the balance was payable at the Kissell offices in monthly payments of one dollar on the hundred dollars of the balance due. The interest rate was fixed at 6 percent. One

SALE TOMORROW

IT IS CERTAIN

That lot prices will never be as low again at

RIDGEWOOD

As they are today

As the property develops additional value will be given to every lot and we cannot lay too deep emphasis upon the importance of immediate selection to those who have the buying of a home site in mind.

You'll learn more about this beautiful property by a visit than we can tell you here in a whole page—and there is no better time for you to go there than right now—today.

The man who makes an investment in RIDGEWOOD will get more for his money than is offered elsewhere, and it will be valuable always. He will be protected by restrictions that will defend his home and his family against undesirable invasion, and he will live amid surroundings that are as healthful and as beautiful as the best available engineering and artistic skill can make them.

RIDGEWOOD

"IN THE COUNTRY CLUB DISTRICT"

OWNED AND OFFERED BY

THE KISSELL IMPROVEMENT CO.

721 to 724 FAIRBANKS BUILDING. SPRINGFIELD, OHIO.

OFFICE IN RIDGEWOOD ON FOUNTAIN BOULEVARD

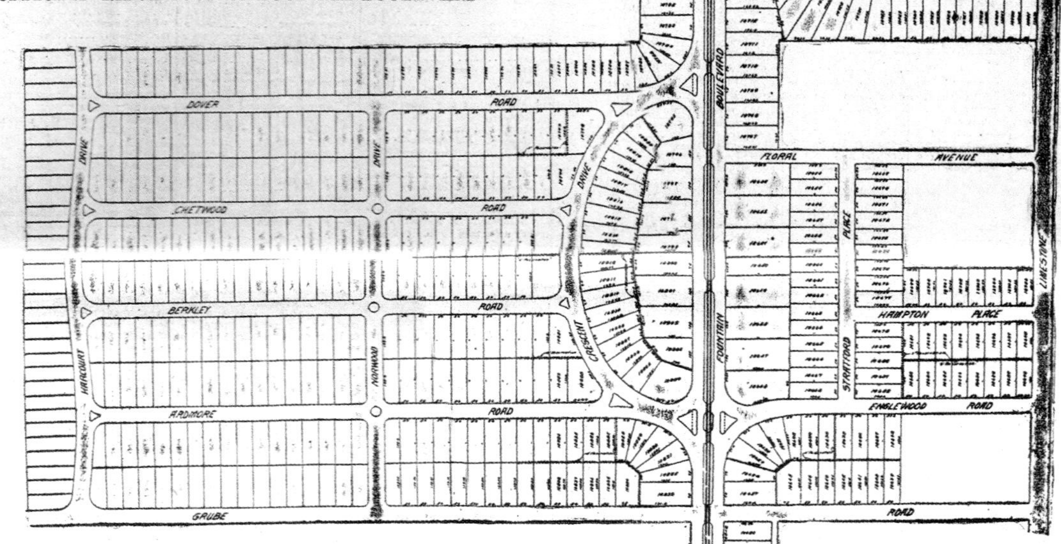

"THE RESTRICTIONS ARE WORTH THE PRICE OF THE LOT"

PLEASE READ CAREFULLY

RESTRICTIONS COMMON TO ALL STREETS

Premises to be used for residence purposes only and not for any purpose of business or trade.

Free or open space shall be left on each side of every building on said premises. The aggregate width of the free spaces on both sides of any building must not be less than thirty per cent of the width of the building, and not less than two-fifths of this free space must be left on either side of the building, but these free spaces may be encroached upon by one-story porches, steps, terraces or other one-story extensions.

No building or erection of any kind, excepting eaves, cornices, one-story bay windows, one-story verandas, one-story portecocheres and structures of a like character (constructed in connection with any dwelling house erected inside of said building line) shall be erected or maintained on any portion of said premises which lies outside of said building lines herein specified.

No fences shall be erected on said premises nearer to the street than the building lines herein described. If the within described lot is a corner lot, no fence other than an open construction ornamental fence shall be constructed or maintained nearer to the side street than the building line on such side street; and no fence shall be constructed more than six feet high anywhere on said premises.

All sanitary drainage must be effected by proper connection with the sanitary sewer.

Intoxicating liquors shall not be manufactured or sold on said premises.

No bill boards or advertising boards shall be constructed or maintained for the posting, painting or printing of signs or advertisements upon said premises.

RESTRICTIONS COMMON TO ALL STREETS EXCEPTING FOUNTAIN BOULEVARD

Only one single or double private dwelling house or residential apartment building with necessary outbuildings shall be erected or maintained on one lot. Special side building line restrictions for all corner lots.

FOUNTAIN BOULEVARD

Minimum price, $4,500. No double or duplex or apartment house and only one single private dwelling house with necessary outbuildings shall be erected or maintained on one lot. Front building line, 55 feet (some exceptions).

KENSINGTON PLACE—NORTH AND SOUTH

Minimum Price—Single houses, $3,000; double houses, $4,500. Front building line, 40 feet.
10743 and 10744 single house only, minmum price $4,000.

CRESCENT DRIVE

Minimum Price—Single houses, $3,000; double houses, $4,500. Front building line, 40 feet (some exceptions).

ENGLEWOOD ROAD—SOUTH SIDE, EXCEPT 10637 AND 10638

Minimum Price—Single houses, $3,000; double houses, $4,500. 10637 and 10638, minimum price, single houses, $2,500; double houses, $4,000. Front building line, 40 feet (some exceptions).

ENGLEWOOD ROAD—NORTH SIDE

Minimum Price—Single houses, $2,000; double houses, $3,500. Front building line, 30 feet.

STRATFORD PLACE

Minimum Price—Single houses, $2,500; double houses, $4,000. Front building line, 40 feet.

HAMPTON PLACE

Minimum Price—Single houes, $2,000; double houses, $3,500. Front building line, 30 feet.

ARDMORE ROAD—BERKLEY ROAD—CHETWOOD ROAD—DOVER ROAD

Minimum Price—Single houses, $3,000; double houses, $4,500. 10792 and 10822 restricted to single houses, minimum price, $4,000. Front building line, 40 feet (some exceptions).

GRUBE ROAD—WEST OF FOUNTAIN BOULEVARD

Minimum Price—Single houses, $3,000; double houses, $4,500. Front building line, 40 feet.

GRUBE ROAD—EAST OF FOUNTAIN BOULEVARD

Minimum Price—Single houses, $2,500; double houses, $4,000. Front building line, 40 feet.

Reservations for public utilities of from 4 feet to 8 feet at rear of every lot and at side of some lots.

Lots sell for cash, or, if you prefer, pay 10 per cent down and the balance in monthly payments. If you don't want to build at once on the lot you buy, make an investment.

Springfield's Only High-Grade Restricted Residence District

- Ornamental lighting for all streets.
- Efficient street car service.
- Fountain Boulevard paved with asphalt its entire length.
- All other streets paved with Tarvia macadam.
- Natural gas for every lot.
- Sanitary sewer for every lot.
- City water for every lot.
- Electric lights.
- Storm water sewers.
- Park spaces and flower beds.
- Wide grass plots.
- Cement walks, curbs and gutters.
- Street car waiting stations.
- Proper restrictions.
- No assessments.
- Maintenance fund.
- Public school at entrance.
- Cash or payments.

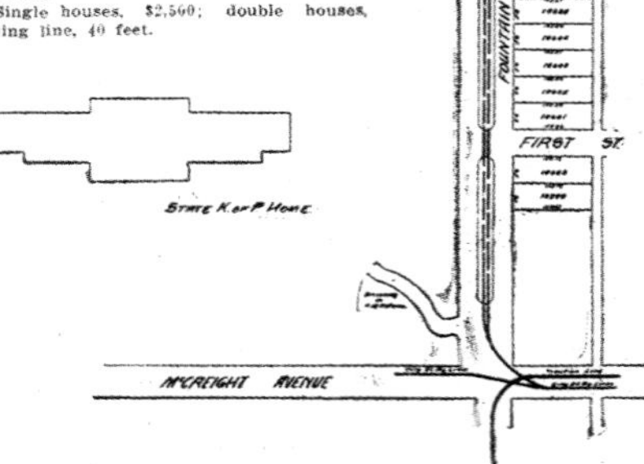

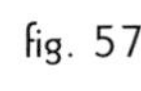

fig. 57

could buy a $3,500 lot with a $350 down payment and a monthly payment of $31.50. Extending financing to buyers represented another major gamble on Kissell's part. By offering a payment plan, he opened up the possibility of buying a lot in Ridgewood to more people, but he also ran the risk of buyers defaulting and sales falling through. Expanding the availability of financing for real estate purchases would become a central component of Kissell's career, but only time would tell if it was, in this particular case, a foolhardy decision or a wise one.

On Wednesday, June 16, 1915, the day before lots went on sale, a nearly full-page ad for Ridgewood appeared in the *Springfield Daily News*. The ad featured a map of the development, and all of the improvements and amenities were noted. For the first time, the deed restrictions were spelled out in detail. The restrictions set minimum prices for houses that could be built on each particular street. They stipulated the percentage of the lot that the house could occupy, as well as the amount of open space required between houses in order to ensure ample fresh air and sunshine for each home. They also banned one-story houses, fences closer to the street than the building line of the house, all billboards and advertising signs of any kind, including "for sale" signs, and all commercial activity. *(fig. 57)*

The map not only showed the original section of Ridgewood, which included most of Fountain Boulevard, Crescent Drive, North and South Kensington Place, Englewood Road, Stratford and Hampton Place, twelve lots on Grube Road, and a few lots on Dover and Ardmore Roads, but it illustrated what was envisioned for the land west of Fountain Boulevard and Crescent Drive. Originally, Kissell had planned for that particular piece of land to be the next phase of Ridgewood. But circumstances would intervene, and it would become the final phase of Ridgewood instead, undeveloped until the autumn of 1922. Like the earlier bird's-eye view map included in the Ridgewood promotional booklet, the map in the newspaper advertisement depicted this future phase of development as being laid out on a rectilinear grid pattern, with regular-shaped lots. Interestingly, the map featured street names, Harcourt Drive and Chetwood Road, that were never utilized.

The placement of this ad on a Wednesday was intentional. Many businessmen and professionals had Wednesday afternoon off, and Kissell and Burleigh were counting on them to take the opportunity to come out that afternoon for a preview of Springfield's most talked about residential property before sales officially commenced the next day. While work was still being completed on some of the side streets, enough of it was done to debut the new subdivision. With vision and nerve—and after clearing a myriad of obstacles—this "monument to civic pride and progress," as the newspaper would dub it, was ready to be unveiled. Kissell and Burleigh were anxious to show off what one year of work by hundreds of men and a total outlay of over a quarter of a million dollars, a staggering up-front investment of private capital at the time, had wrought.

Finally the day that everyone had been working feverishly for, the biggest gamble in Springfield real estate history, was here. An ad in the newspaper on the morning of Thursday, June 17, 1915, announced that the "Sale Begins Today" and offered low introductory prices to encourage early building. Lot prices ranged from $725 for some lots on Stratford and Hampton Place, Grube Road, and Englewood Road, to $4,500 for lots on Fountain Boulevard.

The Kissell Improvement Company team stationed themselves at the temporary sales office in Ridgewood. A newspaper reporter was there to cover opening day. At noon, the reporter questioned Harry Kissell regarding a program for the afternoon. Kissell said that this was a different kind of project than others—"There will be no program, band concert, or fireworks," he said. "This is purely a business proposition. The citizens are given an opportunity to come out and inspect the addition and select their lots." While opening day was not marked by much fanfare, the turnout was gratifying. The evening newspaper remarked, "Much interest is being manifested in the sale of lots in Ridgewood. For the last week or more, the citizens have been reading about Ridgewood and its attractiveness. This afternoon a large number went out to inspect the addition and sale of lots which they will use as building sites for homes."

Three days later, on June 20, 1915, Kissell reported to the newspaper that sales during the first week had been better than expected, and that he was "greatly pleased with the number of lots purchased the first week." He added that surfacing of streets, installation of streetlights, and other finishing touches would be rushed. The public, however, was waiting with great anticipation for concrete sales figures.

The following day they got their answer when another large advertisement proudly trumpeted that Ridgewood "had been given the stamp of approval by the citizens of Springfield." On opening day, $42,450 worth of lots had sold. "Our prophecy that the city was ready for a high-grade, restricted residence district has come true and our fondest hopes have been realized," the ad stated. Things were off to a great start. Sales were good, and building activity was already underway. The Kissell Building Company had started the foundation for Harry and Olive Kissell's own home on North Fountain Boulevard. Likewise, the Burleigh house was well underway. Newlyweds Brown and May Burleigh had chosen a lot on South Kensington Place and were erecting a charming Dutch Colonial, scheduled for completion by the fall of that year. And it was expected that ground would soon be broken for several other homes.

A new series of Ridgewood newspaper advertisements was rolled out, which focused attention on the individual sections of the development. In the most moderately-priced section of Englewood Road and Stratford and Hampton Place, lots ranged in price from $725 to $1,800. The smaller, uniform-sized lots and narrower streets made this the most economical area of Ridgewood. The ad copy for this section pointed out that lot owners on these streets enjoyed all the same amenities of Ridgewood that buyers on pricier streets did, but at a more affordable price. Not surprisingly, these lots sold very quickly and most houses erected exceeded the minimums required for price and size. *(fig's. 58 & 59)*

Another new ad featured North and South Kensington Place and publicized these streets as "nearest to the Country Club." Lyrical ad copy described this section: "This beautiful street leaves Fountain Boulevard. And is a seventy-foot thoroughfare opening onto a sixty-foot triangle park space with an ornamental lamp post in its center, to be surrounded with shrubbery and the whole bordered with flowers and grass. At this point Kensington Place divides and by most graceful curves becomes Kensington Place, North and South. These two streets will be beautifully lighted their entire length with the same ornamental lighting as is used for this purpose at all the street entrances on the boulevard." *(fig's. 60 & 61)*

58. The vacant lots on the east side of Fountain Blvd., south of Floral Ave. Homes along the well built-up streets of Stratford and Hampton Place are visible in the background., circa 1925.

An ad featuring Crescent Drive revealed that the inspiration for it had

61. The north side of N. Kensington Pl., taken from the southwest corner of N. Limestone St. and N. Kensington Pl., circa 1925.

come from the road in Snyder Park that curved gently around the park's playground area. Lots on Crescent Drive were the second most expensive lots after Fountain Boulevard. Only Crescent Drive and a very small portion of Ardmore and Dover Roads were completed west of Fountain Boulevard in the first phase of development. Curb cuts were made on the west side of Crescent Drive for two streets planned for a later phase—Berkley and Chetwood Roads. However, Chetwood Road was never constructed after plans for the later phase evolved in the years between its initial planning and actual construction. *(fig's. 62, 63 & 64)*

Another lyrical narrative illustrated this section of the development: "Ardmore Road and Crescent Drive leave the boulevard on either side of the first streetcar waiting station, divide on the triangle, then they become one street and divide again, Crescent Drive taking a northwesterly course and Ardmore Road the west. Six beautiful triangular park spaces, similar to those on Fountain Boulevard, planted with shrubbery and each having an ornamental lamp post, will be found on Crescent Drive. (The triangular spaces were eventually reduced to five when the plan for Chetwood Road was abandoned.) By a most graceful curve Crescent Drive joins Dover Road and leads out to the boulevard at the second waiting station in the same manner as it entered further down." The ad also called attention to

59. View of the intersection of Fountain Blvd. and Englewood Rd, circa 1925.

60. The northwest corner of Fountain Blvd. and Broadmoor Blvd., looking southeast down Kensington Pl., circa 1925.

the unique irregularly-shaped lots in this area, making possible "the artistic placing of homes on spacious lawns."

On July 13, 1915, an ad ran with a headline that trumpeted, "Character of Ridgewood Has Been Established." The Kissell Improvement Company was able to happily report that over $101,225 worth of lots had been sold in just over three weeks. Kissell and Burleigh were ecstatic. It was a mark that the sales department had not projected to reach until January of 1916, and they took it as affirmation that their instincts were right: "It shows that there is a demand for a high-grade protected residence section in Springfield and that we have met that demand." They further maintained, "We believe the picture of a modern home, built broadside on a broad lot surrounded by shrubbery and open spaces exists in the minds of a great many in Springfield." Thus far, the gamble had paid off. However, there was new competition on the horizon.

In 1915, in an effort to alleviate the housing famine

63 (above). The section of Ardmore Rd. completed in the initial phase of the development of Ridgewood, looking northeast toward Fountain Blvd. The Kissell home at 1801 N. Fountain Blvd. is barely visible to the left, circa 1925.

64 (left). The small section of Dover Rd. completed in the first phase of Ridgewood, taken from the southwest corner of Dover Rd. and Longview Dr., looking east, circa 1925.

62. Looking south down Crescent Dr., circa 1925. The Hutchinson home, at 1812 Crescent Dr., and the Talbott home, at 1824 Crescent Dr. are visible to the left.

in Springfield, residential building was going on in all directions of the city, but a decidedly northward trend was becoming increasingly apparent. The oldest sections of the city lay south of Buck Creek, and most of the residential building in the nineteenth century took place there. As the city expanded, however, it naturally started to spread to the abundant empty land that lay north of Buck Creek. By the early twentieth century, the north side was quickly starting to become fashionable, especially with the arrival of Ridgewood on the scene. This northward trend would only gain momentum as time went on and would persist throughout the twentieth century.

One of the most popular residential developments contemporary to Ridgewood was Northern Heights, which was platted in 1913 and offered for sale in July of 1914, just as development work was getting in full swing in Ridgewood. Northern Heights featured 265 building lots and was located off the east side of North Limestone Street, north of the upscale Rogers Place Addition along East Cassilly Street and south of McCreight Avenue. The development officially fronted on McCreight Avenue with a view of the

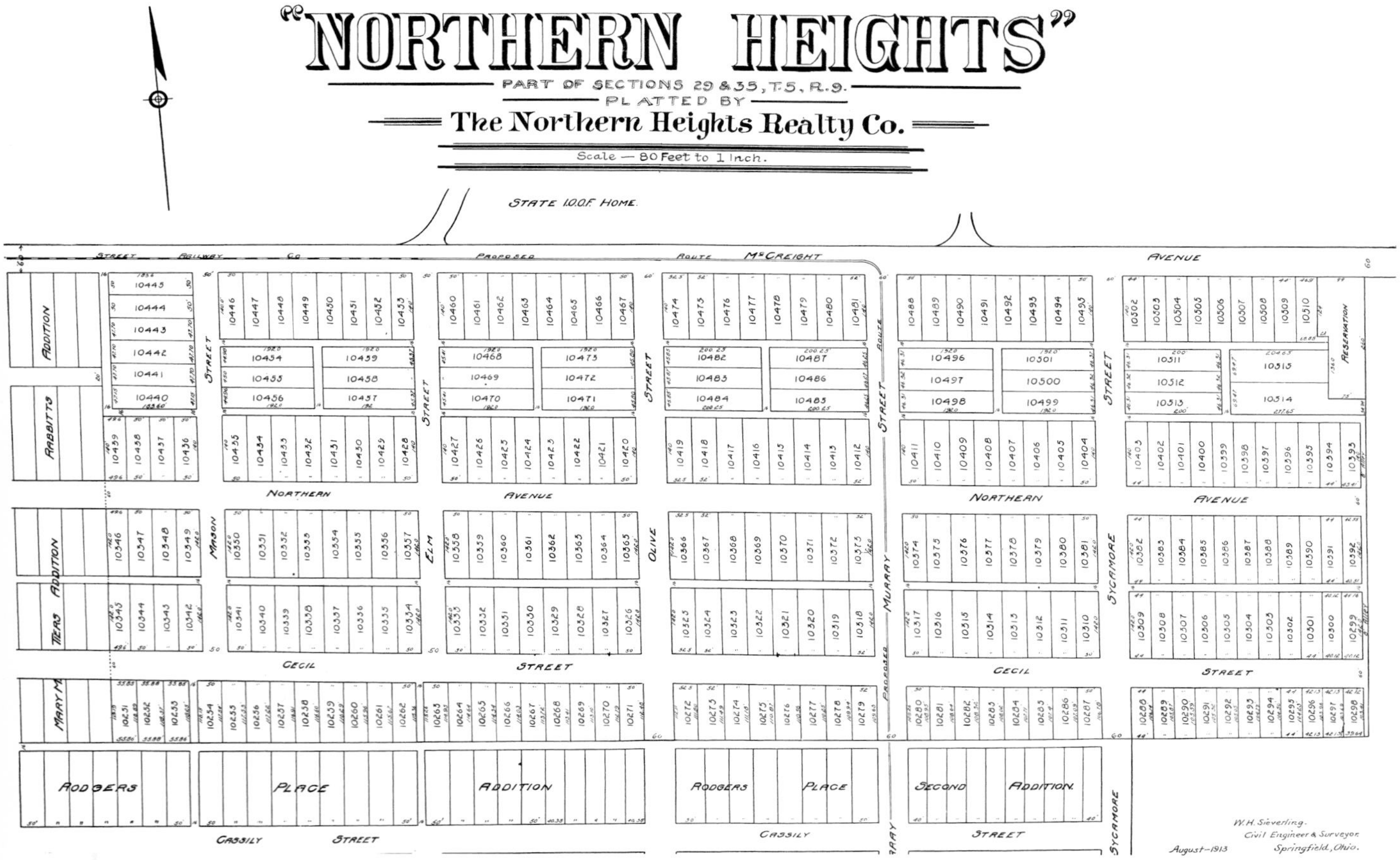

"NORTHERN HEIGHTS"
PART OF SECTIONS 29 & 35, T.5, R.9.
PLATTED BY
The Northern Heights Realty Co.
Scale — 80 Feet to 1 Inch.

fig. 65

beautiful I.O.O.F. Home. However, it was Northern Avenue, known locally as "Maple Row"—due to the gigantic maple trees that formed an arch over the entire length of the street—that was featured most often in advertising. *(fig's. 65 & 66)*

Mature trees were in short supply in most new developments that had previously been cultivated agricultural land, so trees were a great selling point. Ads for Northern Heights reminded buyers that in this development, "You do not wait for shade trees—they are there in all their glory." The site on which Northern Heights was developed had originally been the grounds of the old Clark County Infirmary, and the beautiful maple-lined Northern Avenue was once the tree-lined lane going back to the infirmary building. The infirmary building itself was later converted for use as the Northern Heights School.

Northern Heights was sufficiently removed from the ills of the city but was still easily accessible. Streetcar service was available at McCreight Avenue, or it was a twenty-minute walk from Main Street, which was considered a reasonable walk in those days. Advertisements played up its suburban location with the slogan, "Out of City Rush—Not in the Country Hush." Like Ridgewood and other suburban developments, it offered a compromise between city and country life. And like Ridgewood, one of its most appealing attributes was that there were no railroad tracks to cross in order to get to Northern Heights. Northern Heights also boasted cement streets, curbs and gutters, electricity, city water, natural gas, and storm sewers, but not sanitary sewers initially.

Although Northern Heights offered many of the same amenities

66. A September 30, 1915 newspaper ad for Northern Heights.

as Ridgewood, it was aimed at buyers with average income levels like skilled laborers and low-level managers. Lots were laid out on the rectilinear grid and were narrow, requiring the inclusion of back alleys in order to access garages, and there were no comprehensive deed restrictions. Lot prices ranged from $612 to $1,362. Payment plans were available with only $25 down. Homes in Ridgewood were typically designed by an architect, but most homes in Northern Heights were usually planned by a builder who oftentimes consulted one of the many home pattern books popular in this era. Mail order homes from Sears and Roebuck, Montgomery Ward, and Aladdin were also popular in this neighborhood. Early twentieth century house types that were in vogue at the time, including the bungalow and the American Foursquare, predominated. Northern Heights was a popular and successful development from the start but not a competitor for the high-end buyers that Kissell was targeting with Ridgewood.

Kissell's first real competitor was about to emerge on the horizon, however. In early 1915, two successful Columbus real estate developers, Theodore Weyant and P.J. Guthrie, purchased an eighty-acre tract of land along Saint Paris Pike, north of Ferncliff Cemetery, with the intent of developing it into a residential neighborhood. The land, which had been part of a farm owned by James and Mary Sheaff, but had never been put under cultivation, featured rolling topography and virgin forest. Weyant and Guthrie called their new venture "The Home Improvement Company," and Guthrie hired a sales force and set up offices on the eighth floor of the Fairbanks Building, one floor above The Kissell Improvement Company.

The land they acquired was uniquely beautiful, boasting towering oak and elms trees, verdant knolls, and scenic ravines, all of which made for a rustic, sylvan oasis that would have made Andrew Jackson Downing and Frederick Law Olmsted proud. Theodore Weyant, who had financial backing from an investor in Saginaw, Michigan, filed a plat in June of 1915, and aptly named the new development Hills and Dales. Weyant's plan was for Hills and Dales to be an upscale allotment that, like Ridgewood, provided a variety of price options and would cater to the widest number of potential buyers in the high-grade market. The southernmost portion of the plat was flatter and would feature straight streets and more regular shaped "bungalow" lots starting at $300. But the rest of the development would play up the natural beauty of land. *(fig. 67)*

Excavation for streets in the hilly section would be extremely limited because they were to be located in the meandering valleys that curved around the wooded knolls. The goal was to preserve as much of the natural contours of the land as possible. Preservation of trees was a priority as well. The trees of the old-growth forest had been there since before Springfield was populated by white settlers and would remain untouched. Only underbrush and dead timber would be removed. Many of the large "estate" lots in this hilly section would be irregularly shaped to lend to the natural appearance of the plat. The winding drives were to be of Tarvia macadam. Hill and Dales would boast many of the same amenities as Ridgewood including cement walks, deed restrictions, water, gas, electricity, and storm sewers, but no sanitary sewers at the time. Streetcar service could be had by walking several blocks south to McCreight Avenue and catching the K of P car.

Meanwhile, advertisements for Ridgewood continued to run almost daily until the end of July 1915. This later wave of ads shifted the focus away from the amenities, which had already been presented in great detail, and focused instead on persuasive arguments that appealed to both the practical nature and personal aspirations of potential buyers. A July 19, 1915, ad appealed to the manly ambitions of the family breadwinner, stating that home ownership "develops the best that is in a man." Even in the male dominated society of 1915, however, Kissell regarded women as the true decision makers in the

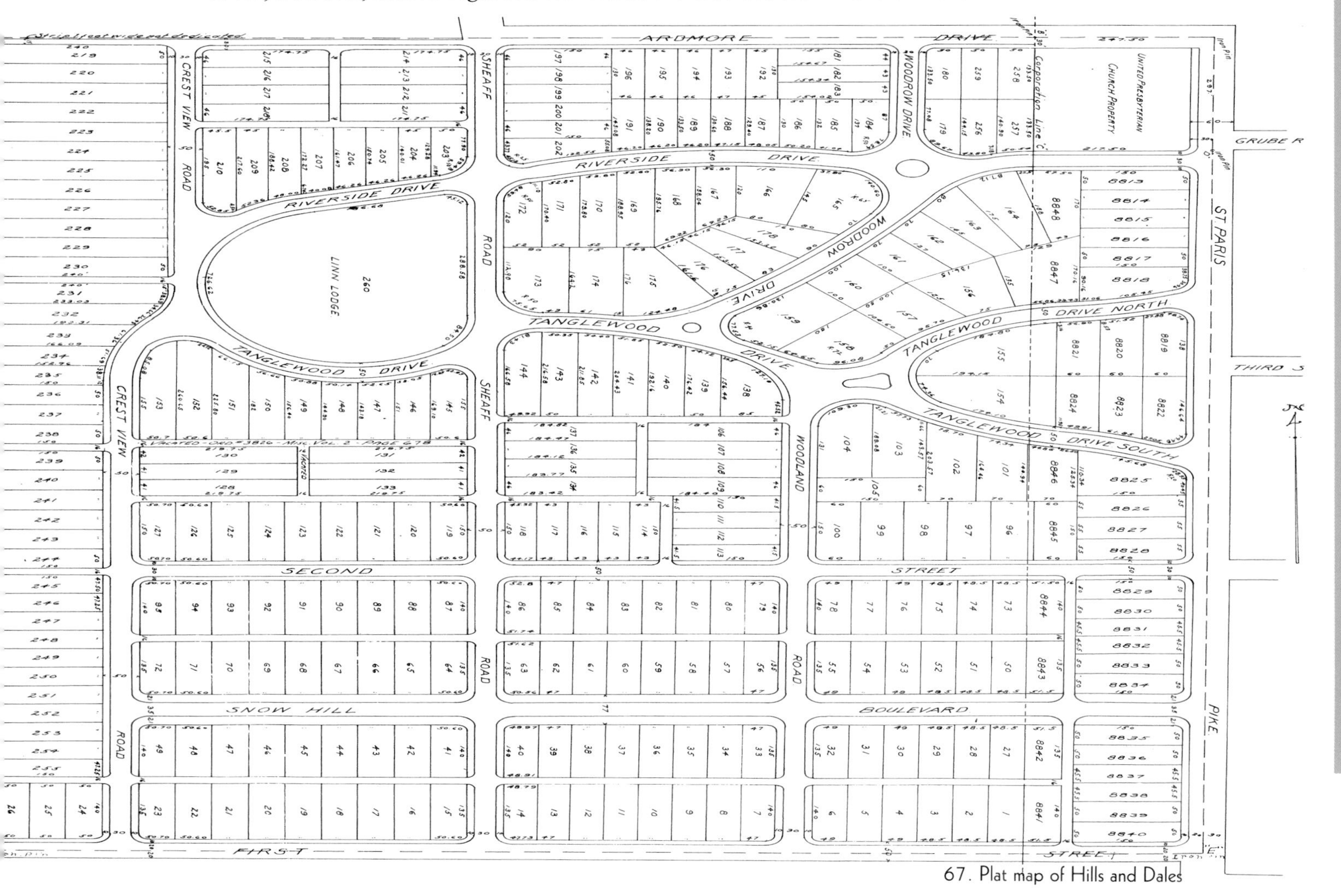

67. Plat map of Hills and Dales

home. He addressed a number of ads to "Mrs. Homemaker" and made a habit of placing all ads near the society columns in the newspaper in order to catch the ladies' eyes. He told a group of fellow real estate men, "There is always some one person that decides the sale; the husband may think he is deciding the sale, but he often is not deciding it, it is the wife . . . not always, but ninety-nine out of a hundred it is."

On August 15, 1915, two weeks after the Ridgewood ads ceased, The Home Improvement Company ran its first advertisement for Hills and Dales even though very little work had been done in the development at the time. Storm sewers and roadwork had started as soon as the plat was accepted, but these were still in their earliest stages. This first ad featured a map of the proposed development and explained all the amenities that were planned. The advertisement also featured photos of the abundant trees in the area, a practice that would be routine in future ads in order to emphasize the natural beauty of the plat, its biggest selling point. The slogan, "Every Look Means a Lot," underscored the unique beauty of the development and suggested that once you saw it, you were bound to buy there.

Unlike Kissell, Weyant and Guthrie blatantly encouraged speculative buying in Hills and Dales as an easy way to make money. They were also deliberate in their effort to equate themselves with the quality of Ridgewood, stating in advertisements that Hill and Dales "compares most favorably with the now popular subdivision of the same character artistically planned and wisely restricted."

70 (top). Entrance foyer and living room of the Burleigh house, 1915.
69 (above). The first home completed in Ridgewood, 30 S. Kensington Pl., was occupied by Brown and May Burleigh in the fall of 1915.

But at the same time, Weyant and Guthrie were quick to play up features that distinguished Hills and Dales from Ridgewood, emphasizing the "monarchs of the forest, which take a lifetime to grow," and even taking a direct jab at Kissell by stating, "Nature has done for Hills and Dales what man can but poorly imitate."

By late September, The Kissell Improvement Company was ready to fire back. No ads for Ridgewood had run between the end of July and late September. This was a deliberate decision by Kissell and Burleigh. They could not compete with the mature trees and hilly terrain of Hills and Dales, but they could offer what Hills and Dales could not—a finished product. When ads resumed on September 26, 1915, all the improvements in Ridgewood had been completed and they proudly declared, "Remember, these improvements are not promises, but facts." A bit of skepticism on the part of Kissell and Burleigh about the promises of outside developers with no vested interest, other than financial, in the community was apparent in subsequent Ridgewood ads. The slogan "Making Good on Our Promises" was a frequent tagline. Unfortunately, Kissell and Burleigh's skepticism about Theodore Weyant and P.J. Guthrie's venture would prove prescient.

As the rivalry between Hills and Dales and Ridgewood played out in competing newspaper advertisements, Kissell and Burleigh directed much of their energy to encouraging as much building as possible in the subdivision before winter set in. Completed and occupied homes provided evidence that the neighborhood would be a reality and would help propel lot sales in the slow winter months, a time when much momentum was usually lost in the real

71 (top). View of the dining room in the Burleigh house, 1915.
72 (above). The living room fireplace in the Burleigh house, 1915.

68. South Kensington Place, looking west from North Limestone Street. Taken at the beginning of 1916, it is the earliest known photograph of a streetscape in Ridgewood. Three of the earliest houses in Ridgewood—the Lewis Cooke house, the Brown Burleigh house, and the Douglas O'Kane house—can be seen from left to right, respectively. The pre-existing John Doyle house, now 2215 N. Fountain Blvd., can be seen in the distance to the right. The desolate looking landscape in the early days of the subdivision make it abundantly apparent why Harry Kissell and Brown Burleigh had such an up-hill battle in trying to lure potential Ridgewood buyers away from established neighborhoods.

estate business. The Kissell Building Company had recently closed a deal with Lewis H. Cooke, the treasurer of the American Trust & Savings Bank, to erect a Colonial-style home at 107 South Kensington Place for Cooke and his wife, Nina, and was rushing construction in order to have the house under roof by December. Brown and May Burleigh's house, at 30 South Kensington Place, was nearing completion. It would be the first house finished and occupied in Ridgewood. The nearby Douglas and Elizabeth O'Kane house, at 101 North Kensington Place, was also nearly ready for occupancy. O'Kane was a salesman with the Kissell Real Estate Company. *(fig's. 68 – 72)*

Construction on Richard E. and Mabel McDaniel's house at 136 Englewood Road was also close to winding up. Richard McDaniel was the secretary and general manager of another local building company—The Builder of Homes Company. The McDaniel home would feature the latest in exterior home finishes—Rocbond stucco—and would be featured in many of the forthcoming ads of the Rocbond Stucco Company. The company was based in Wren, Ohio, but had just opened a new office in Springfield to capitalize on the abundance of residential building going on in the city at the time. *(fig. 73)*

74. A field tree harvested for transplantation on a Ridgewood lot.

In this era when English architecture was all the rage, stucco was rapidly gaining favor as a building material. It was cheaper than masonry but still gave a look of solidity and offered a great deal of aesthetic charm. However, the use of stucco, in not only the McDaniel house, but many others as well, would prove problematic at a time when war was raging in Europe. Just as the house was nearing completion, construction was held up when a merchant ship carrying the materials was sunk by a German U-boat. This would be the first of many war-related delays for those constructing homes in Ridgewood, but the McDaniel home was still largely completed by the end of 1915.

The first two homes to be built on Crescent Drive, the Frank R. and Ola Talbott home at 1824 Crescent Drive, and the Frank B. and Loretto Hutchinson house at 1812 Crescent Drive were under construction that fall and would be about half completed by year's end. Frank Talbott was the secretary and treasurer of The Victor Rubber Company, and Frank Hutchinson was the sales manager of the Kelly-Springfield Motor Truck Company. *(See fig. 62, page 92)* Two other homes were underway in the neighborhood—the foundation for the Mark M. and Leah Livingston home, at 18 East Grube (Harding) Road, was done by early December, and the Nettie Reibold house was in progress at 1763 Stratford Place. Harry Kissell's own home on North Fountain Boulevard was under roof by mid-November.

Many lot buyers, who were planning construction at a future date, prepped their lots that fall with ornamental trees and shrubbery. Most early Ridgewood lot owners employed landscape architects to lay out the grounds surrounding their homes. The beautification movement of the early twentieth century meant landscaping in upscale suburbs was given as much attention as architecture and interior design. Because trees were in short supply in the first section of Ridgewood, lot owners frequently had mature trees, usually maples and elms, transplanted on their lots. Trees that had grown isolated in fields were prized as they got sunlight and air on all sides, making for a better shape than those that grew in clusters in fields and forests. *(fig. 74)*

By the end of 1915, Ridgewood was starting to take shape. Despite the fact that a new competitor in the high-class real estate market had emerged on the scene, there was reason for much optimism about the future of the neighborhood. By all accounts, it was off to a great start.

73. The Richard E. & Mabel McDaniel house at 136 Englewood Rd.

84. The Harry & Olive Kissell house at 1801 N. Fountain Blvd.

4 A BUMP IN THE R

THE YEAR 1916 LOOKED LIKE IT WOULD BE A BANNER ONE FOR THE KISSELL IMPROVEMENT COMPANY.

The business slump that had plagued most of the country from 1913-1915 was starting to recede. There was much anxiety over the bloody trench warfare that had raged in Europe since 1914 between France, Britain, and Russia on one side, and Germany and Austria-Hungary on the other. However, so far, President Woodrow Wilson had managed to keep the United States out of war, and business was going on as usual in the United States.

If building activity was a measure of a city's prosperity, then Springfield was in very good shape. Construction of the new Memorial Hall was nearing completion, several major commercial buildings were going up, and the Hotel Shawnee, Hotel Bancroft, and the Heaume Hotel were all under construction. With new competition on the horizon, the interior of that old stalwart of downtown Springfield hotels, the Arcade Hotel, was even getting a face-lift. Local architects were having trouble keeping up with demand and had to hire extra draftsmen to get out plans and specifications. Contractors were having difficulty in finding enough skilled workers to keep up with the workload and had turned to actively recruiting men from other cities.

In early 1916, fourteen houses were under construction in Ridgewood, including several of the finest homes ever built in the development. For his own home, Harry Kissell had chosen a well-known architectural firm

from Dayton, Ohio. He would later tell a group of fellow developers that he had done so because he felt that in Springfield, "the architects have gotten in a rut, and they simply revamp old stuff, and the people take whatever they give them." For two speculative homes that The Kissell Building Company was erecting in Ridgewood, Kissell chose a Cleveland, Ohio, and a Louisville, Kentucky, architect to produce the plans. Apparently, this had the desired affect as Kissell later affirmed that, "it took just that touch to wake up architects of the town to the fact that they had to get busy."

Kissell secured the venerable Dayton, Ohio, architectural firm of Schenck and Williams to draw up the plans for his own family's home. The principals of the firm, Harry I. Schenck and Harry J. Williams, who had offices in the Dayton Arcade, designed many notable buildings in downtown Dayton throughout the course of their careers. Their commissions included the now demolished Rike-Kumler building, the Spanish Revival-style Central YMCA building, and the modern-style Mutual Home & Savings Association Building, which was Dayton's tallest building from 1931 to 1969. The latter two are extant and listed on the National Register of Historic Places. *(fig's. 75, 76 & 77)*

One of Schenck and Williams's most interesting downtown buildings is the Engineers Club of Dayton. Prominent Dayton inventors and engineers Colonel Edward A. Deeds and Charles F. Kettering founded the Engineers Club in 1914, and by 1917, a permanent home for the group was under construction on Monument Avenue

76 (top). The Central YMCA Building.
77 (middle). The Mutual Home & Savings Association Building.
75 (left). The Rike-Kumler Building.

overlooking the Miami River. During this period, Dayton was gaining a national reputation for scientific research and was regarded as a leading industrial city. The new Engineers Club became a hotbed for innovation, offering a place where the city's many engineers and technicians could exchange ideas and listen to speakers imported from all over the country. Aviation pioneer and Engineers Club member Orville Wright accepted the keys for the new club on behalf of the membership at the February 2, 1918, dedication. *(fig. 78)*

Schenck and Williams also designed Orville Wright's home, Hawthorne Hill, which was completed in 1914 in the Oakwood neighborhood of Dayton and is designated as a National Historic Landmark. That same year they finished Charles F. Kettering's home in Oakwood. Kettering was a prolific inventor who founded the Dayton Engineering Laboratories Company (Delco), and invented the self-starter for automobiles. Kettering's Tudor-style house, called Ridgeleigh

79 (top). Hawthorne Hill.
78 (middle). The Engineers Club of Dayton.
80 (above). Rear view of the Charles F. Kettering house.

Terrace, was also declared a National Historic Landmark, but a disastrous fire in the 1990s destroyed much of the original fabric of the home. *(fig's. 79 & 80)*

In addition to Charles Kettering's home, Schenck and Williams were responsible for a number of other Tudor-style buildings in Oakwood, including the Municipal Building, Oakwood Manor, Oakwood High School, and the Oakwood Memorial Public Library. They would make a foray into modern architecture in the 1930s when they designed the famed Art Deco-style NCR Building 26. It was in Building 26 that engineer Joseph Desch would later design the equipment that helped hasten World War II's end by deciphering the Enigma code transmitted by German U-boats. Schenck and Williams were also responsible for another important Springfield building—the Spanish Mission-style Tuberculosis Sanitarium, built in 1923 in Springfield at 3130 East Main Street. The building would later become the home of Clark County, Ohio, government offices and was renamed the Springview Government Center. *(fig's. 81, 82 & 83)*

It was Schenck and Williams's work in the Tudor style that captured Harry Kissell's fancy. The Kissell house, at 1801 North Fountain Boulevard, bears a striking similarity to the Charles F. Kettering home in Oakwood. The Kissell Building Company handled the actual construction of the Kissells' monumental home. The façade of the house featured the typical Tudor-style architectural elements of brick and stucco, with half-timbering of rough chestnut, and was capped with a striking green tile roof. The interior of the 4,000 square-foot house was finished with magnificent mahogany woodwork. *(fig. 84, page 104)*

81. Oakwood High School.

One of the distinctive

features of the home was that it had a fireproof, two-car garage underneath the house. An entrance from the garage to the first floor of the house afforded the family, and their visitors, protection from the weather. At the time, an attached garage was a novelty and quite controversial. In this era before smoke detectors, when great conflagrations seemed an all-too frequent occurrence, fire was one of most people's greatest worries. Early automobiles were unpredictable at best, and burning wires and a host of other potentially dangerous malfunctions had left people wary of their inherent safety. Add to that the combustible materials that were typically stored in a garage—oil, extra gasoline, and oil-soaked rags, and possibly an owner or chauffeur smoking a cigarette—and one had a recipe for disaster. *(fig. 85)*

To compensate for the risk, insurance companies of the period often charged three times as much for premiums for homes with attached garages, especially if there was a communicating door from the garage to the interior of the house. However, Kissell felt an attached garage would make the backyard look tidier and went forth with the idea. Some of the other larger homes in Ridgewood would also have attached garages, but this was the exception as only the most affluent residents were willing to accept the higher insurance premiums. Most early Ridgewood homes would have detached garages placed at a safe distance near the rear of the lot. *(fig's. 86 – 89)*

Another landmark house that was under construction in 1916, the Harry V. and Juliet Bretney home at 1602 North Fountain Boulevard, remains one of the most distinctive houses ever built

82 (top). NCR Building 26.
83 (above). The Springview Government Center.

in Ridgewood given its imposing size and eclectic style. Harry Bretney was the president and general manager of the successful H.V. Bretney Company, manufacturers of leather goods. The Bretneys were residents of South Fountain Avenue when they decided to follow the "northward trend" and build a home in Ridgewood. Their new home was designed by Mason Maury, one of the most prominent residential and commercial architects in Louisville, Kentucky. Among Maury's most notable buildings were Louisville's first skyscraper, the six-story Kenyon Building, constructed in 1886, and the Kentucky State Building constructed for the World's Columbian Exposition in Chicago in 1893. Maury was particularly known for his use of the "Chicago School" style of architecture in his commercial buildings.

For the exterior of the nearly 5,000 square-feet Bretney home, Maury utilized tapestry brick and an interesting mix of Tudor and Neoclassical elements, accented with rectilinear bands of windows that had been popularized by Frank Lloyd Wright and the "Prairie School" of architects. The reddish brown roof tiles were flecked with green in order to downplay its newness and, instead, offer a rustic "moss-like" effect. The Bretney house had a detached garage designed in a companionable style to the house. *(fig. 90, page 115)*

William Poole served as the contractor for the construction. During the early twentieth century, Poole was perhaps Springfield's most prolific builder. He served as contractor on many upscale homes including the Frank Lloyd Wright-designed Burton J. and Orpha Westcott house at 1340 East High Street, completed in 1908. The Bretney home contained eight spacious rooms for the family, a glass-enclosed living porch with an open fireplace, servant quarters, and a sleeping porch. Many Ridgewood homes had sleeping porches in this era before central air conditioning. Some homes had more than one. On a muggy summer's night, many of the men in the neighborhood could be found snoozing on a cot on the sleeping porch.

86 (top). Olive and Mary Lu Kissell in their newly finished home on N. Fountain Blvd., 1916.
85 (above). The garage of the Kissell house.

Women sometimes utilized sleeping porches, but were less likely to do so out of modesty concerns unless the porch was well concealed. Children were often barred from the sleeping porches out of safety concerns.

Also in the spring of 1916, one of the finest houses ever constructed in Ridgewood, the Louis E. & Nell C. Bauer house, was started. Louis Bauer was vice-president of the Bauer Brothers Company, a well-regarded local manufacturing interest. Bauer and his wife were East High Street residents before they constructed their new home in Ridgewood. Bauer engaged the architectural firm of Meade and Hamilton of Cleveland, Ohio, to design the house. F.B. Meade and James Hamilton designed a number of noteworthy homes in historical revival styles in Cleveland's most prestigious suburbs, including Shaker Heights and Cleveland Heights, as well as a number of mansions on Cleveland's famed "Millionaires Row"—Euclid Avenue. They also designed the home of five-and-dime store magnate S.S. Kresge in Detroit's Boston-Edison neighborhood, where the city's economic elites lived. The Kresge house, completed in 1914, was very similar to the Bauer house. They each shared the same unassuming exterior, and both were very wide, but not very deep houses. *(fig's. 91 & 92)*

To accommodate his Ridgewood home, Louis Bauer purchased three lots that fronted on the west side of Crescent Drive and stretched from Ardmore

87. Harry Kissell in a rare moment of repose at home.

Kissell family life

88. The foyer of the Kissell house. Note the two telephones on the table.
89. A three-year-old Mary Lu Kissell in front of the massive Tudor arch doorway of 1801 N. Fountain Blvd.

Road to Berkley Road. Once completed, the sprawling house stretched over 109 feet wide, with a depth of only twenty-nine feet. The first floor boasted a large entry hall, an enormous living room, a dining room complete with a fireplace, a sun room, a breakfast room, a kitchen with a separate ice room and pantry, and a powder room. The second story had four bedrooms for family and guests, including a master suite with a full bath and a dressing room. There were also two maids' rooms, a sewing room, and four full baths on the second floor. The rambling house was equipped with a number of bells and buzzers so servants could be summoned from anywhere in the house. As utilitarian spaces go, even the basement was grand. A laundry, storeroom, fuel room, heater room, and workroom were pleasantly finished and well equipped. In fact, the house was renowned locally as being outfitted with virtually every modern convenience that was available at the time. Like the Kissell house, the Bauer house had an attached garage. *(fig's. 93, 94 & 95)*

Construction of the elaborate home went relatively quickly. Contractor William Poole and Louis Bauer staked out the foundation on March 30, 1916, and Poole was able to complete the house by the end of the year. When the home was finished, the expansive yard was landscaped to look like a park. Louis Bauer hired the eminent Cleveland landscape architecture firm of Pitkin and Mott to lay out the incredible gardens. The Bauers lived there happily for the next nine years and were an integral part of life in Ridgewood. Mr. Bauer had the distinction of serving as the chief of the "Ridgewood District Weather Bureau." He owned a fine barometer, and each morning he would signal his fellow Ridgewood residents

92 (top). The Detroit home of five and dime store magnate—S.S. Kresge.
91 (above). The Louis E. & Nell C. Bauer house at 1735 Crescent Dr.

90. The Harry V. and Juliet Bretney home at 1602 N. Fountain Blvd.

THE BRETNEY'S

what to expect for the day's weather by running various colored flags up a sixty-foot metal flagpole. Each home in Ridgewood had been furnished with a key that explained the weather signals. Neighbor Brown Burleigh boasted in an article that he wrote for the *National Journal of Real Estate* that Bauer's predictions had a 90 percent accuracy rate.

Unfortunately, however, Bauer's home, one of the finest ever built in Ridgewood, would meet a sad fate. In 1925, Louis Bauer traded his house to J. Harris Thiebaud in exchange for Thiebaud's farm and home on the corner of Urbana Pike and Willow Road. After Harris Thiebaud's death in 1950, the house on Crescent Drive would sit vacant for several years before being purchased by a developer in 1953, who demolished the deteriorating home. The developer then sold off the three original lots that composed the property, and three new homes would later be built on them.

In the spring of 1916, the rivalry between Hills and Dales and Ridgewood heated up again and played out in competing newspaper advertisements. The Kissell Improvement Company chose to highlight the construction going on in Ridgewood and began utilizing images of homes that were completed or under construction. Some of the ads took implicit jabs at Hills and Dales—

93 (top). The living room of the Louis & Nell Bauer house.
94 (above). The dining room of the Bauer house.

"Ridgewood is the product of local men. Men who have always lived in Springfield and who without question will continue to make their home here. Their pride and integrity is at stake. Under no condition could they permit a single representation not to materialize." The Home Improvement Company stuck to using images that featured the natural beauty of Hills and Dales.

While both companies continued to expound on all the attributes of suburbia, they radically departed again when it came to emphasis on the investment quality of lots. One Kissell ad read, "Ridgewood is the sort of home location for the real home lover, not those desiring to make a mere speculative investment in land. Ridgewood is the place in which to live." However, many developers of the era did not share this philosophy. King Thompson, one of the developers of Upper Arlington in Columbus, Ohio, once told fellow developers, "I did not enter the land business some years ago because I had any theories of city building to work out, but merely because I thought I could make a living at it."

Harry Kissell was very much a community builder, however. He subscribed to the philosophy that home ownership brought out the best in a man because it made him a stakeholder in his community with a vested interest in its future prosperity. Kissell further believed that home ownership promoted stable communities. At the beginning of the twentieth century, owning a home was beyond the means of most average people. A mortgage in that era usually required a 50 percent down payment. Buyers then made semiannual interest-only payments, and the balance was due in a lump sum, typically at the end of a five-year term.

Throughout his career, Kissell would work to make mortgage financing available to more people. He helped organize the American Trust and Savings Bank in Springfield for that purpose.

95. The fireplace in the Bauer dining room.

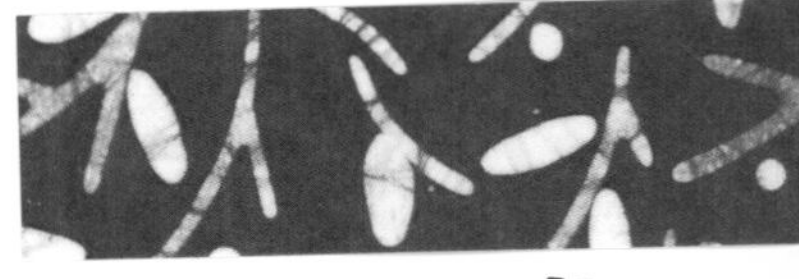

It would later merge to become part of The First National Bank, and he served continuously on the directorate of both institutions and made the extension of better mortgage financing a staple of his tenure. That commitment was paying off. By 1916, Springfield could boast that it had the highest percentage of home ownership of any city of its size in the United States.

But the developer of Hills and Dales, Theodore Weyant, had a different perspective. While he sometimes stated in ads that his development was a monument to civic pride, he had no real ties to the community, nor, understandably, any interest in its future. Despite The Kissell Improvement Company's opposition, the reality was that real estate speculation was a huge game in the wake of the Industrial Revolution as cities, and later suburbs, grew at astonishing rates. For Weyant, Hills and Dales was purely an economic proposition. His motive was simply to sell lots, so he continued to stress the investment quality of lots in his subdivision, assuring speculators that they were "sure to return big profits." And his strategy was working. Lots were selling well in Hills and Dales, but there was virtually no home construction going on. Buyers were simply buying and holding. By April 1916, approximately one-third of the lots were sold even though improvements were still in the earliest stages.

In contrast, The Kissell Improvement Company tried to encourage building within one year of the sale of a lot. Kissell felt that if a person did not build in a year, nine times out of ten they would not build at all. Brown Burleigh instructed his salesmen to size up a man's ambition to actually build, and build reasonably soon, feeling that there was no reason to try to induce a man to buy a lot if he was not ready to build. This divergence in approach likely accounts for the reason that a development of such rare primeval beauty as Hills and Dales got off to a rough start. Because Weyant outright promoted speculation, few houses were built in Hills and Dales for years. It would not

96. The Ridgewood tennis courts at night.

reach its potential and grow into the lovely neighborhood it became until a number of years later when it was finally in local hands.

97. J. Warren James.

On June 18, 1916, The Kissell Improvement Company proudly celebrated the one-year anniversary of Ridgewood lots first going on sale to the public. The occasion was marked with a newspaper advertisement that announced that seventeen homes were completed or nearing completion in Ridgewood and a number of others were in the works. "This is a record which has not been equaled in the first year by any other development proposition in Ohio," the ad stated with great satisfaction. A year ago, Ridgewood had been a barren development. Now it was transforming into a real neighborhood. The Kissells had moved into their own home in April.

The anniversary ad also announced that The Kissell Improvement Company had completed one of the most popular amenities that it would offer. "Owl tennis" was now available to all residents and lot owners in Ridgewood. The company had built two tennis courts on the empty land on the west side of Crescent Drive, at the corner of Crescent and Dover Road. Later the Walter B. and Elsa Kleeman house (1905 Crescent Drive) was constructed on the lot. The new tennis courts were lighted with four 1,000-watt lamps to accommodate the schedules of the men of the neighborhood, hence the name. "If your business forbids you outdoor exercise during the day, 'Owl Tennis' will supply you with necessary recreation at night." There was even a convenient drinking fountain. The Ridgewood courts would be a wildly popular evening entertainment in the neighborhood for years to come. *(fig. 96)*

Throughout the summer, lot sales would continue to flourish in Ridgewood. However, the summer of 1916 was also the year that Harry Kissell's most ardent competitor for the high-class real estate market, J. Warren James, emerged on the scene. J. Warren James was born in Springfield in 1880. And like Kissell, he had followed his father, John A. James, proprietor of The James Real Estate Company, into the family business. Back in 1914, just as work on Ridgewood was starting, J. Warren James also cast his lot

98. The intersection of N. Fountain Ave. and McCreight Ave., looking west down McCreight. J. Warren James' house is to the left.

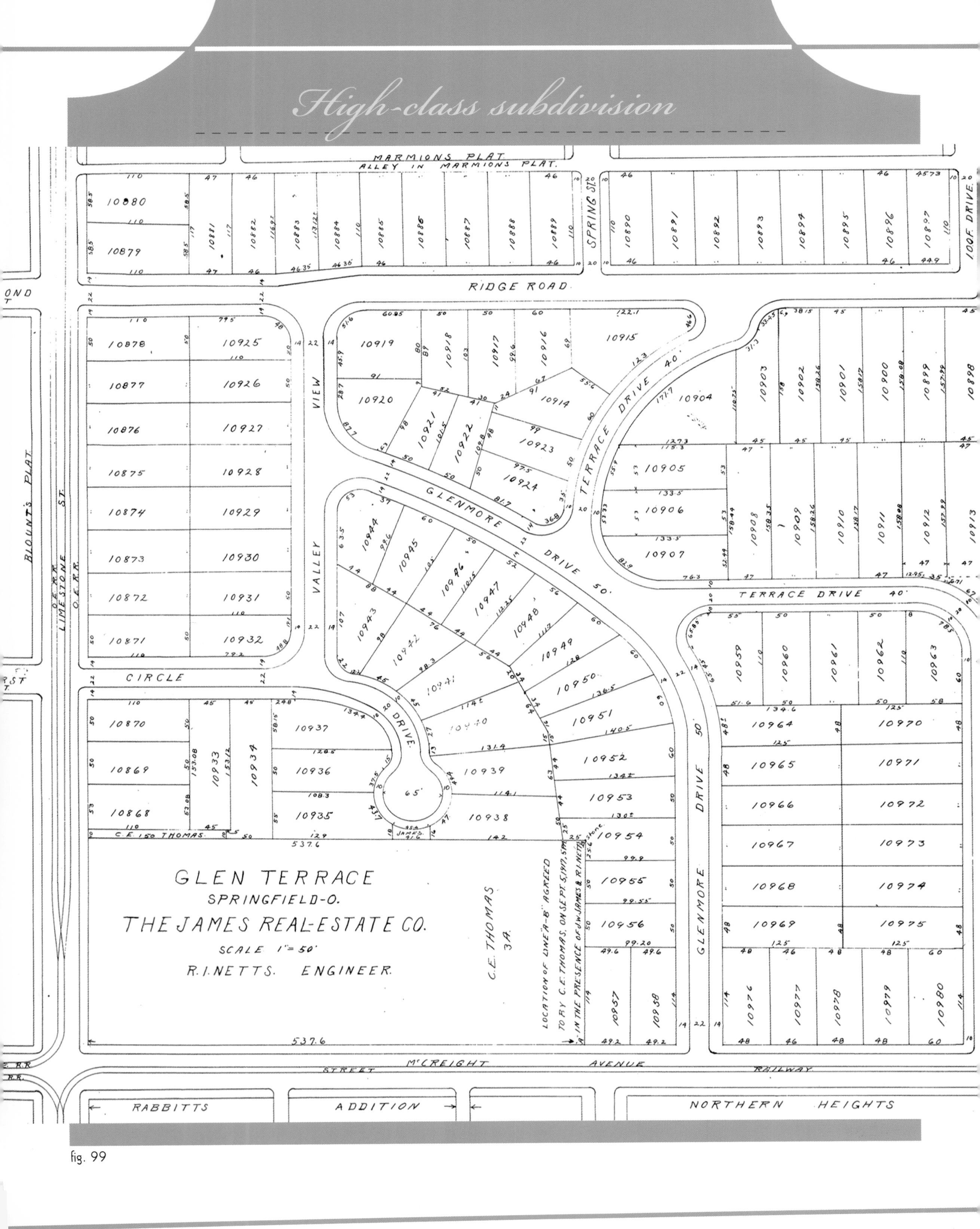
MARMIONS PLAT
ALLEY IN MARMIONS PLAT.
SPRING ST.
100F. DRIVE
RIDGE ROAD
BLOUNT'S PLAT
LIMESTONE ST.
O.E.R.R.
VIEW
VALLEY
CIRCLE
GLENMORE DRIVE 50'
TERRACE DRIVE 40'
DRIVE
GLENMORE DRIVE 50
GLEN TERRACE
SPRINGFIELD-O.
THE JAMES REAL-ESTATE CO.
SCALE 1"=50'
R.I. NETTS. ENGINEER.
C.E. THOMAS 3A.
C.E. 150 THOMAS
M^cCREIGHT AVENUE
STREET
RAILWAY
RABBITTS ADDITION
NORTHERN HEIGHTS

fig. 99

with the emerging "northward trend" and built a charming Dutch Colonial home at 1133 North Fountain Avenue, right across from the new entrance to Ridgewood. Between 1914 and 1916, he built a number of homes on speculation in the Northern Heights subdivision, but he had set his sights on entering the high-class real estate market. So in August 1916, he purchased twenty acres of land, the old Charles P. Thomas homestead, on the northeast corner of North Limestone Street and McCreight Avenue with plans to turn it into a small, upscale residential development and build a new home for himself and his wife there. *(fig's. 97 & 98)*

James engaged a well-known Cleveland landscape architect, Louis Brandt, to lay out the plat. Brandt accentuated the gently rolling land with curving drives and created access points to the tract from both North Limestone Street, via Circle Drive, and McCreight Avenue, via Terrace Drive. On September 24, 1916, J. Warren James made a pre-opening announcement in the newspaper that lots in his new subdivision, Glen Terrace, a "high-class subdivision at moderate prices" were available for sale. *(fig. 99)*

James would have success with his first foray into the upscale real estate market. It was the first time that he competed directly with Kissell for the high-grade market but not the last nor the most disconcerting for Harry Kissell. But that was in the future, and, to Kissell's relief, the first full building season in Ridgewood had come to a successful close. Ridgewood's success now seemed assured, even among those who had originally doubted the proposition. However, the winds of the war in Europe were blowing stronger, and America's continuing isolationist position was being threatened. The first major bump in the road for Ridgewood was in the offing.

When spring dawned the following year, 1917, The Kissell Improvement Company debuted a new advertising slogan: "Ridgewood— The Children's Paradise." A new series of ads focused on the influence a neighborhood could have on a child and featured sentimental arguments that appealed to a parent's sense of responsibility for providing the right kind of nurturing environment. Ridgewood, the ads offered, was a healthful environment where children would make the right kinds of friends, and an idyllic place to make childhood memories, with plenty of space to run and play.

Prospects looked good for another successful year in the Children's Paradise and elsewhere. Much residential building was planned to try to satisfy the ongoing housing famine in the city. The newspaper estimated that home seekers and speculative builders would start over 200 new houses that year to satisfy the demand. At the time, 104 of the original 252 building lots in Ridgewood had sold, and a number of houses were going up, with many more planned. *(fig's. 100, 101 & 102)* Several major homes on North Fountain Boulevard were being completed. Workmen were laboring on the interior of the English-style home of James S. and Lucy Webb. Prolific Springfield architect, Robert C. Gotwald, designed their home at 1802 North Fountain Boulevard. The home of Gardner Hazen, at 1850 Crescent Drive, also designed by Robert C. Gotwald, was newly finished. And the striking Herbert W. and Juanita Eakins home at 1220 North Fountain Boulevard was well under way. *(fig's. 103 & 104)*

The Eakins house was one of the most visually arresting in all of Ridgewood in that it was the first house one saw upon entering the development, and it sat isolated on three large lots on the east side of Fountain Boulevard, just beyond the entrance to Ridgewood. The Eakins' huge lawn stretched from McCreight Avenue to First Street and gave the impression of a small estate. The Eclectic-style house featured a Neoclassical entry and Frank Lloyd Wright-inspired casement windows. It remained

101 (top). House at 1902 N. Fountain Blvd. under construction, 1917.
100 (above). The Fannie M. Raup house at 1845 N. Fountain Blvd., under construction in 1917.

one of the most well known houses in Ridgewood until it was demolished toward the end of the twentieth century. *(fig's. 105 & 106)*

On April 1, 1917, a newspaper article captured the optimism that was prevailing in Springfield's real estate and building circles. It stated that despite a precipitous, war-related rise in prices of building materials, a busy building season would prevail in 1917. But on the very next day, April 2, 1917, President Wilson asked Congress for a declaration of war. America's isolationist position had unraveled when it came to light that the German Ambassador to Mexico was proposing a German-Mexican Alliance against the United States. The American public was outraged and President Wilson had little choice.

The following month, Harry Kissell traveled to Kansas City, Missouri,

102 (top). Foundation under construction for 120 N. Kensington Place, 1917. Homes along N. Limestone St. can be seen to the right.
103 (above). The James S. and Lucy Webb home at 1802 N. Fountain Blvd, completed in 1917, image circa 1927.

104. The home built by Gardner Hazen, at 1850 Crescent Dr., is visible second from the left in this 1925 image.

for the First Annual Conference of Developers of High-Class Residence Property, which took place May 10-12, 1917, in conjunction with the National Conference on City Planning (NCCP). In addition to attending the conferences of the National Association of Real Estate Boards, many of the biggest and most successful real estate developers in the country attended the annual NCCP conference because they could see a natural symbiosis between planned real estate developments and the burgeoning field of city planning.

It was out of discussions at the City Planning conferences that an elite group of the most influential developers in the country decided they needed to have their own conference to discuss issues specific to high-grade residential developments, and so the Conference of Developers of High-Class Residence Property was born. It was an exclusive, invitation only group, limited to twelve participants. Included in the roster of attendees were Edward H. Bouton of Roland Park in Baltimore, Maryland; John A. Demarest of Forest Hills Gardens, Long Island, New York; King Thompson of Upper Arlington, Columbus, Ohio; Robert Jemison, Jr. of Birmingham, Alabama; Hugh Prather of Highland Park, Dallas, Texas; Emerson Chaille of Brendonwood near Indianapolis, Indiana; and one Harry S. Kissell of Springfield, Ohio. J.C. Nichols, developer of the famed Country Club District in Kansas City, served as chair.

Among this group, Harry Kissell had the smallest development in the smallest city, but it was indicative of the esteem in which Kissell was held by fellow developers, and the quality of his development, that he was invited to join this select group of people who hailed from major American cities. In later advertisements, Kissell would proudly draw comparisons between Ridgewood and developments in larger cities stating, "In New York it is Forest Hills Gardens, in Baltimore it is Roland Park, in Toledo it is Ottawa Hills, in Columbus it is Upper Arlington, and in Springfield it is Ridgewood." The developers present at the First Annual Conference of Developers of High-Class Residence Property discussed everything from sales strategies, to lobbying efforts, to advertising. But the potential impact of the war on their developments weighed especially heavily on everyone's minds.

In June 1917, the first military draft since the Civil War was instituted. Every man between the ages of 18 and 46 was required to register for the draft. Ten million American men would ultimately register under the Selective Service draft law, and 4.8 million men would serve. This loss of manpower was an enormous blow to businesses throughout the course of the war. The Kissell organization was rocked as three of its salesmen went off to war, but their loss was typical of others in the real estate business and building trades. Architect Robert C. Gotwald lost three men from his office to enlistment.

Enlisting was considered the patriotic thing to do, and patriotism was reaching a fevered pitch. A new word had entered the American lexicon—the "slacker." Slacker was a derogatory term for men who attempted to avoid military service, but it was starting to be widely applied to anyone who let their country down. "Don't let your dollars become slacker dollars," a Ridgewood ad implored. This ad made the case that, just as it was the patriotic duty of young men to serve, ordinary citizens had a duty to not hoard money out of fear, but to instead

105. The Herbert W. & Juanita Eakins home at 1220 N. Fountain Blvd. under construction. The home was completed in 1917.

106. The completed Eakins house in late 1917. (See also fig's. 34 & 38.)

EAKINS HOUSE

RIDGEWOOD

conduct business as usual to keep the economy going.

Nevertheless, fear about the war's potential impact on the economy did cause people to tighten their belts, and many were delaying building new homes in hopes that prices would come back down. The cost of labor was skyrocketing due to labor shortages brought on by so many American doughboys heading off to war. Material prices were also rising as more and more resources were diverted to war industries. In 1917, increased costs of labor and materials cut home building by an average of 25 to 50 percent across the country. Even if materials were available, delivery was uncertain due to war-related shipping delays. Fortunately, though, the sale of building lots remained largely unaffected.

By midsummer, Kissell ads could still boast, "During war times we have sold in Ridgewood so far this season $55,000 worth [of lots]." The cost of living nearly doubled during the war as commodity prices soared, but Ridgewood was developed at pre-war prices and Kissell was not interested in profiteering. "We improved Ridgewood before the war when prices of labor and material were at their lowest. We were fortunate in this and we are giving the people of Springfield the benefit. We did not pay the present high prices to improve these lots, and we are not going to charge you a high price," one ad stated.

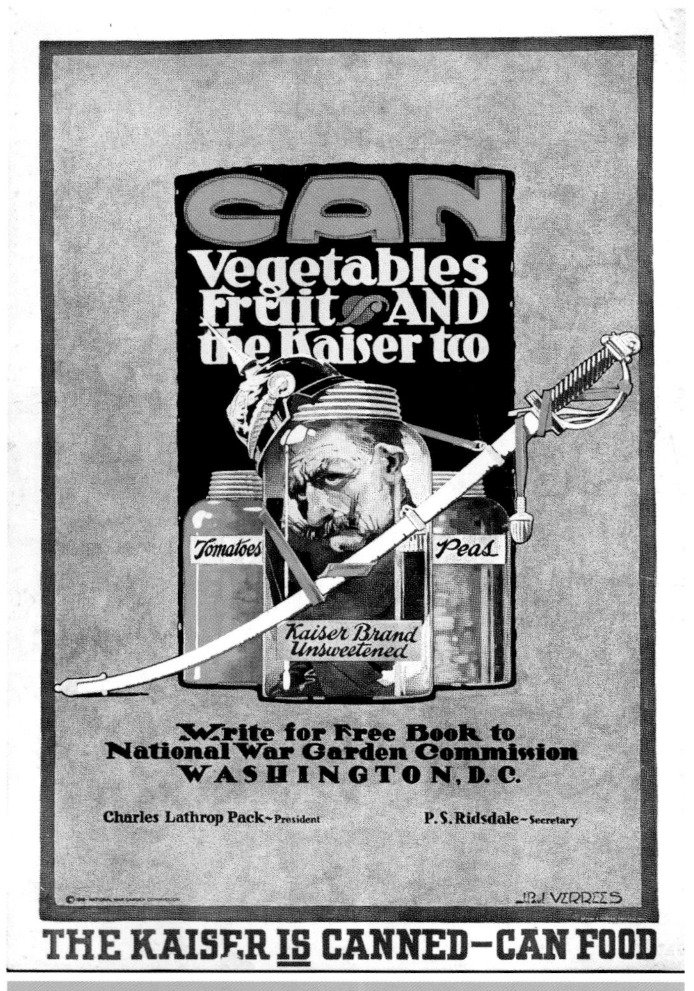

107. WWI poster promoting war gardens and food preservation to help the war effort.

While lot sales remained steady, maintaining the building momentum was another story. Kissell tried to keep things going by erecting speculative homes, a move he hoped would both stimulate home building by others and jump-start areas of Ridgewood that weren't developing as quickly as he would have liked. Building speculative homes was also a good way to set the tone architecturally in the development and influence the architectural choices of other home builders. Kissell made virtually no profit on the speculative houses themselves. His profit came mostly from the lot upon which the house was built. Speculative houses were offered at very attractive prices so they would sell quickly. Having another completed and occupied home in Ridgewood was a boon to the neighborhood, and a quick sell meant that Kissell could get his money back out of it fast and take his profit on the lot. This worked very well, but he had to be cautious about building too many speculative homes. Overbuilding could be worse than no building at all. It tied up capital, and a new home sitting empty for a sustained period seemed somehow more ominous than an empty lot.

As the war got into full swing, it began to affect the everyday lives of Americans. Wartime rationing resulted in a change of lifestyle and deprivation that many Americans hadn't experienced in their lifetimes. On August 10, 1917, Congress had passed the Food and Fuel Control Act, which gave the President broad powers to regulate the sale of coal and food. Coal and food resources needed to be mobilized for war but at the same time, an adequate supply had to be assured for the home front. The goal was to prevent hoarding and promote conservation. "Meatless Tuesdays" and "Wheatless Wednesdays" were introduced to promote food conservation, and war gardens were encouraged. Even the Springfield Real Estate Board got into the act by sponsoring a "Best War Garden" contest. The winner received a free building lot. *(fig. 107)*

Wartime rationing also had a dramatic impact on business. In cities across the country, including Springfield, local fuel conservancy boards were set up to ration and prioritize who got coal. Although supplies were extremely tenuous, no local factories had to close because of the coal shortage as they were allocated enough to keep manufacturing going. Citizens had some coal for heating their homes, and, although there was enough to get by, there was constant worry that at some point there would not be.

Homes in which there was sickness got first priority for coal rations, and "Heatless Mondays" were observed to conserve fuel. But, coal was directed first to existing homes and not new construction. By late fall, this was affecting the building industry. As builders struggled to beat the weather, coal shortages hindered their ability to heat new homes in order to dry them out to allow workmen to do the interior finishing over the winter months. This almost completely stalled residential building in Ridgewood and elsewhere in the city. To make matters worse, residents already living in Ridgewood faced transportation issues as streetcar service had to be severely curtailed due to power shortages brought on by coal rationing. It seemed that everything that could go wrong in Ridgewood did go wrong that year. In 1916, it had looked as if Ridgewood's success was assured, but 1917 had been a tumultuous and worrisome year. One could only hope that the war would end soon and that this was just a small bump in the road.

The beginning of 1918 was punctuated by the sudden death of Hills and Dales developer, Theodore Weyant. On January 19, 1918, the 58-year-old Weyant was on his way to join his wife in Florida when he collapsed at the Grand Hotel in Cincinnati and died suddenly from a cerebral brain hemorrhage. The Hills and Dales development had been lying largely dormant since the previous fall when war conditions had started to hamper construction. Approximately half of the lots had been sold, but only eight houses had been built. After Weyant's death, his associate, P.J. Guthrie, took over responsibility for the development on behalf of himself and Weyant's widow, but no effort was made at all in 1918 to restart the improvement work.

While Hills and Dales sat fallow, Harry Kissell and Brown Burleigh were trying to keep up progress in Ridgewood, but that was also proving tenuous, and they had their work cut out for them once the building season began. A March 24, 1918, advertisement proudly declared that over $400,000 worth of houses had been constructed in Ridgewood since its inception, but they had to also acknowledge the elephant in the room. Due to war-related inflation, it now cost substantially more to build a home than it did five years ago. However, they did their best to get prospective buyers to look at the situation from another perspective—that compared to commodities, which had doubled in price during the war, the cost of building was up only 28 percent. But by late spring they had to accept the reality that, for the time being, war conditions were going to continue to hamper building. Reluctantly, they realized that their intense focus on building up the neighborhood as rapidly as possible had to be deferred, and they would have to concentrate on lot sales instead.

In an effort to keep lot sales moving that spring, Brown Burleigh wrote an editorial that appeared in the newspaper on May 5, 1918. In it he expressed confidence that there would be a real estate boom in Springfield after the war. He felt that the city's many and diversified industries would insure continued prosperity. "The war cannot last forever," he said, "and enough money is available to keep real estate moving slowly, until brighter days return and then great prosperity seems assured." In addition, he reminded readers that land prices rose precipitously after the Civil War, and encouraged readers to buy immediately in anticipation of the real estate boom. He pointed out that the ongoing housing famine in the city was amplified by the war's impact on building. Houses and apartments were more overcrowded than ever before. Pent-up demand would surely inflate real estate values after the war, so now was the time to buy building lots.

At the same time Harry Kissell was trying to keep Ridgewood afloat, he was also called to civic duty. He had been named the county chairman of the Thrift Stamps and War Saving Certificates Drive, and he threw himself into this role with typical gusto. "If we are to win the war, we must win it as a united people," he told the newspaper. "The savings of every man, woman and child are necessary if we are to hasten the victorious ending of the war. War stamp savers are life savers." Ultimately, he would raise $1,760,110 for the effort and receive the Distinguished Service Medal from the Ohio War Savings Committee.

Kissell faced an even bigger challenge while trying to stem the rising anti-German sentiment that was rocking his beloved city. People of German descent composed Springfield's second largest ethnic group after the Irish. The city even had a German language newspaper—the *Journal und Adler*. Nationally, people of German descent accounted for about one-fourth of the population, but that did not seem to prevent all things German from being regarded with scorn in the wake of the war. The rhetoric became so heated locally that there was talk of St. John's Lutheran Church and St. Bernard's Catholic Church suspending German language services. But it was the local college with a very German name—Wittenberg—that became the central focus of persecution.

Kissell was deeply disturbed about the negative impact anti-German sentiment was having on his beloved alma mater. In an effort to try to diffuse the situation, Kissell and Wittenberg President Dr. Charles G. Heckert journeyed to New York to enlist the help of none other than former President Theodore Roosevelt. The two men were able to persuade Roosevelt to come to Springfield to address the issue, and the former President arrived via train on Saturday, May 25, 1918. Roosevelt came under the pretext of encouraging the Red Cross war chest drive, but no help was really needed with that. Springfield's war chest was amply filled. *(fig. 108)*

108. Theodore Roosevelt and Harry Kissell during Roosevelt's visit to Springfield, May 25, 1918.

During his visit to

Springfield, Roosevelt stopped briefly at the Hotel Shawnee, then gave three addresses—first at Wittenberg, then Memorial Hall, and finally on the esplanade in downtown. In his oratory, he declared as infamy holding a man's national origin against him. What mattered was his loyalty to America, and Americanism could not be gauged by a name, argued Roosevelt. The only legitimate test to measure if a man was pure American was whether he stood with the Kaiser or not. Roosevelt's visit seemed to have the desired affect, and anti-German sentiment died down. Now if only things in the business sector would start looking up.

A June 23, 1918, newspaper article captured the impact the war was having on the local building industry. The headline read, "Prospects for New Work are Not So Bright—Uncertain Conditions Cause Builders to Hesitate on Building," and documented that builders were simply not bidding on new work because of the difficulty in securing materials and workers. Instead, many of them were turning their attention to farming as they waited for business to come back. And the draft continued to take its toll. Architect Lawrence H. Hall of the firm Hall and Lethly, which designed a number of homes in Ridgewood, was hurriedly finishing his commissions because he was in selective draft Class 1-A and expected to be drafted at any moment. To keep the firm afloat, his partner, Marley Lethly, was working on a government contract in Columbus.

109. May Burleigh with the infant Brown Burleigh, Jr. who succumbed to the Spanish flu epidemic.

By this time in the war, new construction was limited to only "essential" work necessary to keep the economy going and support the war effort. Local contractors had a little work on additions being made to factories that supplied the war effort, but beyond that, they were limited mostly to remodeling jobs. A new trend was emerging in which Springfield residents were converting their homes into duplexes or apartments. This would prove a popular way to survive hard times. It provided extra income, enabled owners to keep their properties up, and addressed the housing shortage that had been critical in Springfield for years. However, it didn't provide enough work for contractors to live on.

To make matters worse, the Spanish flu was raging that fall. The global pandemic would ultimately kill more people worldwide than the bubonic plague and take the lives of more Americans than would die in battle in all the wars of the twentieth century. Harry Kissell's own wife and daughter had been stricken with the flu and were being tended by private nurses. By the end of October, the influenza outbreak would retreat as quickly as it came. It would return again briefly at the beginning of 1919 and claim the life of Brown and May Burleigh's firstborn child, the infant Brown Burleigh, Jr. *(fig. 109)*

However, October 1918 was the deadliest month for the Spanish flu. It spread so rapidly in Springfield that on October 10, 1918, the Director of Public Health issued an order closing all churches, schools, theaters, and motion picture houses until further notice. The notice in the newspaper that day read, "All public or private gatherings of groups or numbers of people indoors or outdoors except in the regular pursuit of business, manufacture or trade are prohibited . . . Congregating or loitering in saloons, pool and billiard halls, dance halls, bowling alleys, drug stores and cigar stores or other business places is prohibited."

The influenza outbreak's impact on local business was dramatic. The Kissell Improvement Company suspended all of its large advertisements for Ridgewood during the months of September and October. There was simply no point in wasting the money. Rival developer J. Warren James would concede to a newspaper reporter that it had been difficult to close sales because of the influenza.

Between the effects of the war and influenza outbreak that fall, things were so slow that, in late October, in the regular Sunday newspaper article that chronicled local building activity, the writer reported the following: Contractor A.B. Smith and architect Roy Gable "have been harvesting their bean crop in the Orchard Place addition. Each planted three acres in navy beans. Mr. Smith has thrashed his crop and Mr. Gable is gathering his vines. Both will have all of the beans and potatoes they can use during the winter months."

Things were about to get better, however. The infusion of American doughboys and America's industrial might had turned the tide in the First World War. From Germany's perspective, America's seemingly inexhaustible supply of men and military equipment could not be overcome, and, in early November 1918, the world was awaiting the news of peace. In this pre-radio era, arrangements had been made in Springfield between the Bauer Brothers

GREATEST WAR IN ALL HISTORY IS ENDED

MY FELLOW COUNTRYMEN: The armistice was signed this morning. Everything for which America fought has been accomplished. It will now be our fortunate duty to assist by example, by sober friendly counsel and by material aid in the establishment of just democracy throughout the wo ld. (Signed) Woodrow Wilson

THE NEWS

Final Edition

SPRINGFIELD, OHIO, MONDAY, NOVEMBER 11, 1918.

TREMENDOUS EVENT ANNOUNCED; YANKS FIRE PARTING SHOT

(By The Associated Press)

The greatest war in history ended Monday morning at 6 o'clock Washington time after 1,567 days of horror in which virtually the whole civilized world has been convulsed.

Announcement of the tremendous event was made at the state department at the capital a 2:45 o'clock Monday morning and in a few seconds was flashed throughout the continent by The Associated Press.

Details of the terms dictated by Marshal Foch on Friday forenoon to the German armistice delegates have been given out by President Wilson before a joint session of congress.

The terse announcement of the state department did not tell anything of the scene at Marshal Foch's headquarters at the time the armistice was signed. It was stated, however, that at 5 o'clock Paris time, the signatures of Germany's delegates were affixed to the document which blotted forever the dreams which embroiled the world in a struggle has cost at the very lowest estimate 10,000,000 lives.

The announcement was made verbally by an official of the state department in this form:

"The armistice has been signed. It was signed at 5 o'clock a. m. Paris time, and hostilities will cease at 11 o'clock this morning Paris time." (According to Springfield time hostilities ceased at 5 a. m.)

When the war begun the Teutonic alliance was headed by two of the proudest houses in history the Hohenzollerns and the Hapsburgs. Today, William II, of Germany, is a fugitive in Holland and Charles I, of Austria, while he may be still in his country, has been stripped of power and has seen his empire shattered to pieces. Ferdinand, of Bulgaria, another of the rulers in the Teutonic combination, has fled from his country, and Mohammed V, of Turkey, who also joined in the attempt of Germany to dominate the world, is dead, slain, it is said, by the hand of an assassin.

While the curtain was rolling down on the most stupendous tragedy in mankind's history, events were moving with terrible swiftness in Germany, the nation about which revolved the plot and counter-plot of the drama. Berlin, Leipsic, Stuttgart, Cologne, Hamburg and Frankfort are in the hands of the revolutionists who last week raised the red flag at Kiel. Germany's navy apparently is scattered into disjointed units, each seeking sanctuary in Danish ports or waiting in German harbors for the latest turn of events.

Crowds singing the Marsellaise are marching through the streets of autocratic Berlin, and a soldiers' and workmen's council has taken over the government of the empire.

By The Associated Press

WITH THE AMERICAN ARMY ON THE SEDAN FRONT, Nov. 11—2:00 P. M.—Thousands of American heavy guns fired the parting shot to the Germans at exactly eleven o'clock this morning.

WITH THE AMERICAN ARMY IN FRANCE, (2 p. m.) The line reached by the American forces at 11 o'clock today was being staked out this afternoon.

The Germans hurled a few shells into Verdun just before 11 o'clock.

PARIS, Nov. 11.—Official announcement of the signing of the armistice and the termination of hostilities at eleven o'clock this morning was given to the Paris press at 11:30 o'clock. Flags speedily began to appear and preparations were begun for a monster demonstration.

PARIS, Nov. 11.—(11:50 a. m.)—Marshal Foch was received by Premier Clemenceau at 10 o'clock this morning.

LONDON, Nov. 11.—(10:50 p. m.)—Marshal Foch, according to a French wireless dispatch received here has notified the German commander-in-chief that hostilities will cease on the whole front from November 11 at 11:00 o'clock a. m. (six o'clock Washington time).

The allied troops will not, until further orders, go beyond the line reached at that date and hour.

LONDON, Nov. 11.—(10:21 a. m.)—It is offibially announced that the armistice between the allies and Germany has been signed.

The announcement was made by Premier Lloyd George, who said:

"The armistice was signed at five o'clock this morning and hostilities are to cease on all fronts at 11 o'clock today.

LONDON, Nov. 11.—The period given for the evacuation of the left bank of the Rhine by the German forces has been extended by twenty-four hours, according to a French wireless dispatch received here.

(By The Associated Press.)

PARIS, Nov. 11.—(8:17 a. m.)—Announcement is made that the German delegates signed the armistice terms at six o'clock (French time) Monday morning.

Hostilities will end at 11 o'clock this morning.

The official announcement from Washington early today said that the armistice terms were signed at five o'clock French time. The London announcement fixed the same hour of signing.

LIGHTLESS NIGHT ORDER SUSPENDED

WASHINGTON, Nov. 11.—Fuel Administrator Garfield today suspended the lightless night order for tonight only for celebrations of peace throughout the country.

COMPLETE PACT ENDING WAR IS TOLD BY WILSON

WASHINGTON, Nov. 11.—The terms of the armistice with Germany were read to congress by President Wilson at one o'clock this afternoon. Assembled in the hall of the house, where nineteen months ago senators and representatives heard the President ask for declaration of war, they today heard him speak the words which heralded the coming of peace.

The strictly military terms of the armistice are embraced in eleven specifications which include the evacuation of all invaded territories, the withdrawal of the German troops from the left bank of the Rhine and the surrender of all supplies of war.

All allied vessels in German hands are to be surrendered and Germany is to notify neutrals that they are free to trade at once on the seas with the allied countries.

Among the financial terms included are restitution for damage done by the German armies, restitution of the cash taken from the national bank of Belgium and return of gold taken from Russia and Rumania.

The terms also provide for the abandonment by Germany of the treaties of Bucharest and Brest Litovsk.

The military terms include the surrender of 5,000 guns, half field and half light artillery; 30,000 machine guns; 3,000 flame throwers, and 2,000 airplanes.

The naval terms provide for the surrender of 160 submarines, 50 destroyers, six battle cruisers, 10 battleships, eight light cruisers and other miscellaneous ships.

The surrender of 5,000 locomotives, 50,000 wagons, 10,000 motor lorries, the railways of Alsace-Lorraine for use by the allies and stores of coal and iron also are included.

The immediate repatriation of all allied and American prisoners without reciprocal action by the allies also is included.

In connection with the evacuation of the left bank of the Rhine, it is provided that the allies shall hold the crossings of the river at Coblentz, Cologne and Mayence, together with bridgeheads in a 30 kilometer radius.

The right bank of the Rhineland, that occupied by the allies, is to become a neutral zone and the bank held by the Germans is to be evacuated in 19 days. The armistice is for 30 days, but the president spoke of the war as "coming to an end."

German troops are to retire at once from any territory held by Russia, Rumania and Turkey before the war.

The allied forces are to have access to the evacuated territory, either through Danzig or by the river Vistula. The unconditional capitulation of all German forces in East Africa within one month is provided.

The repatriation within 14 days of the thousands of unfortunate civilians deported from France and Belgium also is required.

Freedom of access to the Baltic with power to occupy German forts in the Kattegat is another provision. The Germans also must reveal location of mines, poisoned wells and like agencies of destruction and the allied blockade is to remain unchanged during the period of armistice.

German troops which have not left the invaded territories, which specifically includes Alsace-Lorraine within 14 days become prisoners of war.

These are the "high spots" of the terms as the president read them to congress.

Germany's acceptance of them, he said, signalized the end of the war because it made her powerless to renew it.

All ports on the Black Sea occupied by Germans are to be surrendered and the Russian war vessels recently taken by the German naval forces also are to be surrendered to the allies.

The president made it plain that the nations which have overthrown the military masters of Germany will now attempt to guide the German people safely to the family of nations of democracy.

The president spoke as follows:

"Gentlemen of the Congress:—

"In these anxious times of rapid and stupendous changes it will in some degree enlighten my sense of responsibility to perform in person the duty of communicating to you some of the larger circumstances of the situation with which it is necessary to deal. The German authorities who have, at the invitation of the supreme war council, been in communication with Marshal Foch have accepted and signed the terms of armistice which he was authorized and instructed to communicate to them. Those terms are as follows:

"'1—Military clauses on western front. Cessation of operations by land and in the air six hours after the signature of the armistice.

"'2—Immediate evacuation of invaded countries, Belgium, France, Alsace Lorraine, Luxemburg, so ordered as to be completed within fourteen days from the signature of the armistice. German troops which have not left the above mentioned territories within the period fixed will become prisoners of war. Occupation by the allied and United States forces jointly will keep pace with the evacuation in those areas. All movements of evacuation and occupation will be regulated in accordance with a note annexed to the stated terms.

"'3—Repatriation beginning at once and to be completed within fourteen days of all inhabitants of the countries above mentioned, including hostages and persons under trial or convicted.

"'4—Surrender in good condition by the German armies of the following equipment: Five thousand guns (two thousand five hundred heavy; two thousand five hundred field), thirty thousand machine guns. Three thousand minenwerfers, two thousand aeroplanes (fighters, bombers—firstly D. seventy-three's and eight bombing machines).

"'The above to be delivered in Simmatu to the allies and the United States troops in accordance with the detailed conditions laid down in the annexed note.

"'5—Evacuation by the German armies of the countries on the left bank of the Rhine. These countries on the left bank of the Rhine shall be administered by the local authorities under the control of the allied and United States armies of occupation. The occupation of these territories will be determined by allied and United States garrisons holding the principal crossings of the Rhine-Mayence, Coblenz, Cologne, together with bridgeheads at these points in thirty kilometer radius on the right bank and by garrisons similarly holding the strategic points of the regions. A neutral zone shall be reserved on the right of the Rhine between the stream and a line drawn parallel to it forty kilometers to the east from the frontier of Holland to the parallel of Gernsheim and as far as practicable a distance of thirty kilometers from the east of stream from this parallel upon Swiss frontier.'"

"'Evacuation by the enemy of the Rhine lands shall be so ordered as to be completed with a further period of eleven days, in all nineteen days after the signature of the armistice. All movements of evacuation and occupation will be regulated according to the note annexed.

"'6—In all territory evacuated by the enemy there shall be no evacuation of inhabitants; no damage or harm shall be done to the persons or property of the inhabitants.

"'No destruction of property of the inhabitants. No destruction of any kind to be committed. Military establishments of all kinds shall be delivered intact as well as military stores of food, munitions, equipment not removed during the periods fixed for evacuation. Stores of food of all kinds for the civil population, cattle, etc., shall be left in situ. Industrial establishments shall not be impaired in any way and their personnel shall not be moved. Roads and means of communication of every kind, railroad, waterways, main roads, bridges, telegraphs, telephones, shall be in no manner impaired.

HAND OVER RAILWAYS.

"7—All civil and military personnel at present employed on them shall remain. Five thousand locomotives, fifty thousand wagons and ten thousand motor lorries in good working order with all necessary spare parts and fittings shall be delivered to the associated powers within the period fixed for the evacuation of Belgium and Luxemburg. The railways of Alsace-Lor-

(Continued on Page 5, Column 1)

Fair tonight and Tuesday, continued cool tonight, warmer Tuesday.

EDITIONS COMBINED

In order that The News employes may take part in the great parade celebrating the end of hostilities, the regular home edition and five o'clock edition of The News today has been combined into the final edition.

After a vigilance since early Saturday, without rest, employes of The News are taking part in the occasion. They have guarded the incoming news in order to present it to the public with all possible dispatch, and starting with the first extra shortly after 1:45 o'clock Monday morning, a total of eleven extras were issued.

The final edition, is the last edition for Monday.

OVERTIME ON GOVERNMENT WORK STOPPED

WASHINGTON, Nov. 11.—Orders stopping all overtime and Sunday work on government war contracts were authorized today after a conference of Secretaries Baker and Daniels and Chairman Hurley of the shipping board.

LOCAL PHONES ARE SWAMPED

Both local telephone companies were swamped with calls all day Monday. It was impossible to give satisfactory service on the most urgent calls. It appeared that everyone with a phone deemed it expedient to visit with a relative or acquaintance without taking into consideration that the telephone exchanges are compelled to work with insufficient help due to the scarcity of operators. Monday of all days should have been the day for subscribers to have given the operators the opportunity to handle the urgent business with despatch, was a claim made.

The request is made by both exchanges that the phone be used just as little as possible the remainder of the day and evening for social calls.

DEMONSTRATION IS WITNESSED IN WASHINGTON

WASHINGTON, Nov. 11.—President Wilson's first public appearance today was in response to calls from war trade board employes, who, headed by Chairman Vance McCormick and a band paraded to the White House at noon. The president waved his hand from the portico.

The fuel administration employes followed the war trade board workers and with crowds assembling from everywhere joined in the demonstration before the White House.

TRUTH BRINGS COMPLIMENT

Springfield's second newspaper, evidently flushed with its success in fooling the public Thursday, takes another whirl at it today by claiming to have first given to Springfield the news of the signing of the armistice. This is an absolute untruth for the News through its first extra and the Bauer Bros. and Light Company whistles gave the city its FIRST information and with several minutes to spare.

However the News at this time of joy and thanksgiving is not disposed to further argue so trivial a matter, but on the contrary gladly dispenses with further refuting proof to take in the interest of journalism the welcome opportunity of congratulating the Sun on the fact that it finally did get out an extra that in spite of some glaring misstatements in part was at least based on the TRUTH.

PRESIDENT WILSON—

STINSON

VOL. LXVI, No. 74. PRICE—TWO CENTS.

OUTSTANDING DRAFT CALLS CANCELLED BY PROVOST MARSHAL

WASHINGTON, Nov. 11.—By order of President Wilson, Provost Marshal General Crowder today directed the cancellation of all outstanding draft calls, stopping the movement during the next five days of 252,000 men and setting aside all November calls for over 300,000 men.

A small number of men in eastern states commenced entraining at six a. m. today for cantonments under the calls, and the cancellation comes too late to affect their status. They will be considered as in the army until demobilized. Men not yet entrained, but specially inducted or assembled by general call for whom the day and hour of service has been set by draft boards, will be considered honorably discharged and so paid.

Calls for the navy and marine corps are not affected by the cancellation, and entrainments of men for these services will continue as ordered. Draft boards will continue classification of registrants of September 12.

Secretary Baker later announced that so far as practicable all men who have been called and who have not completed their training will be immediately turned back to civilian life.

Mr. Baker made this statement after a conference which included the heads of practically every important bureau of the war department. He said more comprehensive announcements concerning the situation would be made later.

"All that can be said now," he said, "is that further calls and inductions under the draft have been suspended and that so far as we can, those men who have been called but who have not completely passed through the camps will be turned back to civilian life."

"To the extent that we can, we will turn back those men who have been entrained and who have not reached training camps."

PEOPLE GIVE VENT TO JOY OVER END OF WAR

The citizens of Springfield welcomed the news of the signing of the armistice and the cessation of hostilities as the greatest event the world has known. Their joy over the ending of the world catastrophe was unbounded. Many were elated beyond expression.

The News asked a number of citizens how they felt about the capitulation of Germany and the ending of the war, and their replies were as follows:

H. E. Titus, grocer and Civil war veteran: "As an old soldier, this is one of the greatest days I have ever seen. Our little trouble back in 1861-65 was not of much consequence in comparison with the conflict just ended. I felt that the Germans should have been given a little more of their medicine, but it is far better in the interests of humanity, that it should end in this way."

Max L. Kleeman, merchant: "Elated, a wonderful victory for democracy. The people should not forget, however, the greatest part of the work is yet to come. The funds for the United War Work campaign which started this morning should be greater than the total of the fourth Liberty loan."

Mayor C. F. McGilvray: "More than pleased. The ending of the war is the greatest thing that could happen to this country as well as foreign countries. The United States will have five of the best years of business we ever saw."

Fred J. Green, president of the Springfield Terminal Railway and Power company, and president of the Chamber of Commerce: "Hooray! Too happy for utterance. I have always

(Continued on Page 5, Column 4)

111. Front page of the Springfield newspaper on Armistice Day, November 11, 1918.

Company and Springfield, Light, Heat, and Power Company to announce the news of an armistice by blasting their big factory whistles. On Saturday, November 9, 1918, the newspaper published a key to the blasts. One long blast would mean that Germany had signed an armistice; two long blasts would mean that they had rejected it. Whistles would blow ten times each at one-minute intervals to repeat the code.

Word of the Armistice came over the telegraph wires at 1:45 a.m. on Monday, November 11, 1918. Springfield's own Corporal Leon Roth, a dispatch rider with the 319th Signal Battalion had carried the message announcing the Armistice twenty-five harrowing miles on a motorcycle across the Western Front and delivered it to the head of the American Expeditionary Force. *(fig. 110)*

110. Corp. Leon Roth

Springfield residents who lived within earshot of the whistles were awakened in the early morning hours by one long whistle blast repeated every sixty seconds for more than an hour. Word quickly spread via telephone to those out of earshot, and pandemonium erupted. Church and school bells rang and factory whistles blew. Any bell, whistle, horn, or other noisemaker was pressed into service. By dawn, newsboys were hawking the first extra of the day, which announced the Armistice and described the early morning revelry as an ear-splitting din that engulfed the entire town. *(fig. 111)*

People began descending on the downtown area around 8 a.m., and the crowd soon turned into, according to the day's newspaper, "a seething mass of humanity." People shook hands, waved flags, and marched in impromptu parades. Mayor McGilvray shut down City Hall and declared the day a holiday—"Liberty Day." Someone tacked a sign on the door of City Hall that read, "Nobody Home." Courts adjourned and factories, businesses, offices, and stores followed suit and closed their doors. City Commissioner Burton J. Westcott told a newspaper reporter, "I could not get into any place this morning. I had some business to transact at the bank. I found all of them closed. Then I went to the office of The American Seeding Machine Company and it was closed." He gave up and joined in the merriment.

The city's factory owners volunteered their trucks, and workers filled them to overflowing, waving whatever kind of flag they could secure and banging on drums, anvils, dishpans, and skillets as they made their way downtown. Two planes from Wilbur Wright Field amplified the jubilation by doing stunts over the city that morning. At noon, the members of the Rotary Club dined at the Hotel Bancroft as part of their regular Monday meeting, then brushed aside their regular program and went out into the street. They formed a column behind the Robbins and Myers Company band and paraded through the streets.

A formal parade was organized for 3 p.m. It would feature four divisions—one of schoolchildren, organized by teachers and superintendents; one of Red Cross workers; one of factory and business units, organized by superintendents; and one of floats, motor trucks, and automobiles. Boys from the Pythian orphanage band led the Red Cross unit. Harry Kissell's wife, Olive, a Red Cross volunteer, donned her uniform and marched with the unit. Every fraternal organization was represented, as were the Daughters of the American Revolution and the YMCA. The parade made its way east on High Street from Plum Street to Fountain Avenue. It then marched all the way to Ridgewood, then countermarched back to Main Street and headed west to Yellow Springs Street, where it disbanded. A 4-year-old Mary Lu Kissell joined her mother as the parade passed her grandfather's downtown drugstore and marched until they reached the Fountain Avenue Bridge. The last automobile in the lengthy parade did not leave the starting point until 4:30 p.m., an hour and a half after its start. Thousands marched and rode in the parade and many more thousands watched the spectacle. Boy scouts assisted police officers in keeping the crowds at bay. *(fig. 112)*

A "Meeting of Thanksgiving" was planned for two days later—Wednesday, November 13, 1918— at Memorial Hall. The newspaper announced that "Patriots of every creed and faith will join in a mass meeting to return thanks to God for victory and the coming peace." On that evening, the Robbins and Myers Band led Springfield citizens on a march from the downtown esplanade to Memorial Hall where the reverent but joyous celebration took place. Catholic priests, Protestant ministers, and a Jewish rabbi gave thanks for peace and a victory for humanity. Ridgewood resident James S. Webb led a rousing community sing-along.

The euphoria would persist for some time. Everyone was hopeful that the hardships of war would soon be over and life would return to normal. By the end of the first week of December the Kissell Real Estate Company was able to announce that listings were already more plentiful and that inquiries and sales had picked up. The high prices and building restrictions during the war had conspired to deal a serious blow to the real estate and building businesses. By the end of the year, however, the government had lifted all building restrictions, which fueled optimism that better days were ahead. Mayor McGilvray predicted that in the aftermath of the war, "The United States will have the five best years of business we ever saw." Only time would tell if he was right.

The year 1919 opened with a peculiar mix of hope and uncertainty in real estate and buildings circles. The building restrictions that had all but killed business were gone, but the specter of high materials and high labor costs still hung over their heads. Business was better, but many people who wanted to buy or build a home were still holding off in hopes that prices would come down in the aftermath of the war. Most people in the know, however, thought that while there might be some relief, prices would never again recede to their pre-war levels.

Meanwhile, the serious housing crisis that had plagued Springfield since the first decade of the twentieth century was worse than ever. Although the city was continuing to grow, and many people felt that a population of 100,000 was not out of the question in the next few years, lack of housing was becoming an obstacle to growth. The city could not continue to attract new businesses or recruit new employees from other areas if there was no place for workers to live. Lack of workers also meant higher labor costs, and higher labor costs made people reluctant to build new homes and free up older housing for people with lower incomes. It was a vicious cycle and a problem that had to be solved.

112. There are known photos of the celebration in downtown Springfield marking the end of World War I on Nov. 11, 1918. However, this image captures a similar revelry one year later on the first anniversary of Armistice Day.

The housing crisis was so severe in Springfield that the chamber of commerce was actively trying to solve it. In 1911, the precursor of the chamber of commerce, the Commercial Club, had platted Warder Park, a subdivision of nice working-class housing lying at the eastern edge of the city. Warder Park's southern boundary was Hillside Avenue and it expanded north to Columbus Avenue. It was bounded to the east and west by Burnett Road and Belmont Avenue. The Commercial Club had no desire to engage in real estate development, but the future growth of the city depended on having adequate worker housing. A corporation of Commercial Club members, including local manufacturers, businessmen, and other citizens who were mutually interested in Springfield's economic progress, floated the funds to build houses in the development. *(fig. 113)*

The location of Warder Park was chosen because it was within easy walking distance of ten of the biggest industries in Springfield—The Robbins and Myers Company; The James Leffel Company; The E.W. Ross Company; The Trump Water Wheel Company; The Ohio Steel Foundry Company; The International Harvester Company; French and Hecht; The Safety Emery Wheel Company; The Hoppes Manufacturing Company; and The McGregor Brothers Company. Streetcar lines also ran on two sides of Warder Park, providing convenient transportation.

Warder Park got off to a good start but cooled somewhat over anxiety about the economic downturn of 1914. Even though Springfield weathered much better than the rest of the country, there was some reluctance by manufacturers to increase production and add new workers. The war further stunted the project. House construction in Warder Park stopped and lot sales were suspended for the duration of the war.

After the war, in 1919, the chamber of commerce decided to renew its efforts in Warder Park. Richard E. McDaniel, a Ridgewood resident and manager of The Builders of Homes Company, was commissioned to construct fifty new homes in the addition. McDaniel had built numerous speculative homes in Ridgewood. The Kissell Real Estate Company would handle the sales in Warder Park. Brown Burleigh's advertising strategy for this working class neighborhood was naturally markedly different from that of Ridgewood. He created advertisements to appeal to the financial concerns of the working man—"Have your own garden. It enables you to cash in on your spare time. Your back yard in Warder Park, if you put in a garden, will produce for you $100.00 worth of vegetables each season, with an hour's work a day." "Keep chickens. Your wife can make them earn for you $75.00 a year. A small

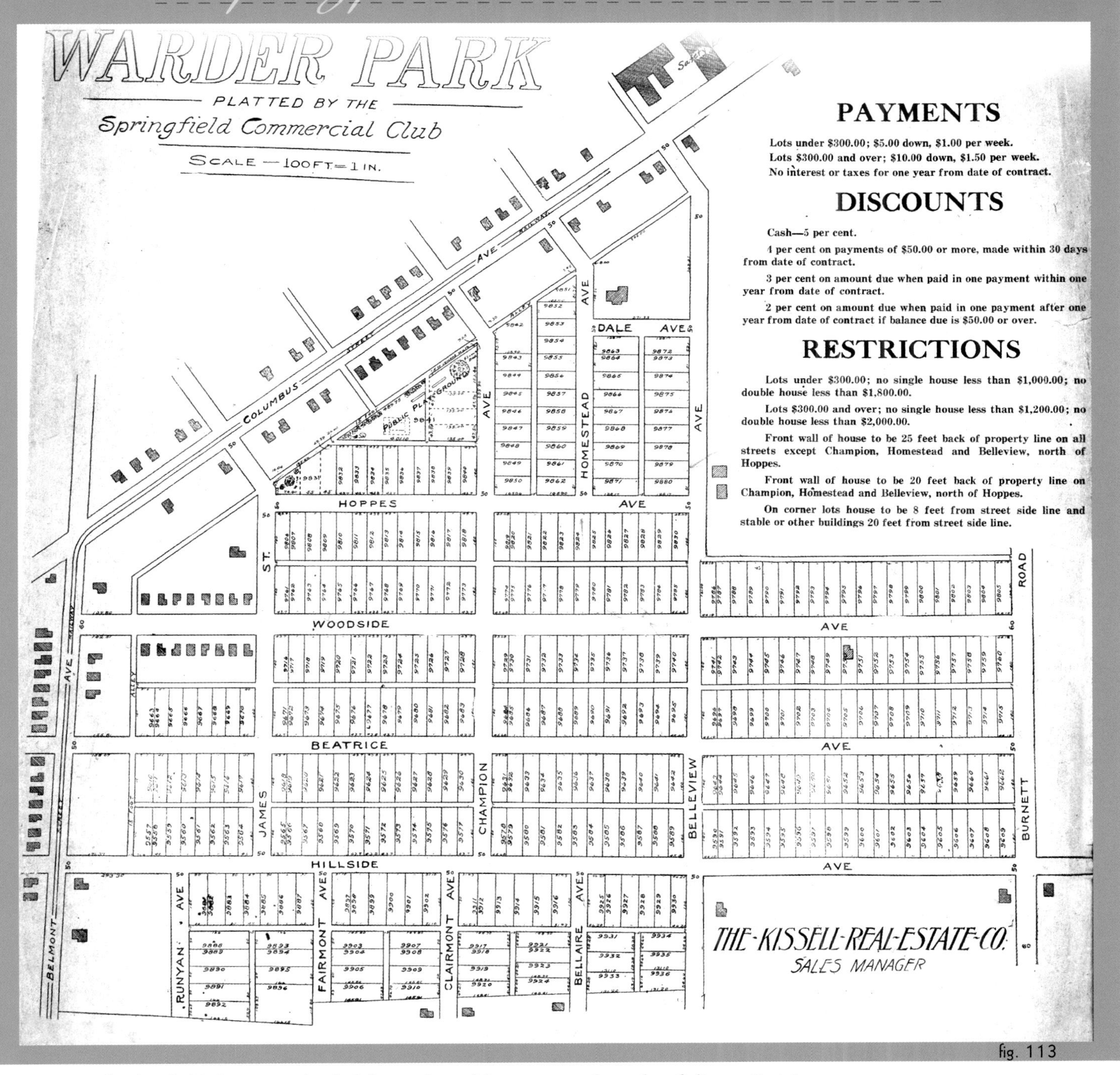

fig. 113

flock of chickens can be fed from the table waste and garden foliage. Raising chickens is very interesting. The care of a small flock is not hard work."

The sales office for Warder Park was open in the evenings to accommodate the schedules of buyers in an era when a six-day workweek was still routine for many laborers. In Warder Park, one could buy a two-bedroom home on a full-sized lot for $3,200, payable in installments, with a complete bath, a well-equipped kitchen with hot and cold running water, and electric light fixtures. The quality construction materials and techniques were heavily publicized. Harry Kissell told the newspaper, "There is no room any more for a shantytown section in any city, and building well at this time, the unsanitary and inconvenient shack will become a matter of yesterday in our city." Demand was so great that houses sold before the roofs were even on.

While the working class housing issue was being addressed in Warder Park, Springfield Real Estate Board members launched an aggressive campaign in 1919 to get people of middle and upper incomes to build and buy houses without delay. Andrew A. Hellmuth of the Link and Link Real Estate Company served as publicity director. A series of newspaper advertisements ran throughout spring, persuasively spelling out all the advantages of buying real estate and owning a home. The Kissell Improvement Company's own advertisements hammered away at the message that building prices were unlikely to ever come down and played up the fact that lots were still available at pre-war prices. Kissell had told fellow developers at the Third Annual Conference of Developers of High-Class Residence Property, held in February 1919 in Birmingham, Alabama,

115. The Dock's second Ridgewood home at 36 Dover Rd.

116. The living room of the Dock house at 36 Dover Rd.

that he had sold 60 percent of the lots in Ridgewood, but that people were now so gun-shy about building that he was considering giving a discount on lots if they agreed to build immediately.

Gradually, however, some people and businesses reluctantly came to the awareness that higher prices were here to stay and began to let contracts for their homes or commercial buildings. On June 22, 1919, the newspaper reported, perhaps somewhat prematurely, that the "period of hesitancy had passed." By late July, the real estate and building trades were getting work again. Local real estate men claimed that they had never had such brisk business. In comparison to the complete drought brought on by the war, it must have seemed that way. At the beginning of the war, real estate companies were devastated by the loss of men in their office going off to war, but as the war took its toll on business there was little need to replace them. Now, with business starting to come back, they were hiring again. Brown Burleigh added three new salesmen to the Kissell Real Estate Company's sales force that summer. And to Harry Kissell's delight, twelve new

114 (left). Frank E. & Helen Dock's first Ridgewood home at 112 S. Kensington Pl.
118 (middle). The sun room of the Dock house, 36 Dover Rd.
117 (above). The dining room of the Dock house on Dover Rd.

houses were going up in Ridgewood. However, the economic impact of the war would have a more lasting impact than anyone thought. In comparison to the complete drought of the past year and a half, this sudden upturn in business was cause for rejoicing, but it would be some time before the economic boom that everyone was predicting would begin in earnest.

Psychologically, though, the dark days of the war times were receding, and life was beginning to return to normal in the Ridgewood. In late May, the City Championship tennis tournament was held for the first time on the Ridgewood courts. Most of the clubs and athletic associations in town fielded players, and good-sized crowds gathered to watch. The newspaper reported on the tournament throughout week.

The men in the neighborhood who had gone off to war were starting to return. One of them was Frank E. Dock. Dock and his wife, Helen, had barely moved into their new home at 112 South Kensington Place in early 1918, when he was drafted into the Army. *(fig. 114)* Like many wives who were left behind when their husbands were drafted or enlisted, Mrs. Dock rented out their home and in her husband's absence went to live with her family. When Frank Dock returned home in the spring of 1919, the Docks decided to sell their original Ridgewood home and build a new one at 36 Dover Road. *(fig's. 115-118)* While the Docks were the first family to build a second home in Ridgewood, many others would follow as their financial status improved, their tastes changed, or their families outgrew their original Ridgewood home.

In mid-August, The Kissell Improvement Company launched a "clean up" sale of unsold lots on North and South Kensington Place, Grube Road, Stratford Place, Hampton Place, and Englewood Road. Lots on Fountain Boulevard were not included in the sale, and the lots available in the first phase of the development of Crescent Drive were sold out. Back in the spring, Frank Talbott had purchased the last unsold parcel on the street. It adjoined the lot upon which his home at 1824 Crescent Drive sat, and he planned to beautify it with a sunken garden. The handful of lots that were available on Ardmore and Dover Roads in the initial phase of Ridgewood was also sold out. By the end of September, only twenty-one out of the original 252 lots in Ridgewood remained unsold. The first section of Ridgewood was a success. In the beginning, Ridgewood had looked like a pipe dream to some, but a mere five years later it had even exceeded the expectations of its proponents, despite the setbacks caused by the war. Now Harry Kissell could fully turn his attention to the next phase of Ridgewood.

Meanwhile, work was finally resuming in Hills and Dales. In 1919, Theodore Weyant's widow and his former partner, P.J. Guthrie, sold the development to a large real estate company out of Chicago. The Fraser Real Estate Company, a Springfield interest, took over the improvements on behalf of the Chicago firm and restarted street work in the development by mid-June. At the time work had stopped due to war conditions in 1917, only about 60 percent of the improvements had been completed. After a long delay, work was starting again and houses were going up in Hills and Dales. By late August, a huge sales push, offering some prime lots as low as $450 dollars, was on. The period of zero activity was over, but because Hills and Dales got off to such a shaky start, it never really posed the type of competition for Ridgewood that it could have. It did, however, kindle in Harry Kissell the desire to offer a wooded section of his own.

Much of the land in the original section of Ridgewood had been pasture or was under cultivation when Kissell bought it and, consequently, had few trees. Lack of trees had not deterred buyers, but Kissell wanted Ridgewood to be the quintessential high-grade residential development in Springfield, and a wooded section would complete his vision. Now he had his eyes on a wooded tract that was part of the Knights of Pythias land at the entrance to Ridgewood.

In 1892, the Pythians had acquired an eighty-four acre tract that laid to the west of the old Blount plat, and between McCreight Avenue to the south and Grube (Harding) Road to the north. The land had been part of the old McCreight estate and would be the site for the Pythians' new state orphanage. Construction on the first building began in 1894, and it opened in 1895. An administration building and separate dormitories for boys and girls were completed in 1897. These three castle-like brick buildings were constructed in the Gothic style and featured dramatic turrets and gargoyles, making them quite a striking landmark in the area. *(See fig. 30, page 33)* Once completed, between a hundred and two hundred children lived in the Pythian orphanage at any given time. (The Pythians also ran a state home for the aged in Springfield. In 1914, they bought the massive Phineas P. Mast house on West High Street for that purpose.)

On the orphanage campus on McCreight Avenue, about twenty-five acres were occupied by buildings and their grounds, seventeen acres were planted with gardens, which supplied much of the food for the orphanage, and forty-two acres at the rear of the property was primeval forest, known locally as Pythian Woods. Pythian Woods was exquisitely picturesque with its towering old-growth trees, but it served no useful purpose for the orphanage. Therefore, in the spring of 1919, the Pythians agreed to sell it to Harry Kissell. Plans to develop the land west of Fountain Boulevard and Crescent Drive as the next phase of Ridgewood were deferred, and instead "The Woods," as he would christen it, became the

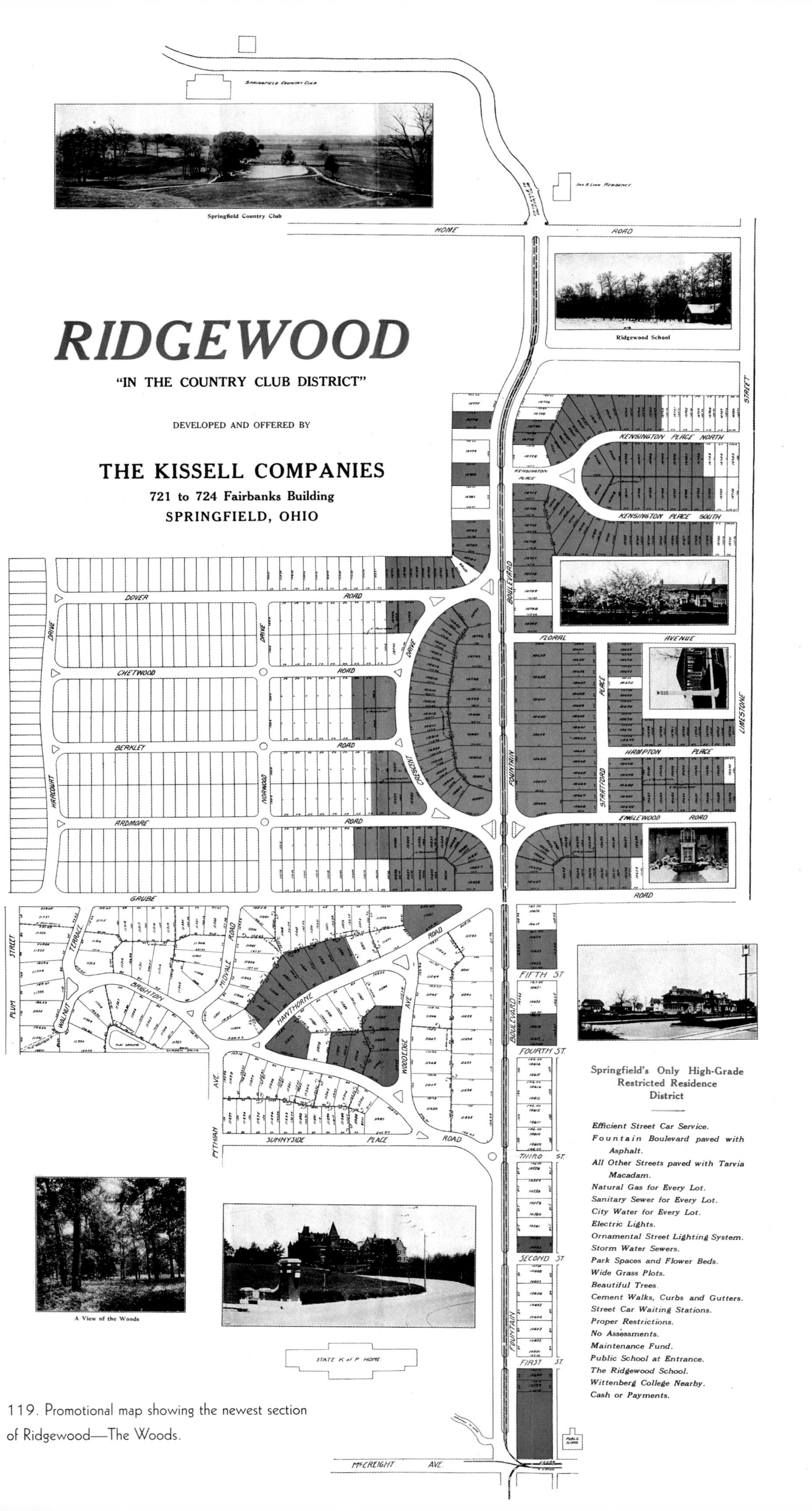

119. Promotional map showing the newest section of Ridgewood—The Woods.

second section of Ridgewood to be developed and offered for sale. The Woods plat, however, was officially known as Ridgewood Phase III, because the original section of Ridgewood had been composed of both Phase I, the land north of Grube Road, and Phase II, the Blount land between McCreight Avenue and Grube Road that was platted at a slightly later date.

For the design of The Woods, Kissell chose the landscape architecture firm of Pitkin and Mott, who had a practice on Euclid Avenue, in Cleveland, Ohio. Before securing the Kissell contract, William Pitkin, Jr., and Seward H. Mott had received a few other landscaping commissions in the region, including the Louis E. and Nell Bauer house on Crescent Drive in Ridgewood, as well as in Upper Arlington, King Thompson's suburb in Columbus, Ohio. But they also boasted an extensive resume of work for many big name clients in Detroit, Toledo, Cleveland, Cincinnati, Columbus, Rochester, Buffalo, and New York City. Two years later, in 1921, they would design the master landscape plan for Wittenberg College, and William Pitkin would serve for a number of years as a member of the college's Advisory Board of Architecture and Campus Planning. Before that time, the placement of buildings and drives at Wittenberg had been hit or miss. But Pitkin developed a long-term, comprehensive plan for landscaping and future building sites. It was through their work on the wooded section of Ridgewood in 1919 that Pitkin and Mott came to the attention of Wittenberg administrators.

During the third week of September 1919, Pitkin and Mott paid a visit to Springfield to make final suggestions regarding The Woods plat. The plat was accepted by the city commission on December 8, 1919, but demand for this new section was so hot that the first advertisement for it ran a mere nine days later, on December 17, 1919, before the first shovel of dirt had been turned over. The Kissell Improvement Company had received so many requests to see the plat map that they were making it available for inspections at the Kissell offices in the Fairbanks building the following day. *(fig. 119)*

In a marked departure from the way they had handled sales of the original section of Ridgewood, Harry Kissell and Brown Burleigh agreed to allow buyers to inspect the site and buy before any work was done. They had simply staked off the lots and marked where the streets would be. They could not even finalize prices because it was impossible to know what the development costs would ultimately be. Instead, they set a minimum price for each lot, and buyers agreed to pay whatever the final cost. The Woods section presented a rare opportunity that affluent customers jumped on. Not only was the section uniquely beautiful, it would be part of an established neighborhood that had already acquired cachet in Springfield. Ridgewood was fashionable and a known quantity, and eager customers bought with confidence.

In addition to winding up sales in the original section of Ridgewood and starting the development of The Woods section, 1919 was the year when Harry Kissell would promote a project that he later told fellow developers was one of the smartest moves he ever made. It helped build the Ridgewood brand and provided a valuable amenity to the neighborhood that he genuinely loved. Since the inception of the Ridgewood development, Kissell had tossed around the idea of having a private school in the neighborhood. His cohorts playfully chided him that his true motivation was a desire to be able to put a red tam on the head of his beloved little daughter, Mary Lu, so as to monitor her progress from the windows of his house as she made her way to school. The doting father could not really disagree with them.

At the time, there were several young ladies in the community who were teaching kindergarten or tutoring small groups of children, but there was no organized private school. In the spring of 1919, now that the war was over and much of the first section of Ridgewood was sold, the timing seemed right, and the conversation began again in earnest among the small group that included Harry Bretney, Fred Wallace, Dr. Harrie Martin, Carl Fried, Elwood Myers, Warren Myers, Allen Nolte, and Armin Kelly. Kissell generously offered up a lot in the new wooded section of Ridgewood as a site for the school. The triangular-shaped piece of ground located just west of Fountain Boulevard and bounded by Grube and Hawthorne Roads, was valued at $6,000. To further sweeten the pot and get things going, Kissell threw in $1,000 in cash towards construction.

Kissell and his associates tapped Miss Marthena Winger to promote the venture. The 29-year-old Winger was a first cousin of Harry Kissell's wife, Olive, and had been educated at Wittenberg and Ohio Wesleyan. At the time, she was engaged in private tutoring in Springfield and had long expressed an interest in starting a private school. With Miss Winger on board, the group of men called a meeting at the Hotel Bancroft and invited eleven more of the city's most prominent men—leading businessmen, manufacturers, doctors, and lawyers—to join them. At the meeting, Miss Winger outlined the proposition for the private school. And, perhaps most persuasively, she made

120. Artist rendering of the design proposed for the Ridgewood School building.

the argument that most cities of Springfield's size had two or three private schools but since a seminary on East High Street had closed several years ago, Springfield had none. Not about to let the Best 60,000 City in America be outdone, the group agreed to incorporate a new private school with capital stock of $10,000 with the intent to begin the process of erecting a building as soon as possible.

The plan for the new Ridgewood School was to accept up to fifty students and initially offer instruction from kindergarten through fourth grade. Miss Winger would be employed as principal and the teacher of first and second grades. Miss Jeane Hatch was hired as kindergarten teacher, and Miss Nellie Myers would serve as the third and fourth grade teacher. Another grade would be added each year until it was possible for children to receive all their education at Ridgewood School until they were ready for junior high school.

A building committee, formed to oversee the school's design and construction, engaged the local architectural firm of Hall and Lethly to draw up the plans. Hall and Lethly were responsible for the design of many homes in Ridgewood, and the committee was confident that it could produce a design that was architecturally harmonious with the rest of the neighborhood and would not look like a commercial building. The new school would have three classrooms, an auditorium with a stage, ample cloakrooms, and a luncheon room in the basement. The exterior of the building was originally to be of the English cottage type, finished in stucco with a half-timbering effect, but the design was later revised to make the exterior brick. Hall and Lethly were so successful in making their design fit seamlessly into the residential neighborhood that, for years to come, it was not unusual for a salesman to mistake the school for a home and knock on the front door.

The land on which it was to be situated was heavily wooded, which inspired the school's slogan, "Ridgewood—The School in the Woods." A June 15, 1919, newspaper article made the first public announcement of the school's formation and featured an artist's rendering of the proposed building. Hall and Lethly had the plans and specifications done and were ready to receive bids from contractors by the last week of June. Construction was set to start July 1, and it was hoped that the building would be ready for occupancy by the end of September, in time for the start of the school year. Meanwhile, Miss Winger repaired to Lake Chautauqua in New York State to take a six-week preparatory course prior to the opening of the school. *(fig. 120)*

George Cogswell, of the Cogswell Building Company, would handle the construction and was under orders to rush completion as fast as possible without compromising quality. The foundation was excavated the last week

121. Ridgewood School, shortly after completion, 1919.

of July and, by the third week of September, the building was under roof and workmen were plastering the interior. Nevertheless, it was quickly becoming apparent that, despite an ambitious schedule, the building would not be ready for the planned opening day of the school year. As a result, school had to be held in temporary quarters until Monday, October 20, 1919. However, even after students and teachers occupied the building, there were frequent interruptions as finishing work was still being completed. The total cost of the project, including the value of the lot was $25,000. A clause was inserted into the deed that if the building ever stopped being used as a school, the property would revert to the Kissell Real Estate Company, and Harry Kissell would settle any financial obligations of the school at the time. *(fig's. 121 & 122)*

Tuition at every grade level of Ridgewood School was set at $125 a year per pupil. Children would be promoted by subject at their own pace to higher grades or "groups." Because of the school's location in a grove of forest trees, nature study was an important component of instruction at Ridgewood from the beginning. When weather permitted, students took nature walks and studied flowers, trees, insects, and birds, and gathered seeds and berries.

There was an especially heavy emphasis on outdoor activities in kindergarten. Ridgewood kindergarten was based on the Froebelian method. Friedrich Froebel was a pioneer in early childhood education who had opened the first "kindergarten," or children's garden, in Germany in 1837. Before Froebel's ground-breaking work, most people felt that children under the age of 7 did not have the ability to develop cognitive skills. However, Froebel believed that children could learn through play and directed activities, a revolutionary idea at the time. Further, he saw the role of a teacher of young children as that of a guide, not a lecturer. To that end, Froebel developed the concept of gardens for children where they could participate in growing and harvesting food, and, in turn, develop cognitive skills and a love and incentive for work. Kindergartners at

124. The Ridgewood School May queen, Lucille Schaefer, flanked by her attendants—John Harwood & Marjorie Jane Myers, May 22, 1921.

Ridgewood maintained a school garden where they planted a variety of seeds and bulbs, then tended the growing flowers and vegetables. They even studied food preservation. Children between the ages of 3½ and 6 years old could be admitted to the Ridgewood kindergarten.

In other grades, the traditional subjects of arithmetic, spelling, reading, geography, history, music, art, and French were taught, and special emphasis was given to practicing the Palmer method of penmanship. This popular, early twentieth-century method taught a uniform system of cursive writing that focused on using arm and shoulder movements instead of finger movements, to increase legibility. Chapel services were held three mornings a week in the school's auditorium, and students participated in physical training five days a week. Physical training generally involved folk dancing and a variety of games, but Miss Eula Wilcox of the YWCA came once a week to teach the students gymnastics. Whenever possible, physical training was held outdoors.

All of the holidays were marked with great enthusiasm at the school. Children crafted valentines, participated in Easter egg rolls, and arrived in costume to celebrate Halloween in the school's auditorium, which was decorated each year with leaves and cornstalks. At Thanksgiving, students collected food, clothing, and money to be distributed to the needy through the Young Woman's Mission and the Social Service League. Christmas was a time of much merriment at the Ridgewood School. A huge tree was erected in the auditorium, children made gifts for their parents, and Santa Claus always paid a visit. May Day was celebrated each year with a pageant performed by students and held outdoors on the lawn under the trees. The annual pageant became a big social event in the neighborhood for years to come. *(fig's. 123, 124 & 125)*

126. Mary Lu Kissell and Adelaide Bretney at the Kissell home, Christmas 1919.

Even when classes were not in session, the little brick school remained a center of activity in the neighborhood. When Kissell donated the land and money towards construction, it came with a stipulation that children in the neighborhood could use the school's playground after hours even if they did not attend the school. The

122. The first class of the Ridgewood School, fall 1919. Mary Lu Kissell is seated in the first row, second from the left.

125. The Ridgewood School pageant, Spring 1921.

auditorium of the school was utilized by various organizations for meetings. The Ridgewood District Association, the official neighborhood association of Ridgewood, held all its meetings there. The Ridgewood Mothers' Club met there once a month and discussed educational and general childhood issues. On occasion, an eminent psychologist would be engaged to address the group, and the meetings were followed by a very popular social hour.

Of the forty-two students enrolled during the first year of Ridgewood School, only two lived in Ridgewood—Mary Lu Kissell and Adelaide Bretney. At the time, there were only thirty-seven houses completed or under construction in Ridgewood and less than forty children under the age of 18 living in the neighborhood. The majority of the rest of the children enrolled at Ridgewood School came from affluent homes on North Fountain Avenue, South Fountain Avenue, and East High Street. Many of them arrived each day in chauffeured limousines. *(fig. 126)*

No matter where the students lived, the school did much to raise the profile of the Ridgewood name throughout Springfield. The roster of attendees was published at the beginning of each school year in the newspaper, and events at the school were usually covered in the society column. As time went on, and more houses were built in Ridgewood, the composition of the student body would change. By the 1927-1928 school year, approximately half of the students lived in the neighborhood. And there was no doubt that proximity to their children's school was a consideration for many parents who chose to buy in Ridgewood. Students who did not live in the neighborhood carried the Ridgewood name home with them each day as they returned from school.

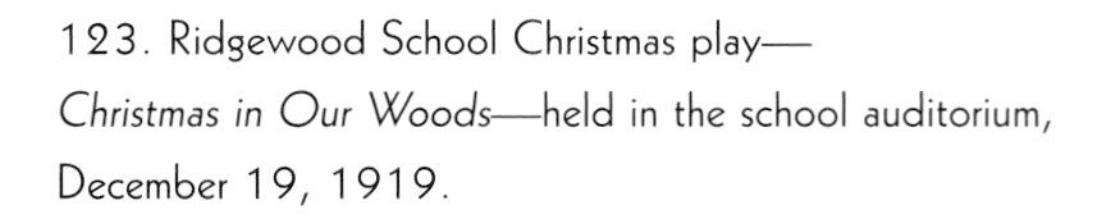

123. Ridgewood School Christmas play—*Christmas in Our Woods*—held in the school auditorium, December 19, 1919.

Our beautiful school in the woods
We love with all our might
And that is why we are so good, so happy, and so bright
Ridgewood, Ridgewood, happy, happy Ridgewood
Ridgewood, Ridgewood, best in all the land.

127. The then vacant lot on the northwest corner of N. Fountain Blvd. and Sunnyside Pl. The original fountain is visible on the triangular parklet to the left.

5 A GOLDEN AGE O

THE ERA KNOWN AS THE ROARING TWENTIES REALLY STARTED WITH MORE OF A MURMUR.

With the greatest war in human history behind them, Americans were full of optimism about the future. In the aftermath of the war, however, business conditions in the United States had still not returned to normal. The building trades were still being plagued by high labor costs and high materials costs, which were continuing to rise. Wholesale prices on building materials peaked in 1920 at 147 percent above 1913 prices. In addition, a severe lumber shortage threatened to exacerbate the situation. While everyone seemed to agree that prosperity was imminent and that the greatest building boom in history was just around the corner, people were still putting off building in hopes that prices would come down.

To complicate things further, credit was becoming tight for those who were willing to build or buy. The credit crunch was fueled by the new craze of investing in stocks and bonds, once the province of only the affluent, and it was having a serious effect on real estate and building. Money that average Americans would have ordinarily deposited in savings accounts at banking or savings and loan institutions was being diverted to play the stock market. As a result, there was less money available to lend for mortgages. And the long-standing safe haven for investors—real estate—was falling out of favor as more and more people were looking to make a quick buck in the stock market. Taken together, these circumstances conspired to create the perfect storm that

F PROSPERITY

dampened the housing market and frustrated real estate agents, builders, and home seekers.

Springfield had been in sound economic shape going into the war. For the most part, the city had escaped the worst of the economic recession of 1914-1916 and was poised to recover faster than many American cities after the war. But the housing famine still stood in the way of the city's progress. The war had almost completely shut down new residential building, and every year, the housing stock was further diminished as some houses were destroyed by fire, some were demolished to make room for new commercial buildings, and some were converted to other uses. And plenty of work in local factories meant that the population continued to grow and any vacant housing that was available was quickly absorbed. One thousand men were employed at the Lagonda plant of the International Harvester Company, with plans to add a thousand more when the plant began to manufacture motor trucks in 1921. Robbins and Myers employed 3,000 men at three plants. The continuing housing famine, however, threatened to make it hard to attract and retain workers. In early 1920, Robbins and Myers took the drastic step of purchasing fifty homes that the chamber of commerce had under construction in Warder Park, as well as all the empty lots left in the development, with the plan to erect a hundred more homes and offer financing to their workers just to ensure an adequate workforce.

The estimate was that it would take five years of normal building to catch up with the pent-up demand for homes. People's inability to find suitable housing was so acute that they were resorting to putting their furniture in storage and living in hotels. Multiple families sharing a house were commonplace even if there was no familial relationship between them. Even those who were in a position to buy a house often couldn't find one available. Homes that were offered for sale often sold repeatedly, each time at an escalated price, as people sought to profiteer in a market of low supply and high demand. In the overheated market, landlords would sometimes sell houses right out from under tenants.

In the local newspaper, Harry Kissell expressed optimism about the dire situation. "There must be an enormous amount of building done in Springfield," he said. "As soon as things become normal again, which we hope and believe is coming to pass soon, people will want to be relieved of their congestion, families will wish to go to themselves, old desires for a home which have been stifled for five years or more will again assert themselves, and Springfield will see the largest amount of home building which it has ever seen in any one year."

In the spring of 1920, despite lingering worries about the economy, Kissell was forging ahead with the improvements in the new wooded section of Ridgewood. Only one announcement had ever appeared in the newspaper about The Woods, and that had run the previous December. However, by May 2, 1920, The Kissell Improvement Company could proudly state in the newspaper that over $50,000 worth of lots had been sold in the section and those sales were almost solely by word of mouth.

The buzz was huge on this exclusive new section of Ridgewood and the company chose to play up that exclusivity in its advertising. Beginning on May 29, 1920, The Kissell Improvement Company ran a series of cryptic newspaper advertisements, the first of which was a small ad that read simply: "90." The next day they followed with one that said, "90—Not a cigarette." By the third day, they had thoroughly piqued the curiosity of the town, and the new ad stated, "90—Not a cigarette, not a breakfast food." On June 1, "90—Not a cigarette, not a breakfast food, or a patent medicine," appeared. By June 2, the suspense was nearly over. That day, readers were directed to "See tomorrow's news." No mention was made in any of this series of advertisements that they were placed by The Kissell Improvement Company.

Finally, on June 3, 1920, the intriguing mystery was solved when the company announced in a newspaper advertisement that the mysterious "90" referred to the limited amount of lots available in the desirable wooded section of Ridgewood. Only ninety families in a city of 60,840 people could call this select area home, and only ninety families could enjoy its rare natural beauty. "No other "wooded tract—all virgin forest trees—is located like this, within the corporation limits of Springfield," the June 3 advertisement read. At the time, Hills and Dales was still outside the city limits, and its location required a substantial walk to the nearest streetcar line. However, The Woods had the same rural ambience as Hills and Dales with closer proximity to the city, access to city services, and more easily accessible public transportation.

"Indeed I had no idea that a town of 60,000 people could make such a tremendous showing, and support such a well designed and laid-out development as Ridgewood. I want to congratulate you on the work you are doing."

—John M. Demarest, New York City.

In an effort to keep costs down in the postwar inflationary period, The Kissell Improvement Company was handling its own construction for this section of Ridgewood. Initially, it had put the work

128. Looking northeast down Sunnyside Pl. at the rear of the Shawver house at 101 Brighton Rd. Note the way the curbing was redirected in order to preserve the tree.

out for bid by contractors, but when the bids came back too high, Kissell decided to purchase construction equipment and hire his own men to complete the project. Not only did this give him the ability to avoid a contractor's markup, it gave him more control over making sure the work was done to his exacting specifications. The Woods section would be developed in two phases. Hawthorne Road, Woodedge Avenue, a section of Brighton Road, and eight lots on the south side of Grube Road just west of Ridgewood School, would be the first part to be developed, with an initial offering of fifty-four lots. Sunnyside Place, Midvale Road, Walnut Terrace, and the remaining portion of Brighton Road would be constructed and lots offered at a later date. The later offering would also include six lots on Pythian Avenue.

In the spring of 1920, workers were busy in the first phase of The Woods trenching for sewers, excavating for streets, and laying water and gas pipes. Improvements were being rushed as much as possible while still maintaining quality. Harry Kissell and his little daughter, Mary Lu, made the rounds each morning in his automobile to inspect the progress. Several triangular parklets were also being laid out, a design element from the original Ridgewood plat, which landscape architects Pitkin and Mott had carried over to the new section. Kissell was planning to erect a third streetcar waiting station on the triangular parklet where Sunnyside Place and Brighton Road left Fountain Boulevard, but this was later changed when he decided to install a fountain instead. The same ornamental lighting standards that were used in the original section of Ridgewood would also be used in The Woods. However, unlike much of the original section of Ridgewood, the streets in The Woods would follow the curvilinear form and meander in a naturalistic manner, resulting in many picturesque, irregularly shaped lots. Pitkin and Mott also made every attempt to preserve as many trees as possible, which influenced the way streets and lots were laid out and where sidewalks were located. *(fig's. 127, page 160 & fig. 128, page 164)*

Following the mysterious "90" ads that ran at the end of May and the beginning of June, Brown Burleigh followed the same marketing strategy that the company had utilized with much success for the original section of Ridgewood. He launched a series of large advertisements for The Woods that ran virtually every day in the newspaper throughout the month of June. One unique ad, which

"I want to tell you how keenly I enjoyed my visit to Springfield. I think your citizens have a very wonderful proposition offered to them in your new Woodland district."

—Edward H. Bouton, Baltimore, Maryland.

appeared on June 6, 1920, featured a persuasive letter from Harry Kissell to Brown Burleigh, written while Kissell was presiding over the National Sub-Dividers Conference in Kansas City, Missouri, which was part of the Annual Convention of the National Association of Real Estate Boards. (The National Sub-Dividers Conference was the descendent of the series of Conferences of Developers of High-Class Residence Property that had taken place from 1917-1919, of which Harry Kissell had been a part.)The clever piece of advertising warned potential buyers that a rise in lot prices was imminent and cautioned them that they should buy at once.

(fig. 129)

Subsequent advertisements continued to hammer two of the primary themes used to market this section of Ridgewood—exclusivity and prestige. One ad did not mince words about the social status a home in The Woods would convey to its owner—"Just as surely as a man is judged by his associates, his success is determined by the place in which he lives." The Kissell sales force would even show interested parties which lots had been sold and tell them who had bought them, so buyers would know whom their neighbors would be. And the company assured potential buyers that all the people who bought lots in the new section were community builders like themselves, with a vested interest in the future prosperity of Springfield.

In addition to exclusivity and prestige, advertisements for The Woods focused on all

Hotel Muehlebach
Whitmore Hotel Co.
Lessee

Kansas City, Mo.
June 2, 1920.

Mr. Brown Burleigh
Secy., The Kissell Companies.
Springfield, Ohio.

My dear Burleigh:

After talking with a number of the more prominent sub-dividers who are attending the convention here, I find that it is the consensus of opinion that the biggest market which we have ever known in the sale of vacant lots is ahead of us. The very good reason given is that vacant property is the only thing we know of that has not suffered price inflation, and before long, when building materials are reduced to a price that warrants construction on a large scale, vacant lots must necessarily advance - by reason of their shortage and the great demand that will follow. In the meantime, houses have reached such high prices that relief must be found in the construction of new homes. And the same demand for homes from an increased population, which has brought about these conditions in the improved property market, must shortly increase vacant property prices through increased demand for building space.

There is such a tremendous shortage of houses that as soon as the financial condition of the country warrants, we will face the greatest building boom in history. The people must have places to live. There is today a limited amount of restricted vacant property available in Springfield. A study of the local situation proves that there is very little property which can be developed, and what is now available will be taken up quickly even from the ordinary increase in our population - to say nothing of the tremendous shortage occasioned by some four years of inactivity in building.

Tell Strauss to push construction work in Ridgewood with all possible speed; and tell Fiske that he need not be a bit afraid to advise any of his prospective customers to buy at once.

Yours very truly,

H. S. Kissell

fig. 129

130. Triangular parklet at the intersection of Brighton Rd. and Woodedge Ave., looking northeast at the east side of Woodedge where the homes at 1520, 1530 and 1600 Woodedge Ave. would later be built.

the gifts that Mother Nature had bestowed upon it. Almost every type of Ohio wildflower and a variety of towering hardwood forest trees could be found in the new section. Squirrels frolicked and bird lovers could delight in the many bluebirds, martins, wrens, thrushes, robins, cardinals, and many other warblers that abounded. Some advertisements waxed poetic when describing the pastoral appeal of the new section, even quoting Longfellow—"This is the forest primeval." Other ads promoted the spiritual connection with nature that a home in The Woods would provide: "In the evening you can sit in the open, and see the beautiful sunsets, and watch the candles of heaven lit one by one, and your children can figure out the Seven Sisters and the Big Dipper, and wonder what it all means." The Kissell Improvement Company promoted the new section as a "residential masterpiece" that nature had created. With the assistance of landscape architects, they had preserved that beauty, and now they declared that The Woods was Springfield's "residential place de luxe," a marked departure from the older, affluent residential sections of Springfield.

Another marketing strategy that was employed for the first section of Ridgewood was revived for The Woods. Advertisements were crafted that directly targeted the unique interests and desires of men or women. Wives, the

131. Looking northeast along Hawthorne Rd. before many houses were built. Homes along W. Harding Rd. are visible in the background. Ridgewood School is visible to the right.

ads stated, could enjoy entertaining their friends in their modern new homes. The Children's Paradise theme was also resurrected to appeal to the motherly instinct. In the summer of 1920, 162 people lived in Ridgewood and 30 percent of them were children. Ridgewood was promoted as a safe place for children to play with the right playmates during their formative years. According to the ads, a mother did not have to worry about threats to her children's physical safety or their character development in Ridgewood. And, of course, the proximity to Ridgewood School was always a persuasive argument. Advertisements targeted at men promised them that they could associate with their peers and enjoy recreation on the Ridgewood tennis courts and golf at the country club. And, perhaps more significant, they could have a private drive for their machine. "There are no alleys in Ridgewood," the ads boasted.

For the first time ever in a Kissell Company promotion, the June ad campaign stated that lots in Ridgewood were a good investment, noting that people who sold their lots had doubled their money. In the past, the company had avoided promoting the development as an investment. While it was quick to clearly state it still did not encourage speculation, the reality was that it was competing like never before with the stock market for people's dollars. And it

132. View of the west side of Woodedge Ave., circa 1925. The Dr. Robert C. & Jessie Rind home, 1601 Woodedge Ave., is to the left.

took the opportunity to remind potential customers that real estate was "the safest investment on earth. It is real."

Despite the competition, however, in June of 1920, lot sales in The Woods continued to do well, and only a handful of lots were still available in the original section of Ridgewood. Sales had gone so well in the original section that the sales office on the east side of Fountain Boulevard, opposite the streetcar waiting station at Dover Road and Crescent Drive, was being dismantled and the lot on which it sat was being offered for sale.

By late July, Brighton Road, Woodedge Avenue, and Hawthorne Road were taking shape and one could actually see what up to this point had only been described and buyers had to visualize. Throughout the summer and into the fall, The Kissell Improvement Company pushed the work to try and finish as much as possible before cold weather set in. By mid-September, the sewer system was almost finished and curbing and gutters were under way. On occasion, additional day labor was needed in order to hasten the completion of some part of the improvements. When this was necessary, The Kissell Improvement Company ran an advertisement in the newspaper stating how many men were required and instructing them to board a truck that would leave the following morning at 6:15 a.m. from downtown at the corner of Columbia and Limestone Streets. Work proceeded into the winter. By the end of the year, all the curbing and guttering was completed in the first phase of The Woods, and gravel had been applied to the initial streets. The final course of Tarvia and pea gravel would be applied in the spring. *(fig's. 130, 131 & 132)*

All of the construction activity in The Woods was an indicator that life was getting back to normal, and the hardships and shortages of the war were over. Right in the midst of it sat the little school in the woods. That year, Christmas at Ridgewood School was celebrated in fine style. A large tree was erected in the center of the auditorium, and miniature trees and balloons of every hue were placed in each of the classrooms. A child danseuse, little Miss Verna Fulton of Columbus, Ohio, was brought in to dance for the children. Afterward they engaged in a rowdy peanut hunt, followed by the telling of a Christmas story. Ice cream, in the shapes of animals, and cookies were served. And, most excitingly, Santa Claus visited in the personage of Frank Dock. A year ago, Dock was just returning from serving in the war. Now he was back and building a new home on Dover Road, and he had exchanged his military uniform for a Santa suit. *(fig. 133)*

The year 1921 was when the economy finally turned the corner. The price of materials and labor was coming down a little, giving a much-needed boost to new construction. At the opening of the building season in March of 1921, new building permits were up in Springfield 167 percent over 1920 rates. By the end of April, they were up 354 percent over the previous year. That month, the Kissell Company launched an aggressive advertising campaign in an effort to take advantage of the modest dip in prices. The ads made the case that the decline in prices might be fleeting, and, if construction costs did stay low for awhile, then demand would increase and ultimately drive up prices again. Either way, the Kissell ads argued that this was a small window of opportunity if one was in the market for a new home—"Any Springfielder who contemplates ever owning his own home should select his site, and make his purchase without further delay. The time has come when waiting longer will cause a loss instead of a saving."

Springfield's citizens seemed to agree with that assessment. In 1921, there would be over a million dollars in new construction in Springfield. About a third of it was in the north end, the fastest growing section in the city with the biggest increase in property values. Another third of the construction took place downtown, with the remainder spread over the other areas of the city. In April of 1921, the Harshman addition, later known as Parkview Acres, was under development adjacent to Snyder Park. However, the west end would see the least amount of construction that year. The complete lack of paved roads in the west end was a deterrent to growth. When Maiden Lane was finally paved several years later, the area would start to see increased development. Nevertheless, in the spring of 1921, everyone was rejoicing that business conditions were at long last returning to normal, and the city was once again experiencing the kind of growth it had seen before the war. *(fig. 134)*

The spring of 1921 would also be one of the defining moments in Harry Kissell's professional life. By all accounts, Kissell was not a man given to personal pride, but his pride in his hometown was ample. And it was with the greatest satisfaction that in April of 1921 he welcomed the biggest, most successful real

fig. 134

RS
RS

133. The Ridgewood School Christmas party, 1920.

WORLD'S NEWS RECEIVED OVER ASSOCIATED PRESS WIRE

SPRINGFIELD DAILY NEWS

16 PAGES TODAY

VOL. LXVIII, No. 80. Home Edition SPRINGFIELD, OHIO, WEDNESDAY, APRIL 6, 1921. PRICE—TWO CENTS.

NEW MANDATE NOTES ARE SENT TO ALLIES BY U. S. GOVERNMENT

Communications Cover All American Rights Growing Out of World War, It Is Learned.

WASHINGTON, April 6.—New notes on the subject of mandates have been sent by the American government to the governments of Japan, Great Britain, France and Italy.

The notes are understood to be very similar, but the occasion for preparing them is said to be the receipt of Japan's reply to the original American note protesting against Japanese mandates over the former German island on the Pacific north of the equator.

State department officials refused to discuss the documents, but it was learned that they were broad enough in terms to cover all American rights growing out of the world war.

The notes form a part of the series begun by Secretary Colby and in which the United States insisted upon its full rights as one of the allied and associated powers and also the right to pass finally upon all mandates before their adoption.

RIGHTS OF U. S. ARE AFFIRMED

SENATE IS DIVIDED ON RESOLUTION

Separate Peace Proposal Expected to Precipitate Long Wrangle.

BY DAVID LAWRENCE

PROMINENT REALTORS VISIT SPRINGFIELD

—Photo by The News.

Members of the National Sub-Dividers' Conference, one of the strongest organizations of real estate men in the country, are shown here. They are holding one day's session of their annual meeting in Springfield, where they are guests of H. S. Kissell, of the Kissell Improvement Company, a member of the conference. They represent 10,798 acres of highly developed allotment property, representing millions of dollars. They are: Front row, reading from left to right, John M. Demarest, Forest Hills Gardens, New York City; Edward H. Bouton, Baltimore, Maryland; J. C. Nichols, Kansas City, chairman of the conference; J. E. George, Omaha, Nebraska; Emerson W. Chaille, Indianapolis, Indiana. Second row, reading from left to right: Brown Burleigh, Springfield; Hugh Prather, Dallas, Texas; Benjamin Thompson, Columbus, Ohio; Judson Bradway, Detroit, Michigan; King Thompson, Columbus, Ohio; Harry S. Kissell, Springfield; Duncan McDuffie, San Francisco, California, and Robert Jemison, Birmingham, Alabama. The conference opened its sessions in Columbus Monday.

HITCH DEVELOPS IN PROPOSED PARLEY TO END BRITISH STRIKE

Announcement Made by Lloyd George—Transport Workers to Support Miners.

(By The Associated Press)

LONDON, April 6.—A hitch developed this evening in the proposed resumption of negotiations between representatives of the striking coal miners and the mine owners, it was announced in the house of commons by Mr. Lloyd George, the prime minister.

Decision to support the British miners in their strike was reached by the transport workers' federation at a meeting held here this morning.

The vote taken by the transport workers was unanimously in favor of lending aid to the miners. It was decided to meet in conference immediately with delegates of the national union of railway men and the miners' union for the purpose of securing action on the strike situation by the "triple alliance."

At the conclusion of the conference, Robert Williams, general secretary of the transport workers, said:

"On recommendation from the executive committee, the conference has decided to give all assistance in our power to whatever extent necessary to help the miners and at once to enter into negotiations with the railway men and the miners for the purpose of taking joint action throughout the remainder of the contest."

DAUGHERTY TO CONTROL PATRONAGE

Attorney General Made Arbiter in Disputes Over Federal Plums.

SEMAPHORES TO BE DISCARDED

COLUMBUS, April 6.—Use of semaphores by traffic policemen will be discontinued here within the next two weeks. Chief of Police French says that the use of hand signals in regulating traffic will serve to greatly decrease congestion. With the semaphores will go the traffic booths and umbrella stands.

DELAYS IN CITY PLANNING COSTLY CONFERENCE TOLD

Sub-dividers Meet in Springfield—Chairman Impressed With Growth of City.

City planning so as to take care of the practical needs of the citizens in the most economical way is advocated as an imperative requisite of city expansion by J. C. Nichols, Kansas City, chairman of the National Sub-Dividers' conference, and who developed the largest high-class residential sub-division in the world. Eleven members of the conference were present at the session of the annual meeting which was held here Wednesday. They came from all parts of the country. The conference opened its sessions in Columbus Monday.

Chairman Nichols expressed himself as being favorably impressed with the growth of Springfield and its future possibilities. It has passed the stage of uncertainty in its growth, he said, and is sure now to develop into a really large city.

Being on the threshold of a bigger development, both in industrial lines, and in residential districts, now is the time, he declared, ...

MAGISTRATE IS UNDER ARREST

YOUNGSTOWN, April 6.—Justice of the Peace James Quigley is held in the county jail here today following his indictment by the grand jury yesterday for embezzlement, based on charges that he failed to account for fines he collected and that he extorted money from East Youngstown foreigners, whom he had arrested for liquor law violations.

TWO KILLED WHEN TRUCK IS STRUCK BY FAST EXPRESS

POST IS TO BE ACCEPTED BY HERRICK

"STOCKADE" ON GEORGIA FARM IS DESCRIBED

SENATE ACTION ON DUNN BILL IS POSTPONED

SUSPECT IS HELD IN CONNECTION WITH ROBBERY OF BANK

NOTE OF PROTEST SENT TO GERMANY

JURY TO DECIDE FATE OF ACCUSED WOMAN SELECTED

GENERAL EDWARDS TO BE PROMOTED, IS ANNOUNCEMENT

DEPARTMENT SHOULD HELP IN MARKETING CROPS SAYS WALLACE

THREE MEASURES TO AID DISABLED MEN ARE FAVORED

WOMAN CHARGED WITH VIOLATION OF LIQUOR LAW

EX-EMPEROR IS THREATENED BY AUSTRIAN CROWD

WIDOW'S CLAIM AGAINST SHONTS' ESTATE GRANTED

PASTOR, ARRESTED FOLLOWING GIRL'S DEATH, KILLS SELF

HAMILTON GROCER SHOT BY BANDITS

SENTENCE IMPOSED

135. An April 1921 visit by notable developers was the talk of the town and a source of pride for the community.

estate developers in the country to his beloved city.

The National Sub-Dividers Conference was holding its annual convention in Columbus, Ohio, which convened on Monday, April 4, 1921. The following day, the group inspected King Thompson's Upper Arlington subdivision in Columbus, then traveled to Springfield at the invitation of Harry Kissell. The esteemed group, chaired by J.C. Nichols, developer of the Country Club District in Kansas City, Missouri, represented a combined total of 10,798 acres of high-end residential developments in the United States. Most of their developments were either adjacent to country clubs or had clubs incorporated into the development itself. Among the group were Hugh Prather, Dallas, Texas; Emerson Chaille, Indianapolis, Indiana; Robert Jemison, Birmingham, Alabama; King Thompson, Columbus, Ohio; Edward Bouton, Baltimore, Maryland; and John Demarest, New York City, all of whom had been part of the original group dating back to 1917. Also included were Judson Bradway, Detroit, Michigan; J.E. George, Omaha, Nebraska; and Duncan McDuffie, San Francisco, California. *(fig. 135)*

The group spent Tuesday night in Springfield, and on Wednesday morning, Harry Kissell and Brown Burleigh gave the developers the grand tour of Ridgewood and the Springfield Country Club. The group then lunched at the Hotel Shawnee. At the luncheon, J.C. Nichols spoke glowingly of Kissell and Ridgewood. "The city should give him free rein in developing the property as the whole municipality will benefit from the fruits of the experiments carried out by Mr. Kissell on his property. Such a project constitutes an experimental laboratory where plans for a better city are formulated and tried out. When the city is well planned, the 'city beautiful' will result as a natural consequence."

Conferences were held that afternoon in the new assembly room on the eighth floor of the Hotel Bancroft where the attendees could get a fine view of the city. At the conclusion of the conference, Chairman Nichols shared remarks with the local newspaper that he was suitably impressed by the city, its growth, and future possibilities and declared that Springfield "had passed the stage of uncertainty in its growth, and is sure now to develop

"I cannot tell you how much we were impressed with Springfield and Ridgewood. I have never been in a town the size of Springfield that left such a happy thought with me. It seems so clean and well designed, and the residents whom we met were so extremely hospitable and loyal to their town that Springfield will stand very high in our estimation."

—Emerson W. Chaille, Indianapolis, Indiana.

into a really large city." He also asserted that now was the time in the city's development to plan for its future growth. New York City and Chicago had recently spent hundreds of millions of dollars in tearing down what had already been built in order to start a city planning program, he said. According to Nichols, Springfield had the opportunity to avoid this by setting aside districts for residences and ones for industry. However, it would be five more years before Springfield did pass a zoning ordinance, a dozen years after Harry Kissell had platted one of the early prototypes of city planning, and zoning—Ridgewood.

In the heady aftermath of the conference, Kissell and Burleigh used the testimonials offered by the developers to great effect in a Ridgewood sales campaign that ran throughout the spring. They also capitalized on an assessment that the visiting developers made after inspecting Ridgewood. Taking into account the size of the city, the cost of the raw land and improvements, and costs related to selling, such as advertising, the group unanimously agreed that $100 per front foot was a reasonable price for a Ridgewood lot, and the price one would usually find in similar subdivisions in other cities.

In the original section of Ridgewood, however, lots remained at prewar prices of $30 to $50 per front foot, and lots in the new wooded section were offered for only $50 to $60 per front foot. Kissell had been fairly successful in his effort to keep prices down in the wooded section, even in an inflationary period. He had purchased the land in 1919 and contracted for much of the materials before prices peaked in 1920. All the sewer, water and gas lines, sidewalks, and roads were put in with Kissell's own equipment, eliminating the contractor's profit. Some work, like the installation of sidewalks, was deferred in hopes that there

136. The Charles I. and Elizabeth Shawver house at 101 Brighton Rd.

might be some price relief. The gamble paid off. Cement was $4.65 a barrel in 1920, but by the spring of 1921 the price came down to $2.60 per barrel, and work on the sidewalks proceeded at that time.

The endorsements and cost comparisons of Ridgewood lots with those in other cities paid off handsomely. At the end of May, just as the big spring sales campaign was winding down, Kissell told the newspaper, "The sale here was twice as good as one recently conducted in Columbus in another high-class subdivision. We had the best results of any offering of high-grade lots that I know of. This speaks well of Springfield. I am most gratified over the success of our sale. The lots sold during the sale totaled $77,000." The impressive figures brought congratulations from local businessmen and many in financial circles who breathed a collective sigh of relief and took it as a sign that the tough times were over.

Meanwhile, construction work in the first section of The Woods was winding up. The roadways were being prepared for the Tarvia macadam paving. Sidewalks were going in, and the underground cable for the lighting

138. Looking southeast up Brighton Rd. from the corner of Brighton and Hawthorne Rd. The Shawver house, 101 Brighton Rd., and the Bowlus house, 133 Brighton Rd., are visible through the trees in the center of the image. The Cliff C. & Margaret Corry house, 215 Brighton Rd., is to the right.

137. Looking west down Brighton Rd. from the intersection of Brighton and Woodedge, circa 1925. Three of the earliest houses in "The Woods" section were constructed here in 1921. The Shawver house and the Bowlus house are visible to the left. A glimpse of the Ballinger house is visible through the trees to the right. The Patterson house, 140 Brighton Rd., and the Eipper house, 120 Brighton Rd., both constructed at a slightly later date, flank the Ballinger house to its left and right, respectively.

system had just arrived. Three houses were already under construction in the new section. The Charles I. and Elizabeth Shawver house, one of the landmark houses of Ridgewood, was underway at 101 Brighton Road. Charles Shawver was the owner of The Shawver Company, Manufacturers of Automobile Supplies and Wood Working Machinery. The Shawvers' house was designed by the local architectural firm of Hall and Lethly, who had designed the Ridgewood School and numerous other Ridgewood homes, and it represented the first use of the Mediterranean style of architecture in Ridgewood. The Mediterranean style became extremely popular in the United States in the 1920s, and several fine Mediterranean homes were built in Springfield during that period. *(fig. 136)*

Also under construction in the spring of 1921 was the Colonial Revival-style home of Charles J. and Fannie Bowlus at 133 Brighton Road. Mr. Bowlus was a partner in the Bowlus-Hackett Fruit and Cold Storage Company. And another Hall and Lethly-designed home, the Colonial Revival-style Homer W. and Nellie Ballinger home was going up at 132 Brighton Road. Homer Ballinger was treasurer and general manager of the Clark County Lumber Company. *(fig's. 137 & 138)*

It was a busy spring for architects Lawrence H. Hall and Marley W. Lethly. The little school in the woods had proved such a success that it had reached its maximum enrollment limit in just two years of operation, and more people were clamoring to register their children. In order to accommodate more pupils for the 1921-1922 school year, Hall and Lethly were asked by the board of directors of the school to prepare plans for a four-room addition to the original building. The addition would provide room for up to fifty more pupils. Following the example of Harry Kissell in handling the improvement of the wooded section of Ridgewood, the building committee decided to contract directly with laborers to keep costs to a minimum. By mid-June, the addition was underway and it was ready for occupancy at the beginning of the fall term in September.

That fall, the finishing touches were also being completed in the first phase of The Woods. Concrete and granite was being installed for the new fountain on the triangular parklet at the intersection of Sunnyside Place and Fountain Boulevard. The fountain was being built about an ornamental lighting standard in the center that coordinated with the rest of the lighting standards in Ridgewood. Once the fountain was completed, water would flow in converging streams from three different points. The other triangular parklets in the wooded tract were being beautified with blue grass sod and shrubbery, and Grecian benches were to be placed on them, making each a lovely place of repose for residents. *(See fig's. 127, page 160 & fig. 130, page 169)*

The lighting system was also finished that fall in the first phase of the wooded section, and in newspaper advertisements Springfield residents were invited to come out and inspect the effect: "The Woods portion, the most beautiful portion of all the Ridgewood development will be illuminated every evening for the pleasure of visitors. An ornamental park lighting system, just completed converts the district into a forest fairyland, whose winding roadways and commingling of light and shadow beneath the sentinel trees invite the motorist to an inspiring nighttime drive." Just as the original section of Ridgewood had been, and remained, The Woods would become a popular attraction among local sightseers for a number of years.

Still riding high from the validation received during the visit from the country's biggest real estate developers back in the spring, Kissell and Burleigh bid residents to "Come by any day this week. See the most wonderful property in the most wonderful city of its size in America. We can tell you a lot more about both." If they needed any more corroboration about the quality and appeal of the Ridgewood proposition, the sales figures provided it. Out of the nearly 350 home sites that had been offered so far in Ridgewood, only fifty were left. Seventy-five homes had been built, with a number of new ones under construction, and everyone was predicting that 1922 would be a record-breaking year for building.

For early Ridgewood residents, 1922 would always be remembered as the year of the Springfield Country Club fire. That spring, the board of directors of the country club had contracted with the Cogswell Building Company to make an addition to the clubhouse. The plan was to extend the women's locker rooms and construct new caddy house quarters and a larger refrigeration plant.

Spirits were high that spring at the club as members celebrated the opening of the newly expanded golf course. Going back to the days of the original club at the old McCreight homestead, an eighteen-hole course had been a dream of members. In 1921, club directors had been able to purchase forty-nine acres of land from the Signal Hill property adjacent to the club, which was owned at the time by Wilbur Myers, as well as

"I was most agreeably impressed with your subdivision, the city, hotels and your many progressive citizens whom it was our pleasure and privilege to meet. I know of no city even approximating the population of Springfield which boasts of such a subdivision as Ridgewood, such hotels as the Shawnee and Bancroft and such a progressive citizenship as we met."

—Robert Jemison, Jr., Birmingham, Alabama.

several more acres from Armin Kelly, in order to expand the existing nine-hole course. Once the land was secured, the directors entered into a contract with the renowned golf course architect, Donald Ross, for the design. The long-awaited course was dedicated with a formal opening on Tuesday, May 30, 1922. The club's president, Judge Augustus N. Summers, drove the first ball at the formal opening. One hundred sixteen players teed up that day to play in the country club's first annual spring golf tournament. *(fig's. 139 & 140)*

The excitement over the beautiful new course was quickly muted by tragedy, however. Just over two weeks later, on Wednesday, June 14, 1922, the

139 (top). Putting the finishing touches on the new 18-hole golf course at the Springfield Country Club, spring 1922.
140 (above). The nearly completed golf course and the original Springfield Country Club clubhouse several weeks before fire swept through the building on June 14, 1922.

Springfield Country Club clubhouse went up in flames. The blaze started at 7:30 a.m. when an oil stove exploded in the new refrigeration plant that was under construction. An employee of the Cogswell Building Company was heating tar on the stove in order to coat the cork lining of the refrigeration plant when the explosion occurred, splashing tar all over the ceiling, and igniting the cork lining. The employee fled the room and began screaming to alert others of the fire. The club's new manager, Henry J. Weseloh, immediately grabbed a fire hose that was maintained at the club and attempted to extinguish the blaze, but the water pressure proved insufficient. *(fig. 141)*

Club member William P. McCulloch arrived at the club in his automobile just in time to hear the explosion. McCulloch ran quickly into the clubhouse and telephoned in the alarm. He then went back outside to move his automobile to safety before attempting to go back into the building. However, in the short amount of time it took for him to move his auto, the fire had spread so much that he couldn't safely enter again. Several employees made valiant efforts to salvage whatever they could. John Kieger, who was in charge of the 200 men's lockers, tried to save the expensive golf bags and other contents, but he had to flee when the ceiling began to collapse. Club Manager Henry Weseloh narrowly escaped as well. He had brought out a typewriter and an adding machine and had gone back in to try to salvage furniture when another part of the ceiling fell.

By that time, Engine Company No. 4 was on the scene and Fire Chief Samuel F. Hunter was directing the efforts of his men. When they arrived, flames were already leaping hundreds of feet in the air, and some of the grass surrounding the building was scorched. One firefighter had to be carried to safety by a fellow firefighter after he was struck in the face by the nozzle of a hose line while he was battling the blaze in the basement of the clubhouse. Fortunately, the dazed fireman's injuries were limited to two black eyes and mild disorientation. Once the fire was partially extinguished, Chief Hunter and some of his men entered the building and made a daring effort

141. Aerial image of the gutted Springfield Country Club clubhouse.

Looking west at the Knights of Pythias orphanage at the entrance of Ridgewood, circa 1925. Image taken from the front yard of the Eakins house at 1220 N. Fountain Blvd.

that helped save the records of the club. Another fireman emerged with four trophies, three of which were partially melted.

A newspaper photographer had arrived on the scene by 8 a.m. and was capturing images of the blaze. Word of the conflagration spread as quickly as the fire itself. Ridgewood residents telephoned their friends and families, and then gathered to watch the inferno. Residents of Elmwood and other affluent neighborhoods hopped into their automobiles and came over to join the crowd of spectators that numbered several hundred people.

The fire burned for two hours, destroying the building entirely. However, as soon as the fire was extinguished the chair of the house committee, Fred Wallace, called an executive committee meeting. Plans were immediately hashed out for the automobile shed on the property, east of the clubhouse, to be enclosed and equipped so it could be pressed into service as a men's locker room and shower house. Even the great conflagration was not going to stand in the way of the golf season on the new course. The Cogswell Construction Company was immediately commissioned to salvage whatever plumbing and fixtures they could from the destroyed clubhouse and begin work on the new locker room and shower facility at once. The Crain-Desormeaux Company was contracted to improvise lockers.

Provisions were made as well so that there would be as little interruption in the other activities of the club as possible. Dining accommodations would be made in the old Manor House, which was untouched by the fire. And, by the end of the day, as the acrid smell of the blaze still hung heavily in the air and club members picked through what was left of the contents of their lockers, Fred Wallace was able to report to the newspaper that a new fireproof clubhouse would be constructed as soon as plans could be made for it. With surprising specificity, he announced that, "The new building will be of brick or tile construction with stucco." That evening, after work, hundreds more descended on the site to look at the ruins.

On the morning after the blaze, stoves and a large refrigerator were delivered to the Manor House. The new club manager, Mr. Weseloh, and his wife had been temporarily residing on the first floor of the Manor House since Mr. Weseloh had started his job with the club at the beginning of May. However, the two were now busily moving to the second story so that the first floor could be used for dining and parties. Also that day, a portable dance platform, which had been constructed by the Cogswell Building Company for their wealthy clients to use for lawn fetes at their homes in the summer, was moved to the club grounds so dances scheduled for the summer could go on as planned. Just three days after the fire, on Saturday, June 17, 1922, the temporary quarters in the Manor House and the makeshift locker and shower facility were operational.

The smell of the fire lingered in the area for days, but even a catastrophic event at an institution so central to life in Ridgewood could not dampen the spirits of Harry Kissell because the building boom that everyone had been waiting for was finally beginning in earnest. In March of 1922, new construction in Springfield had broken all records going back to 1914. Records were broken again in April and May, and many more buildings were being planned. Fueling the demand for new construction was the long-awaited stabilization in lumber supplies and materials prices and the easing of credit.

About six weeks later, however, some news broke that surely must have given Harry Kissell pause. He learned that while he was busy working on what he considered to be the showpiece of Ridgewood—The Woods—his aspiring rival in the high-grade residential development market, J. Warren James, and James's new partner, Walter B. Bauer, had managed to acquire a thirty-two-and-a-half acre strip of land from the Adam Grube estate. The two men were now doing business as the James-Bauer Realty Company. James served as president of the new venture, and Bauer served as sales manager. Somehow, the two were able to buy the very piece of property that Kissell was unable to buy at the time he purchased the land for the original section of Ridgewood but had always hoped to acquire in the future. The Grube land adjoined Ridgewood just north of Dover Road and west of Fountain Boulevard. The deal was made public in the newspaper on July 30, 1922, with the headline, "Big Realty Deals are Announced." At the same time, the James-Bauer Realty Company also acquired a thirty-three acre wooded tract just west of the Grube land, owned at the time by Jacob Sientz.

The purchase of the Grube land was simply a shrewd business move on the part of James and Bauer, but it must have been troubling to Kissell. His chief competitor was literally setting up shop right next door. Once the news of the land deal was made public, James and Bauer left immediately for Cleveland to meet with landscape architect Louis

"Springfield is a beautiful city. We were all most agreeably surprised. We came away feeling it is truly 'The Best 60,000 City in America.' It is needless to tell you what we thought of Ridgewood. We were all impressed with it. It is certainly in keeping with your city, and in fact better than any sub-division I know of in any such city twice the size of Springfield."
—J.C. Nichols, Chairman, Sub-Dividers Conference, Kansas City, Missouri.

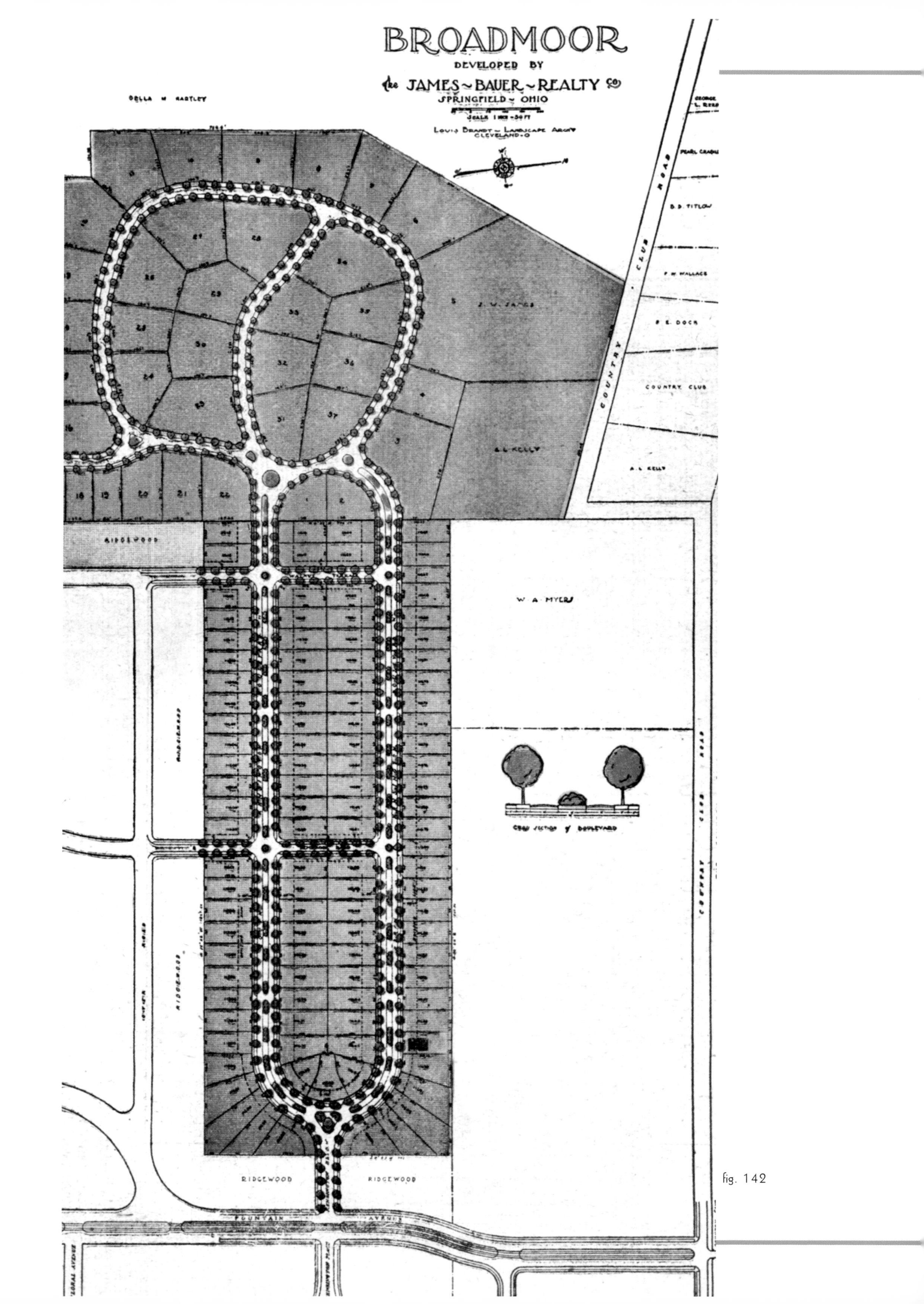
BROADMOOR
DEVELOPED BY
the JAMES ~ BAUER ~ REALTY Co
SPRINGFIELD ~ OHIO
CLEVELAND-O
COUNTRY CLUB ROAD
COUNTRY CLUB
A. L. KELLY
W. A. MYERS
RIDGEWOOD
RIDGEWOOD
RIDGEWOOD
RIDGEWOOD
FOUNTAIN AVENUE

fig. 142

Brandt to discuss the design for the new development. James had previously used Louis Brandt for his Glen Terrace subdivision off North Limestone Street.

Brandt's plan for this new development was to create two boulevards on the Grube land that would run westward from Fountain Boulevard. This section would be known as Beautiful Broadmoor, and, to the vexation of some Ridgewood residents, the two boulevards would originally be named North Kensington Boulevard and South Kensington Boulevard. The wooded section to the west of the Grube land was christened Broadmoor Estates and would be laid out in estate-type lots of three to five acres each. Improvements were set to begin in the early spring of 1923. The subdivision would have all the modern amenities of a high-end suburban development. *(fig. 142)*

Kissell had never really regarded Theodore Weyant and Hills and Dales as a serious challenger for Springfield's high-grade real estate market, but J. Warren James and Broadmoor were another story. Unlike Theodore Weyant, James was a Springfield native, and just like Kissell, he had a long, respectable history in the real estate business. Due to the precarious circumstances surrounding Hills and Dales fate, Kissell didn't really have to worry about losing customers to it, but Broadmoor was a different story.

That fall, though, there was an exciting development that helped soften the blow. Ridgewood was featured in a four-page spread in the September/October issue of the national bimonthly magazine—*Country Homes: Devoted to the Interests of Suburban and Country Life*. The magazine had offices in New York City and Baltimore, Maryland, and featured the finer suburban and country homes and suburban developments in the United States. The article, which was illustrated with numerous photographs of homes and scenes throughout the neighborhood, was entitled "Ridgewood—A High-Grade Suburban Development in a Small City." *(fig's. 143–145)*

The author of the magazine article lavishly praised Ridgewood and lamented the fact that suburban developments outside of large cities were usually "cut up into checker-board plats with very little attention being given to parkways, open spaces, shrubbery, landscaping, and the many other things which lend attractiveness to similar sections in the bigger communities." According to the author, this was not the case in Ridgewood: "It is very refreshing, therefore, to find a city which has a population of about 60,000 in which is located one of the most attractive residential districts which it has been our pleasure to visit. The developers of this tract, which is known as "Ridgewood," and which is located in Springfield, Ohio, certainly believe in their city, and feel that the residents of the smaller cities are just as keen lovers of nature, and take as much pleasure in the surroundings of their homes and in the aesthetic things of life as the home owners of the more populous centers. It has seldom been our pleasure to inspect a more beautiful and a more modern residential section, even in the largest cities of the country."

In addition, it was noted that "It is adjacent to one of the most attractive golf courses which we have ever had the pleasure of playing over." The author also admired the beautifying elements, such as the numerous park-like grass plots, that were the equivalent to other high-class developments like Roland Park. The author was particularly delighted by the "clever handling" of the streetcar system through the main boulevard, with its extensive plantings and the ornamental trolley poles with light fixtures atop. What was typically considered unsightly infrastructure had been transformed into a unique ornamental feature. The fountain, triangular park spaces complete with Grecian benches, and the "delightful little waiting stations" were also praised.

144. Magazine image, looking west down Englewood Rd., across Fountain Blvd., towards Ardmore Rd. and Crescent Dr. Note the enormous tree preserved in the roadway.

The article noted that much building activity was taking place in Ridgewood and that it boasted some "real gems of architecture." Among them were houses ranging in price from $7,500 to $50,000. Landscaping in the development received great praise as well: "It is scarcely possible to find homes which are more beautifully softened and tie into the landscape better than these."

In pre-World War II era Ridgewood, its residents raised landscape gardening to a high art. Neighbors engaged in friendly, informal competitions to try

and out-do one another with their gardens, and the Kissell Company in its marketing effectively utilized the fruits of their labor. Gardening was a popular diversion among the class of people that the Kissell Company wanted to attract to Ridgewood, so advertisements in the spring were geared toward highlighting the particular attributes that made Ridgewood the "beauty spot" of Springfield. Advertisement copy would announce that it was "Lilac Time" in Ridgewood, or "Next Sunday the spirea should be in full bloom in Ridgewood," and invited Springfield residents to drive out and see the "Residential Showplace of Central Ohio."

The author of the *Country Homes* article also applauded the attention paid to attracting birds, a pet project of Harry Kissell. When Ridgewood was first laid out, Kissell bought hundreds of bird boxes and distributed them throughout the neighborhood. After a number of houses were built, he sent out a letter to homeowners telling them of his desire to attract birds to the neighborhood. It stated, "Ridgewood will be more beautiful this year than ever before, and your attention is called to the fact that if you wish birds on your premises, boxes and bird baths are helpful in attracting and holding the birds. You also probably know that if a cat is kept in the neighborhood, it will be next to impossible to get birds to make their nests in your shrubbery."

He repeated this practice every year for the benefit of new residents. According to Kissell, "No matter how much people may like cats, most people like birds better and we have instilled in them the love of birds." The gentle social pressure worked. A few years later, in an article in the *Annals of Real Estate Practice*, the official publication of the National Association of Real Estate Boards, Kissell wrote, "There are two hundred homes in the subdivision and not a single cat." Attracting birds became a unifying pastime for the Ridgewood community. According to Kissell, "Everyone in the community is interested in birds and has a particular choice and puts up his particular kind of box and tells others when his birds have arrived in the spring. We have even used it in our advertising in the spring by saying that 'The martins have come to Ridgewood.'" Kissell must have been delighted when the author of the *Country Homes* article gave him the following accolade: "It seemed much like a bird sanctuary with bluebirds, martins, cardinals, flickers,

145. Magazine image of the ornamental lighting standards and streetcar waiting stations in Ridgewood, 1922.
143(left). The entrance to Ridgewood, from *Country Homes Magazine,* 1922.

orioles, wrens, and numbers of other feathered creatures, which are not usually seen in a residential section."

But perhaps the greatest compliment of all came in the following passage: "The writer, having lived in Roland Park, really had very little trouble imagining that he was back home when he looked at the many features which resembled this wonderful district in Baltimore." For Ridgewood to be favorably compared with the acclaimed forerunner of early twentieth-century, high-class suburban developments—Roland Park—was a singular honor.

Soon after the glowing article appeared in *Country Homes*, Harry Kissell and Brown Burleigh responded to J. Warren James and Walter Bauer's challenge for a piece of the high-grade subdivision market. As soon as they had heard the news back in the summer, Kissell and Burleigh assessed how this new addition would affect their plans for the future development of Ridgewood and decided to react swiftly. Taking into account that the economy was improving, that the original section of Ridgewood was mostly sold out, and that The Woods section was selling well, they decided to forge ahead with the final section of Ridgewood.

Kissell had deferred the development of the land that was west of Fountain Boulevard and Crescent Drive, and north of Grube Road, once he was able to buy the Pythian Woods tract. However, by moving ahead with it now, even though he was not finished with the improvements in The Woods, he could get a jump on James and Bauer and attract buyers that, come spring, he might have otherwise lost to them. Even though very little real progress could be made in either subdivision so late in the year, Ridgewood had a slight advantage over the Broadmoor addition. Ridgewood was a known quantity, so lots in the new section could be offered immediately. Buyers would feel safe in purchasing before any improvements had even been started because all of Kissell's promises had been fulfilled in the past.

Although J. Warren James was a well-known and respected real estate man and would go on to develop several successful suburbs, he was still a relatively new player in high-grade real estate development. Furthermore, this was an era when people were still widely skeptical of any new subdivision venture, given all the land fraud schemes that still proliferated. Buying a house from someone was one thing, but buying a lot in a new subdivision and gambling that the subdivision would evolve into a thriving neighborhood was another. The dubious fate of Hills and Dales had only served to further Springfield residents' trepidation. Kissell knew that once the improvements in Broadmoor were done, though, he would lose any advantage he had over James, so time was of the essence.

That fall, Kissell and Burleigh waxed eloquent as they announced in the newspaper their plans to move ahead with the final section of Ridgewood: "In the golden Autumn of 1922 there is to occur another manifestation of beautiful Ridgewood and perforce of Springfield. The spirit of this occasion has already invaded the hearts of hundreds of home lovers and it is in answer to their hopes and desires that the developers of this now firmly established restricted residential section have decided to unfold at this time the plat of another section of wonderful Ridgewood homes sites. Already plow-shares have turned the furrows which mark the gracefully winding boulevards in this new part of Ridgewood; already the scrapers and shovel men are clearing the drives and preparing for installation of pipes arriving by the car load. Engineers are busy with rod and stake. Soon to follow—curbs and gutters, ornamental lighting system, parkways and landscaping. All done in 'true Ridgewood style.' Progress has been so great and fast in Ridgewood that we are able to do this fully a year before . . . we expected."

The new section, officially known as Ridgewood Phase IV, encompassed forty unbroken acres of land. When Ridgewood was platted in 1914, this section was envisioned with streets laid out on the rectilinear grid system. However, eight years later, the plan had evolved into one featuring curvilinear streets. Advertisements for Phase IV described it as "a series of winding drives that crisscross, somewhat informally at times, to permit enchanting parks and parkways to lend their charm in the general scheme of beauty"—a far cry from the original 1914 plan. Several of the meandering drives in The Woods section, Midvale Road and Walnut Terrace, would continue across Grube Road and wind gracefully through the new section. *(fig. 146, page 198)*

In order to get the jump on Broadmoor, a pre-development sale would commence on Monday, October 9, 1922, and run until October 28. During the sale, buyers would receive a 10 percent discount off the price of their lot. Most lots in Phase IV would be priced at $40 per front foot, with a few in the $45 to $50 range. Kissell and Burleigh decided that the last section of Ridgewood would be improved in two phases, just as they were doing in The Woods section. Initially, eighty-three home sites would be offered in Phase IV. And, as in the other sections of Ridgewood, lots could be purchased with 10 percent down and monthly payments equaling one percent of the balance.

On opening day of the sale, Kissell and Burleigh unveiled in the newspaper the slogan for the final section of Ridgewood. The new tract would be billed as "In the Heart of Ridgewood." Once Phase IV was completed in its entirety, the lots in its western most portion would be the equivalent of four blocks in distance from Fountain Boulevard. In the early days of Ridgewood, this might

147. Before WWII, the most densely built section of N. Fountain Blvd. was a stretch along the west side of the boulevard, north of Ardmore Rd. and south of Dover Rd, image circa 1925.

have been a deterrent for some buyers. However, by 1922, personal automobile ownership had become so prevalent, with some families even owning two, that proximity to the streetcar line was less of an issue. In fact, as the years wore on, home sites removed from the noise of the streetcar line and the increasing automobile traffic on Fountain Boulevard became more desirable, which accounts for why many lots on the boulevard remained unsold for years despite their prestigious location. *(fig's. 147 & 148)*

For the Phase IV sale, Kissell and Burleigh did as they had done when The Woods section was offered for sale, and its improvements were just starting—they plainly marked the future location of streets and lots on the Phase IV land with signs. When the sale began on October 9, salesmen were stationed on the ground and others were standing by at the office, ready to take their automobiles and pick up interested buyers and squire them out to inspect the new section.

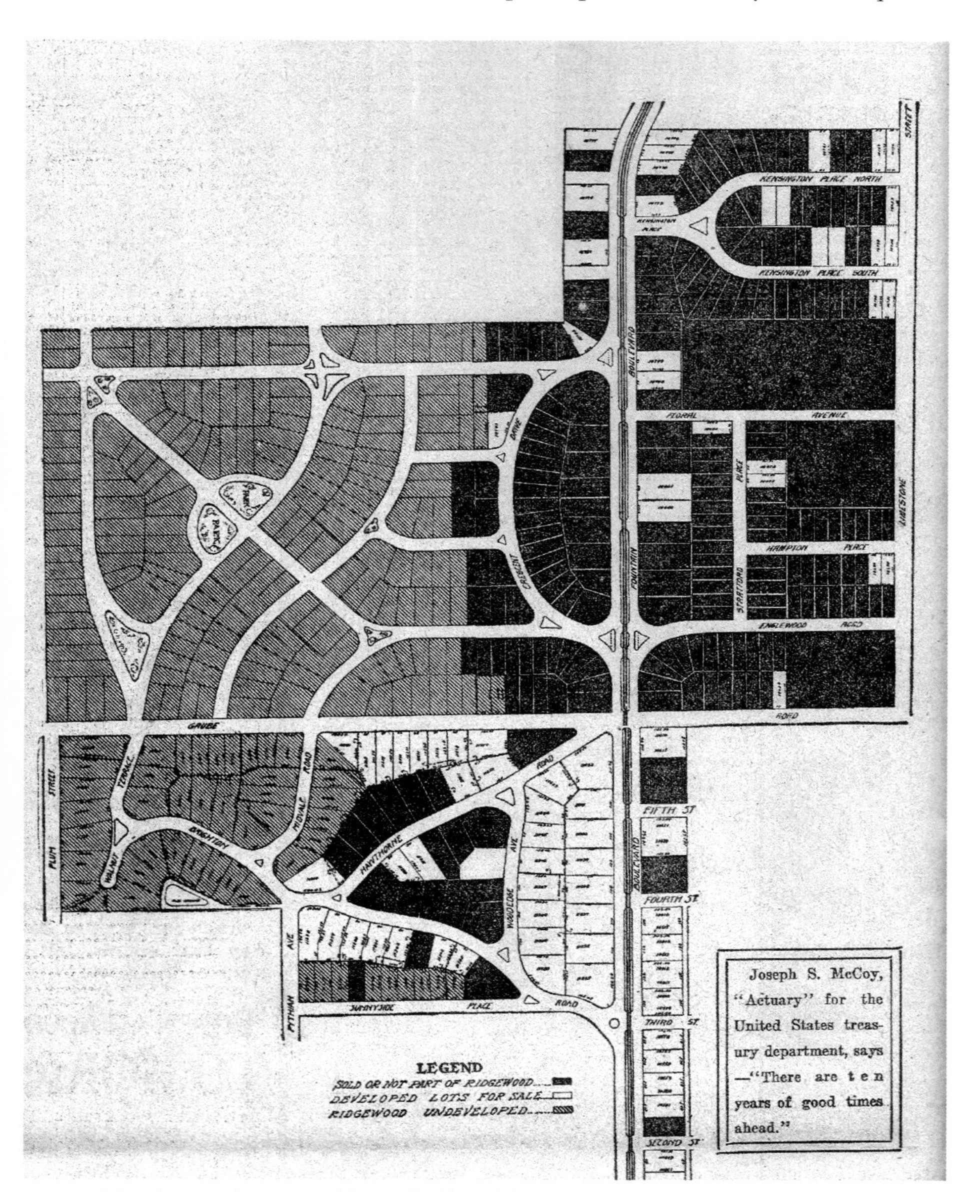

146. Map showing the proposed layout for Phase IV.

Unfortunately, the weather did not cooperate. Torrential rain poured all day on opening day and the following day. "Opening day dawned bleak and cheerless," the Kissell Company acknowledged in an advertisement several days later. However, to Kissell and Burleigh's delight, initial sales were still respectable. They proclaimed that even the "tempest couldn't dampen [customers'] ardor," and were certain that "sunshine will double the enthusiasm." Eight lots, valued at $20,000, were sold in the first two days. Once a lot was sold, it was marked with a diamond-shaped sign that read "Another Happy Family Has Bought."

Good weather did indeed increase buyers' enthusiasm. In the course of the three-week sale, sixty of the initial eighty-three lots offered were sold. The newspaper trumpeted the success of the offering with the headline—"60 Building Sites in One Section Sold." Kissell affirmed to the newspaper that it "was by long odds the biggest sale ever held here," and likened it to the current skyrocketing sales of automobiles. "Sixty lots sold in three weeks is a remarkable record," he stated.

The success of the sale was indicative of the boom everyone had been waiting for. A golden age of prosperity for Springfield—and the nation as a whole—had arrived. As Christmas approached, the Clark County Lumber Company celebrated the return of good times in an advertisement: "The year 1922 will have been more than generous to The Clark County Lumber Co.—a truly banner year, which, from the standpoint of sales volume solely, will have eclipsed any year in its entire history. [This serves as] a monument to progressive citizenship, and convincing testimony to the high morale of the city of Springfield and its vicinity, which, already risen undaunted from the gloomy aftermath of the great national catastrophe, is courageously forging ahead toward the greatest of all goals—a community of self-owned homes."

148. Vacant lots on the east side of Fountain Blvd., north of First St. and south of Third St. Many lots on Fountain Blvd. remained vacant until after WWII. Image circa 1925.

Roosevelt Junior High

149. The Theodore Roosevelt Junior High School on N. Limestone St., constructed in 1923.

THE GOSPEL OF

BY THE SPRING OF 1923, THE BEST 60,000 CITY IN AMERICA HAD OUTGROWN ITS NICKNAME.

The population of Springfield, Ohio, now stood at 65,000 and growing, and it was time for a new slogan that would work when Springfield was a 75,000 or a 100,000 city. The *Springfield Daily News* declared that such a population was within reach, but it could "only be done by everyone of our citizens continually boosting Springfield not only at home, but when traveling or enjoying their vacations, striving at all times to create the impression that we not only have a wonderful city here, but that we ourselves appreciate its greatness and are continually inviting not only new industry, but our friends to move here and enjoy it as our home."

The title of "Best 60,000 City in America" had been both a declaration and a rallying cry for the residents of the city. And it had the desired effect. Despite some rough times, Springfield had continued to grow, prosper, and send its message of prosperity out to the world. Goods manufactured in the city were emblazoned with the slogan and the chamber of commerce, local businesses, manufacturers, and organizations utilized it on their advertising matter, bill heads, letter heads, envelopes, newspapers, and billboards. But now it was time for a slogan that would express the new ambitions of the city.

The Springfield Real Estate Board sponsored the contest to find a new slogan and labeled it as "the opening gun in a campaign to attain a new goal in population." Over a thousand entries were received, and on Saturday, May 12, 1923, the winner was announced. Roll C. Laybourn of 557 Stanton Avenue submitted the

OPTIMISM

winning entry—"Where Prosperity Begins." Laybourn, a Springfield native employed as foreman of the shipping department at the Crowell Publishing Company, told the newspaper how he came to submit the idea. "My daughter Ethel had been reading about the contest and had sent in a coupon," he said. "She asked me why I did not send in a slogan suggestion. I had just returned home and was wearing my old clothes and had taken three pennies out of my pocket. I held out the pennies in my right hand and remarked: 'Where Prosperity Begins' . . . I believe that this slogan means cooperation and ambition. Where there is cooperation and ambition there is bound to be prosperity." Springfield Real Estate Board members presented Mr. Laybourn with a check for $50 at his home that afternoon. The local Automobile Association immediately announced that it would have two large signs printed with the new slogan and placed along the National Road where it entered and left Springfield to the east and west.

Prosperity was indeed returning to Springfield in 1923. Building was booming, up over 50 percent from the previous year. Among the new buildings under construction was the new school on North Limestone Street—the "fireproof" Theodore Roosevelt Junior High. It boasted the city's first electric clock system, and students going to and from class would henceforth be regulated by "the bell." The construction of the new junior high meant that Ridgewood residents could now educate their children, from kindergarten until they were ready for high school, right in their own enclave. *(fig. 149, page 200)*

However, 1923 was also the year that a great scandal rocked the town and threatened its economic recovery. On March 7, 1923, August H. Penfield, the son-in-law of prominent physician Dr. David K. Gotwald, attempted suicide in the garage of the Gotwald home at 505 North Fountain Avenue. Penfield was employed as a cashier at The Springfield National Bank and had been embezzling money in excess of $800,000 from the bank's Liberty Bond account. Bank officials had discovered the shortage that morning, and believing that exposure of his crime was imminent, Penfield attempted suicide by slashing his wrists while sitting in his automobile in the Gotwald family garage. He was found semiconscious, slumped over the steering wheel where the weight of his body sounded the horn and brought curious family members out to investigate the commotion.

The bank was ordered closed that night by the chief national bank examiner of Cleveland, who arrived the next day to assess the situation. Penfield's theft amounted to what was at the time the second-largest misappropriation of funds in the history of the country's national banks. He was convicted and sent to prison fairly quickly, but it took time for bank examiners to sort the matter out, and the bank remained closed for some time. The bank's closing and the losses suffered by depositors unleashed an enormous wave of pessimism and anxiety among Springfield residents.

The new slogan contest had helped combat some of the negative chatter swirling among the city's residents, but Harry Kissell was determined to quash it once and for all and restore the city's confidence. That summer, to combat the pessimism, he unveiled a "We Believe in Springfield" campaign. The series of newspaper advertisements bore no mention of Ridgewood or any other of the Kissell Company's business. Instead, it simply offered facts and figures to bolster Kissell's assertion that both Springfield's financial institutions, and Springfield as a whole, were in sound shape.

In the ads, Kissell reminded everyone that the failure of The Springfield National Bank was due to the misconduct of one man alone, and he challenged the naysayers. "We have other facts and figures in our office which prove to us that Springfield is fundamentally in wonderful condition," he said. "We will be glad to furnish these to anyone interested. If you are not a knocker, then help stop the knockers. Ask them for their proof. Mere generalities are not facts which justify a man in saying slanderous things about his own home city. If you hear a knocker who disputes these facts, bring him to our office and let us prove them to him. The time is past when we should mince words. It is now time to stop the knockers and to fight for Springfield."

He further asserted, "We are among those who believe that when trouble comes we should at once gird our loins and prepare to build a greater structure, just as Dayton did after her flood, or Galveston, or San Francisco, or Japan has done since her earthquake. It is not the time to quit when trouble comes and when the clouds are dark. Then is the time to fight. If we in Springfield will stop listening to every idle rumor that floats, and will determine not to be pessimists ourselves, and will use every possible effort to check the insidious work of the pessimists, then Springfield will go forward and be a greater and better city for having been tried, as she has, within the past couple of years."

In the end, Springfield, according to Kissell, "stood the test like Gibraltar." No factories were hampered, and no merchants went out of business. Once again, he had risen to the occasion when events threatened his city and offered a calming presence and a positive outlook, which he modestly attributed to the fact that "realtors are natural optimists."

The year 1923 was also when the Kissell Real Estate Company moved

The southwest corner of Harding Rd. and N. Fountain Blvd., circa 1925, as improvements of lots on Harding Rd. were being completed. 1665 N. Fountain Blvd. was later constructed here. Homes in The Woods section are visible in the distance.

into new quarters on the ninth floor of the Fairbanks Building. The chamber of commerce previously occupied the suite before it purchased and relocated to the old Lagonda Club building on the corner of Spring and High Streets. Since the Fairbanks Building had opened in 1908, The Kissell Company had occupied offices on the seventh floor, but the business was growing and the new 2,025 square-foot suite on the northeast wing of the building would give the company the largest offices in Springfield devoted exclusively to the real estate business. At the same time, a new electrically lighted sign was erected on top of the building to announce their increased presence. The mammoth sign, measuring sixteen feet high and forty-five feet wide, faced north toward Ridgewood, and its 275 incandescent lights flashed "Kissell Real Estate." The sign would serve as a glowing beacon of downtown Springfield for the next several decades. *(fig. 150)*

150. Looking south down Fountain Ave., towards Main St., in downtown Springfield. The Fairbanks Building, crowned by the Kissell Real Estate sign, can be seen in the distance to the right.

The old cramped quarters of the Kissell organization, on the seventh floor of the Fairbanks Building, had accommodated only four salesmen comfortably, but with improved business conditions, the Kissell sales force was now up to ten. The staff also included an accountant, a rental department manager, an engineer, a construction superintendent, a timekeeper, a filing clerk/stenographer, and a listing clerk/telephone girl, in addition to Brown Burleigh. Burleigh was continuing his duties as sales manager, but by then, he had also been elevated to the position of vice president of the Kissell Companies.

The Kissell organization functioned like a well-oiled machine. Salesmen started each day at 7:45 a.m. with a class in salesmanship and business efficiency led by Brown Burleigh. For the class, Burleigh utilized manuals from the Alexander Hamilton Institute, a popular correspondence type program in the early twentieth century. This was followed from 8 a.m. to 9 a.m. with a sales meeting to go over each man's sales from the previous day and address any concerns. In order to ensure that the Kissell organization received plenty of media exposure, the office maintained a publicity pad like a police blotter, and any sales or rentals were listed on it, and left available for the newspapermen to look over daily. On Friday mornings at 9 a.m., Kissell salesmen emerged from the Fairbanks Building to inspect properties listed for sale with the office since the previous Friday. Every salesman worked both the brokerage and the subdivision ends of the business. Ideally, a Kissell salesman would sell a buyer a lot, then handle the sale of his existing home as well.

151. Harry Kissell at his desk in the Fairbanks Building.

Every Wednesday night at 6 p.m., Kissell and Burleigh hosted for the entire office force a weekly dinner at one of the local hotels, followed by a general meeting back at the offices. The hours for Kissell salesmen were long, but with commission of four to seven percent on each sale, they could make a good living when times were good. A cash bonus was paid each month to the man with the highest sales. And Kissell men never had to work on Sundays. Some developers did conduct Sunday sales, but Kissell and Burleigh always discouraged that. They felt that their men could just as easily get most of their prospects out in the early morning or evenings during the week as they could on Sunday. Sunday was reserved for church and family. And, to Kissell and Burleigh, Sunday sales were the practice of unscrupulous curb stoners and fly-by-nights who came to town, bought a cheap piece of property, drove white stakes in the ground to mark it off , then fled with their profits without ever making any improvements. Men on the Kissell sales force were known for integrity, courtesy, and fair dealing. They were, according to Kissell, "All 'straight shooters' or they would not be associated with us. You can believe what they tell you."

Harry Kissell arrived at the office each day at 8 a.m. and made a point of going around to greet each employee. From his corner office at the top of the Fairbanks Building, he enjoyed a spectacular view of Springfield. According to Kissell, "It would do us all good, if some day we would visit the top floor of one of Springfield's tall buildings and see Springfield . . . From these dizzy heights we are humbled, we become encouraged—if distressed, consoled." From his bird's-eye view, Springfield seemed a hive of activity with all the

152. Northeast corner of Sunnyside Pl. and Pythian Ave. Both streets were completed in the second phase of "The Woods" section in 1923. 212 Hawthorne Rd. can be seen to the left. The rear of 215 Brighton Rd. can be seen to the right. Image circa 1925.

hustle and bustle on the streets below. Moreover, he could look northward to the area of the city that was thriving, due in large part to him. Since platting Ridgewood, he had promoted the "northward trend," and more and more people were moving there, but he was intent on making sure that the Ridgewood brand retained its supremacy. *(fig. 151, page 207)*

"When we speak of the "Northward Trend" we do not refer to Ridgewood alone," he commented to the newspaper. "The home being built on the Urbana Pike for Richard M. Rodgers, Frank S. Anthony's home on the St. Paris Pike, the beautiful residence of A.L. Kelly on the Home Road and that of W.J. Myers north of the Country Club, all show the tendency to move northward. Recent purchases by J.B. Cartmell, Fred M. Wallace, Pearl P. Crabill, J. Warren James, Dr. B.D. Titlow, and George L. Reed, none of which are located directly in Ridgewood, are yet in the Ridgewood district, and are further proofs of what is becoming a fixed opinion in the minds of those who really know, that the North Side is the future residential district of Springfield . . ." The inclusion of J. Warren James in this list of people who had moved to the "Ridgewood District" was just one of the many plays in the always civil but spirited tit for tat between the two business rivals. Ultimately, Kissell's efforts to perpetuate the Ridgewood brand would win out. For many years, Ridgewood and Broadmoor maintained their unique identities. As time passed, however, fading memories and the size of the Broadmoor plat—relative to the much larger Ridgewood plat—caused it to be subsumed under the Ridgewood name in the public's eye.

In the spring of 1923, though, the hearty competition between the two competitors was still playing out and each was hard at work on their respective subdivisions. In Ridgewood, construction on the second phase of The Woods was underway. Large forces of men were busy constructing the roadways and finishing the curb and gutter work in Sunnyside Place, Pythian Avenue, Midvale Road, and the extension of Brighton Road. Lots on these streets were offered for sale in late July of 1923 and they proved just as popular as the initial offering in 1919. The Kissell Company gleefully reported to the newspaper that one lot had sold three times in one day. A salesman had just come into the Kissell office with a contract and check, when in walked a second salesman with a check for the same lot. Two hours later, a third salesman did the same thing. The first one through the door, of course, prevailed to the disappointment of the two other buyers. *(fig's. 152 & 153)*

In addition to the ongoing work in The Woods, construction was also proceeding in Phase IV of Ridgewood, north of Grube Road. Water lines and gas lines were going in, and, now that the economy had improved, the Kissell Company was once again contracting for the work instead of doing it themselves. Sixteen houses were under construction that summer in Ridgewood. Despite the economic boom, however, the real estate business as a whole was still losing out to the stock market for investors' dollars. In an effort to combat this, the Kissell Company was running ads that summer that would prove prescient and a little chilling in hindsight: "Think of your family and their future needs while you are in a position to do so. Remember that money can take wings and fly away, stocks drop in value over night, but a good home-site—Mother Earth—cannot 'burn up or blow away.' Your money is always safe when invested this way."

In the Broadmoor addition, trenching for water and sewer lines was underway. Louis Brandt, the Cleveland landscape architect who had designed the plat, paid several visits that spring and summer to oversee the work and to confer with J. Warren James and Walter B. Bauer about their latest venture—Garden Acres. The new ninety-one acre subdivision for economically priced homes was being developed along the National Road (U.S. Route 40) beyond the eastern limit of the city, near Bird Road. Garden Acres lots were priced at an affordable $495, and marketing for the plat was targeted at those desiring

153. Intersection of Brighton Rd., Midvale Rd., and Pythian Ave., (completed in the second phase of "The Woods," 1923) looking southeast towards the future site of the LeBolt house at 223 Brighton Rd. (See page 259)

154. Image of the west side of Fountain Blvd., north of Dover Rd. One of the homes designed by architect P.E. Robinson, at the entrance to the Broadmoor addition, now 30 Broadmoor Blvd., is visible to the left. To its immediate right is the Electric Home, now 110 N. Broadmoor Blvd. The enormous electric sign, which advertised the Broadmoor addition, is to the right of Electric House.

to build stylish bungalows and cottages with all the modern amenities. Brandt's plan for the plat included setting aside a 100-foot-wide grass plot alongside the National Road to act as a buffer zone between the neighborhood and the well-traveled highway. (Many years later, this grass plot would be sold off and a number of commercial buildings would be erected on it.) At the time, the National Road was second only in the United States in automobile traffic to the Dixie Highway, which ran from Ontario, Canada, to Miami, Florida.

A boulevard effect was planned for the center of the new addition, and there were plans for a park and community center in a wooded area at the rear of the addition. Garden Acres tested the limits of the suburban idea, as it was the first new suburban development in Springfield that did not adjoin an existing part of the city. It was a full ten-minute ride from downtown Springfield, an unusually long commute at the time. But according to James, "It is the common disposition of people today to get to the country, but they refuse to go out without city conveniences," and he was determined to satisfy their desire. He would repeat this experiment a few years later with a slightly less remote suburb—Sunnyland.

Back in the Broadmoor addition, as work on the first phase of construction was coming to a close, a forty-foot wide promotional sign was being erected near the entrance of the addition. The enormous sign was equipped with an electric reflector so that it would be visible at night from Fountain Boulevard. A temporary sales office had been erected in the Broadmoor addition, and the installation of the ornamental lighting system was also being completed. The ornamental lighting standards used in Broadmoor were quite different in appearance from the ones used in Ridgewood, and this difference was one of the few things that distinguished Broadmoor from Ridgewood to the casual observer.

155. 30 Brighton Boulevard, designed by Cleveland architect, P.E. Robinson.

Another thing that set Broadmoor apart from

Ridgewood was the paved streets. James chose to use the more expensive asphaltic concrete paving as Kissell had done on North Fountain Boulevard. The streets in the rest of Ridgewood, with the exception of the busy thoroughfare of Grube (Harding) Road that would be paved with asphaltic concrete the following year, were of the less expensive Tarvia macadam. Kissell, of course, had many more streets to pave in Ridgewood at much greater expense than James did in Broadmoor, but the asphalt roads were definitely an advantage when promoting Broadmoor.

The only other noticeable difference between Ridgewood and Broadmoor was that J. Warren James and his partner, Walter B. Bauer, insisted that all the homes constructed in Broadmoor be of English style. The English style was popular as well in Ridgewood, but diversity was acceptable within certain parameters.

To set the tone architecturally for the Broadmoor neighborhood, the James-Bauer Realty Company had solicited plans by Cleveland, Ohio, architect P.E. Robinson for several homes in the addition. Robinson, along with his partner J.M. Miller, had designed a number of prestigious homes in Akron, Ohio, and in the Euclid Heights neighborhood of Cleveland. The homes that Robinson designed for Broadmoor would resemble old English villas and be constructed with a brick and stucco finish. Three would be clustered right at the entrance to Broadmoor on the curve where the two boulevards diverged. Another one, to be constructed at 222 North Kensington Boulevard (later 222 North Broadmoor Boulevard) would be the home of Walter B. Bauer, sales manager of the James-Bauer Realty Company. At the time, Bauer was living at 141 Englewood Road, in the section of Englewood that was part of the Wilbert's Plat and not part of Ridgewood. *(fig's. 154, 155 & 156)*

156. The home of Walter B. Bauer, 222 North Broadmoor Blvd., another P.E. Robinson designed home. An example of the type of lamppost used in the Broadmoor addition is visible to the right.

157. Image taken from Dover Rd., looking north towards the Broadmoor addition. The Electric Home can be seen to the left, and the three English villas, designed by P.E. Robinson and clustered at the entrance to Broadmoor, are visible in the center of the image.

By the end of the year, six houses were under construction in Broadmoor and eight more were being planned. One of those in the planning stages was a model home, branded as the "Electric Home." The Electric Home would prove to be a brilliant promotion for the new subdivision. It was advertised as a cooperative effort between The James-Bauer Realty Company and the *Springfield Daily News*. In the announcement for the Electric Home, the newspaper sang its praises: "Within the beauty of this new residential district of the city and set off with its own equally beautiful lines of construction the Electric Home is expected to be one of the showplaces of the city for years to come." The involvement of the newspaper would ensure extensive coverage of the home's progress. *(fig. 157)*

The Kissell Company presented its own electric model home, the Electric Cottage, with great success back in 1914, but the Broadmoor house took the concept of an electrically equipped home to a new level as the number of electrical gadgets available for home use had multiplied exponentially in the intervening years. The house was to be constructed on a lot at 110 North Kensington Boulevard (later 110 North Broadmoor Boulevard) using a unique construction technique that utilized cinder blocks for the main construction frame of the home.

This construction method had been popular in England and Germany for several decades and lauded for its weather resistant qualities, but it was relatively rare in the United States. The Springfield Light, Heat, and Power Company would handle the wiring of the Electric Home. Architectural plans for the house would be sent to the National Lamp Works, the headquarters of General Electric's lighting business, located in the company's Nela Park industrial park in East Cleveland, Ohio. There the complete wiring and equipment layout for the home would be designed in detail, so that it could be equipped with every newfangled electrical device available at the time.

Once completed, the home would be open for public inspection with guides to demonstrate all the exciting new "electric servants." Electric homes were a popular concept at the time. Similar homes had been done in Cleveland, Columbus, St. Louis, Boston, Detroit and a number of other cities and had proved wildly popular. In 1922 alone, nearly three million people had visited electric homes in the United States.

The popular local architectural firm of Hall and Lethly was once again tapped to develop the drawings for the Electric Home. In keeping with the theme of Broadmoor, the home would be of the English style, with eight rooms and an attached garage. Construction would be rushed to get the home under roof so that interior work could proceed throughout the winter. However, the stucco would not be applied until the following spring in order to demonstrate the cold-resistant qualities of the cinder blocks that were being utilized in the construction. The newspaper touted the cinder blocks as being damp-proof, frost defying, fire resisting, and a non-conductor of heat and electricity. The goal for construction was to keep costs under control in order to show visitors that a comfortable home, equipped with all the modern conveniences, could be had at a reasonable price. Excavation for the house's foundation was underway by November of 1923.

As winter broke and the building season dawned in 1924, The Kissell Real Estate Company was happily celebrating the tenth anniversary of Ridgewood. To commemorate the auspicious occasion, Harry Kissell penned a piece for the newspaper reflecting back over the last ten years of the development of Ridgewood. In it he acknowledged that he had risked practically every cent he had in the world and his entire reputation to make Ridgewood a reality. Among the city's conservative businessmen, he had faced "almost universal advice that it was too large a project for Springfield." At times, he stated, it looked like the gamble might not pay off as he faced "many hardships and discouragements." First, there was the battle over the location of the streetcar service, then the work of trying to convince the public that property restrictions were really protections, followed by the world war and an almost complete shutdown of building. And, finally, there was the wild postwar inflation in labor and materials prices.

But, now, ten years later, what had been 165 acres of farm fields, pasture, and forest was, according to Kissell, "now one of the most popular and thickly populated sections of Springfield." In 1924, there were 300 lot owners in Ridgewood, 118 houses had already been built and occupied, seventeen houses were under construction, and 114 children lived in the neighborhood. And, among the heads of households there were nineteen salesmen; four bankers; sixteen manufacturers; fourteen merchants; six physicians; one surgeon; four engineers; two lawyers; five realtors; three dentists; four printers; four accountants; and a handful of representatives of other classifications. The composition made for what Kissell called, "A well balanced community of home loving people getting the most out of life."

In the summer of 1924, work in Phase IV of Ridgewood was continuing. The entire length of Harding Road, from Limestone Street to Saint Paris Pike, was being paved with asphaltic concrete. In the latter half of 1923, after the sitting President of United States, Warren G. Harding, died suddenly of a heart

158. The north side of Harding Rd. (originally Grube Rd.) looking east towards Fountain Blvd. These lots were among the twelve lots offered on Harding Rd. during the initial phase of the development of Ridgewood. Image circa 1925.

attack, the road's name had been changed from Grube Road. The renaming offered the chance to honor the deceased president, who was a native Ohioan, and do away with a name that had been tainted by a gruesome suicide. When Ridgewood was originally platted, Grube Road was an already existing road. Its name reflected the extensive land holdings in the area by the Grube family. However, in April 1919, one of the members of the family who had sold land to Kissell for Ridgewood, Charles E. Grube, committed suicide. The 54-year-old Grube had been suffering from failing health and depression and killed himself on April 28, 1919, by placing a twelve-gauge shotgun on one of the twin beds on the sleeping porch of his North Limestone Street home, sitting on the other bed, and pulling the trigger of the shotgun with a clothes hanger. The sudden death of President Harding had provided the opportunity to do away with a reminder of one of the more dreadful events to ever take place in the burgeoning north end.

Initially, when Ridgewood was first platted, only twelve lots were offered on Grube Road. But now building lots on both sides of the newly christened Harding Road, between Fountain Boulevard and Plum Street, were available.

159. Heavily wooded lots on the south side of Harding Rd., between Midvale Rd. and Walnut Ter. 295 W. Harding Rd. would later be constructed here.

(fig. 158) In 1924, Harding Road was still a road to the country, where the beautiful Mad River Valley lay on both sides of the Saint Paris Pike. Ads for the new Harding Road lots described the "avenue of loveliness" in the following manner: "Harding Road with its bright morning sunshine and its long afternoon shadows from the stately oaks of the Woods Tract presents ideal locations for homes of character. It is virtually in the center of Ridgewood north and south, and being a great thoroughfare of great future possibilities, its value will enhance as the years roll by. Sunshine and shadows will vie with each other for supremacy on this, the only thoroughfare that completely crosses Ridgewood. It fringes The Woods tract and is virtually the hub of all drives and boulevards west of Fountain Boulevard. [It is a] magnificent road that possesses the quiet dignity of a forest drive and the gay spirit of the open road—a rare combination indeed." Lots along Harding Road were priced between $3,000 and $4,000. *(fig's. 159 & 160)*

In the summer of 1924, the new double tennis courts opened in Ridgewood just west of Longview Drive, where the two grassy plots on Ridge Mall would later be made. The original Ridgewood tennis courts, on the corner of Crescent Drive and Dover Road, had to be retired once the development of Phase IV was started. Like the original Ridgewood courts, the new ones were illuminated with 1,000-watt lamps with reflectors so that residents could play in the cool evenings and no shadows would be cast on the courts. Kissell noted that the courts were "especially appreciated by bank employees and others who cannot get their afternoons off for golf and other recreations." And just like the old courts, they could be flooded in winter and used for ice skating. Kissell remarked

160. Vacant lots on the north side of Harding Rd. (opposite fig. 159) where 260 and 276 W. Harding Rd. would later be built. Homes along Dover, Ardmore and Berkley Roads and Crescent Drive are visible in the distance.

161. Looking west down Dover Rd. from Fountain Blvd., circa 1925. The second house from the left, the Walter B. & Elsa Kleeman house at 1905 Crescent Dr., was built on the site of the original Ridgewood tennis courts.

that, "We are in a city without any safe places for ice skating, and the flooded courts, where mothers know their children are absolutely safe, are really worthwhile." *(fig. 161)*

This was also the final year that polo was played on the Ridgewood field. Back in 1919, a group of socially prominent young men had organized a hunt and polo club in Springfield. At the time, before Phase IV was developed, Kissell offered a forty-acre plot of ground just west of Crescent Drive for them to play on until they had their own field. The land west of Crescent Drive was, according to Kissell, level as a board, with a splendid strand of grass, and perfect for polo. He offered the land gratis and even put his workmen on the ground to do any little thing necessary, such as changing the location of fences and constructing graveled driveways into the polo field, all of which turned out to be a wise decision. The polo matches became a primary diversion in the neighborhood and drew a number of affluent Springfield residents from other areas of the city to the neighborhood, the type of people Kissell wanted to interest in Ridgewood. The society and sports columns of the newspaper covered the games, which were usually played with teams from Cincinnati, Toledo, Cleveland, and Dayton, giving Ridgewood much free publicity. *(fig's. 162, 163 & 164*

In 1924, however, construction on Phase IV was well underway, and the new Greenwood Hunt and Polo Club was taking shape on the Urbana Pike. The clubhouse would be ready that fall, and work was progressing on the construction of the swimming pool and tennis courts. The club would also offer a trapshooting range, a gymnasium, shower rooms, and a sixty-stall stable. Two polo fields, one for match play and one for practice, were expected to be in condition for the 1925 season.

162. Looking east across the original site of the Ridgewood polo field, towards Crescent Dr. In this 1925 image, Longview Dr. had been completed through the middle of the old field.

The year 1924 would also be the end for a number of other neighborhood activities that had taken place in the empty land west of Crescent Drive before construction on Phase IV progressed. A number of Ridgewood residents enjoyed horseback riding and kept horses in the stable at the country club. To accommodate their hobby, Kissell had designated certain places in the undeveloped section of Ridgewood where residents could ride, and he even had a figure eight path made for beginning riders so they could ride free of danger from automobile traffic.

Five acres of the open land west of Fountain Boulevard and Crescent Drive had also been set aside for park space and playgrounds. A baseball diamond was constructed for the boys in the neighborhood. The bases were made a little closer together than they would be for a standard diamond in order to make play easier and more fun for the boys and to deter adult men from occupying the diamond to the exclusion of the boys. There was even a Ridgewood baseball team, made up of boys from 12 to 16 years old. The Ridgewood team played in the city league with other boys of the same age. Kissell felt that if you "take care of the boys in this way and try to build up a pride in their home section, you will find that there are less broken windows, lamp globes, damaged trees and spoiled shrubbery."

Another popular pastime among the men in Ridgewood during nice weather was quoits. Quoits was a game similar to horseshoes, but one tossed a metal ring instead of a horseshoe. Quoits was often played at night. To keep off the evening dew, Kissell had two canopies built at the proper distance apart, and electric lights with reflectors were placed on them so that the light would be thrown on the pins and not into the eyes

163 (top). 1924 image of the polo field in Ridgewood, the last year polo was played in the neighborhood. Homes along Crescent Dr. are visible in the distance.
164 (above). Early 1920s image of polo at Ridgewood. To the left is starter Manthon Harwood, who lost an eye in WWI and was unable to play. The players are Eddie Greiner, Dick Rogers, Henry Beckley, Harold Prout, and John Westcott.

The northeast corner of N. Fountain Blvd. and Kensington Pl., circa 1925. The Paul D. & Violet Shellabarger house at 2032 N. Fountain Blvd. is to the left.

of the players. The Kissell Company also arranged picnics on the undeveloped land each year for Ridgewood residents and lot owners. The company provided entertainment and ice cream and coffee, and everyone brought a basket of food.

Activities like these reflected a concerted effort by Kissell to build a unique neighborhood identity and a sense of cohesiveness and community spirit among its residents. When one bought a lot in Ridgewood, the buyer did not just get a home site. They were also buying into the Ridgewood lifestyle in a neighborhood that offered plenty of what Kissell termed "community features." Kissell acknowledged to fellow real estate developers, "Of course, many of the features are used for advertising purposes. However, if it is to be a real subdivision the company promoting it must be perfectly willing to spend its money where it will not see a direct return in dollars and cents. It must be willing to promote things which are of real benefit to the community and contribute to the health, pleasure and enjoyment of the residents."

Kissell also believed that an effort in community building needed to be backed by an organization. Therefore, in 1917, when enough families were living there to make it viable, he promoted among them the idea of a neighborhood association. The Ridgewood District Association would be charged with the task of facilitating quality of life amenities in Ridgewood that required a unified, instead of an individual effort. Louis E. Bauer served as the association's first president, and association meetings were held in members'

165. Looking southeast at the rear of the streetcar waiting station at the junction of Fountain Blvd., Crescent Dr. and Ardmore Rd., where the Ridgewood community Christmas tree was always placed. The old Grace Lutheran Church is visible to the left.

homes at first, and later in the auditorium of the Ridgewood School. At the suggestion of Kissell, officers of the association had no connection at all with the Kissell Company. This was a deliberate move so that it would be a true community effort, one that would get residents invested in their neighborhood.

Among the activities promoted by the Ridgewood District Association was an annual Fourth of July celebration. The association took up a collection among members to defray the cost of the celebration, and Kissell always offered to make up any deficit. One year, Kissell purchased over a thousand Japanese lanterns, and the men of the association worked for nearly a week in stringing fine wire between all the trees and hanging the lanterns over the various streets.

Kissell recounted the spectacle in an article he wrote in 1925 for the *Annals of Real Estate Practice*: "On the Fourth of July evening, the whole subdivision was divided into blocks and at a certain hour, various men started on their particular blocks to light lanterns. It was a real job but the result paid for all the effort because I never saw a more beautiful sight than those lighted Japanese lanterns all over the subdivision. There was a regular traffic jam in the subdivision that night and the display was the talk of the city. Of course, we had purchased a great number of fireworks, including set pieces, and employed an expert to set them off. We have not used the lantern feature every year but use the fireworks practically every Fourth of July and enormous crowds come to Ridgewood annually to see the fireworks."

Another popular community feature promoted by the association was the community Christmas tree. Each year in mid-December, a large evergreen was placed to the rear of the streetcar waiting station on the triangular park space where Fountain Boulevard intersects with Crescent Drive and Ardmore Road. The tree was electrically lighted, a children's group sang carols, and Santa Claus always made an appearance. *(fig. 165)*

While the association took care of most of the community features, there were some things that the Kissell Company handled. One of these was arranging for the collection of ashes, garbage, and other refuse in the neighborhood. In the early years, Ridgewood had its own special system of weekly garbage collection. In order to avoid having the unsightly city garbage wagons pass through the neighborhood at objectionable times, garbage was quietly collected at night when residents would not notice the presence of the wagons. Every year, there would also be a spring cleanup week. Letters were sent notifying residents, and they could take the opportunity to get rid of larger items and any yard or landscaping waste. During the winter, the sidewalks in the neighborhood were kept free of snow by means of a horse that pulled a small, wooden, v-shaped plow.

At the inception of the suburb, in order to take care of these more mundane but necessary tasks, the Kissell Company instituted a maintenance agreement that each lot buyer was required to enter into at the time of purchase. The agreement required the payment of an annual fee, based on the size of their lot, in order to fund the maintenance of ornamental parkways, the cutting of weeds on vacant properties, garbage removal, and snow removal. Each agreement was in effect for five years after the date of purchase and amounted to about $45 to $50 a year for the average lot owner.

The Kissell Real Estate Company also handled the community newsletter, *The Ridgewood Bulletin*, which was published monthly, beginning in 1914, while the development was still under construction. Initially, it was used as a promotional piece and mailed to potential customers but, once the subdivision got going, lot owners and residents also received it monthly. The high-quality publication featured photos and progress reports on the development of Ridgewood, as well as various articles of interest to homeowners, including ones on decorating, landscaping, home mechanical systems, etc. The cost of the publication was borne by offering advertising space for local companies. Coal and fuel companies, decorating and furnishing businesses, plumbing and heating companies, lumberyards, and mortgage-lending institutions kept regular ads in the newsletter. Kissell only had to pay for the postage. *(fig. 166)*

166. Cover of the November 1917 issue of the Ridgewood Bulletin.

The Kissell Company welcomed each new Ridgewood family with a bouquet of flowers, whatever kind was in season at the time, delivered on the first Saturday after they moved into their home. A card that accompanied the bouquet read, "The Kissell Improvement Company welcomes you to Ridgewood." This gesture was timed so that the flowers would be on display on the first Sunday after a family moved in. This was the day when guests were typically invited to come inspect a family's new home. The flowers were often sent several years after the company had any real contact with the family. The new residents may have bought a lot a number of years ago and just built on it. In some cases, the Kissell organization had never had any contact with them at all. The new residents may have purchased a lot from another realtor, or an owner who was selling it, or, they may have bought an existing home. Nevertheless, every new resident got the flowers just the same.

Each new resident was also presented with a set of four colored postcards bearing scenes from Ridgewood to use for correspondence. Any Ridgewood resident could request more postcards by calling the Kissell office. While each of these gestures did help promote Ridgewood, Kissell held that "no one of these things are purely for advertising purposes because they instill pride in the minds of people who live in the subdivision."

While the residents of Ridgewood were enjoying their pleasant summer pastimes in 1924, the first section of the Broadmoor addition, Beautiful Broadmoor, was nearly completed and now had a finished look. The lighting system was done, trees that had been removed and transplanted from the adjacent wooded section of Broadmoor, Broadmoor Estates, were now growing sturdily in front of new homes, and all the shrubbery had been planted in the grassy center parkways of the boulevards. The two boulevards in the Beautiful Broadmoor section had recently received their final coating of Tarvia. They had gotten new names as well. When J. Warren James first revealed that the two boulevards in Broadmoor would be called North Kensington Boulevard and South Kensington Boulevard, a hue and cry went up from Ridgewood residents that lived on North Kensington Place and South Kensington Place because of the potential for confusion that this would cause. By July 1924, the issue was amicably resolved when James agreed to change the

167. Looking west down the newly finished Perrin Ave., 1924. The Highlands School is visible to the left.

East side of N. Fountain Blvd., circa 1925. From left to right, 1502 and 1440 N. Fountain Blvd. flank the intersection of Third Street.

names to North Broadmoor Boulevard and South Broadmoor Boulevard.

The Broadmoor offering had been well received by the public. Lots had only been on the market for one year, and the improvements had just been completed, but one third of the initial offering was already sold. In advertisements for the development, the James-Bauer Realty Company touted Broadmoor as "closest to the Country Club" and "as far north as Fountain Boulevard goes." The Kissell Company had also used the "closest to the Country Club" line back when it was first marketing North and South Kensington Place, but at that time, the company was simply trying to put a positive spin on the most remote lots. Interestingly, when Kissell was first developing Ridgewood, he focused on building up the section north of Grube/Harding Road because he feared that those lots that were farthest removed from the city would be the most difficult to sell. Kissell and Brown Burleigh deliberately built their own homes in that section for that reason, and most of the speculative homes that the Kissell Company built were located there as well. In the intervening years, however, as automobile ownership increased, this was no longer an issue and James was using the far north location of Broadmoor as an effective selling point.

168. Looking west down Parkwood Ave. in the new Perrin Woods addition. Lowry Ave. intersects to the right.

Both Harry Kissell and J. Warren James had new competition that year. The W.R. Bush Improvement Company was developing a new residential neighborhood, Perrin Woods, in southwest Springfield. Perrin Woods was located on the periphery of a beautiful section of century old trees. The new development centered on Perrin Avenue, an eighty-foot-wide boulevard platted on land that had been part of the old John Perrin farm. It was conveniently located close to the city and to area schools. The plat adjoined Highlands Grade School and was only a ten-minute walk from Springfield High School, a much shorter commute than was required by high school students living on the north end. Although there was a definite northward trend in residential

Perrin Woods

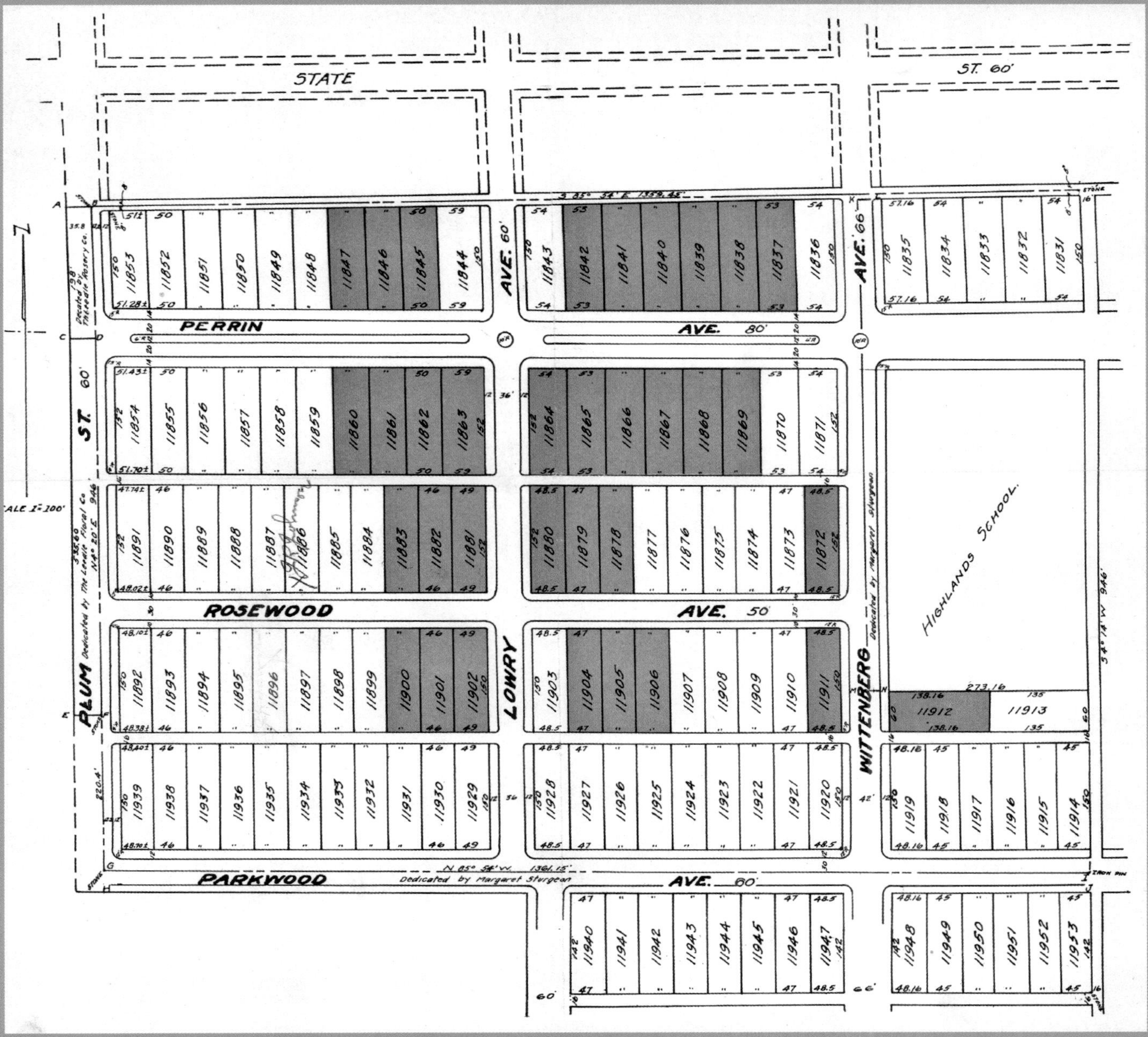

fig. 169

developments in Springfield, Perrin Woods was a success from the start and would be expanded to the south and the west two years later. The Link and Link Real Estate Company would build a number of speculative homes in Perrin Woods, many of which sold before construction was even finished. Over the course of the next several years, residential building activity in Springfield would center in Perrin Woods and Ridgewood.

(fig's. 167, 168 & 169)

In Ridgewood, in the summer of 1924, there was much rejoicing because

170. The second Springfield Country Club clubhouse, completed in 1924, replaced the original one that was destroyed by fire in 1922.

construction of the new Springfield Country Club clubhouse was drawing to a close. During the previous fall, after viewing a number of proposed plans, the building committee of the country club had selected a design created by Cleveland architects Phillip L. Small and Carl D. Rowley, both sons of former Springfield residents. The building committee felt that Small and Rowley's plans were artistic and represented the latest in clubhouse construction. However, what they really liked about the design was that it was well adapted to the needs of the country club and was not, like others they had seen, a monument to the architect. Nor did the design contain lots of useless and expensive ornamentation. The committee wanted an attractive clubhouse of course, but utility was every bit as important as beauty. This was to be a rustic country retreat and not some high-style building in the city. Small and Rowley's plans called for a rambling type building with a first story of brick, and the second of stucco finish with half-timber accents. The clubhouse would have a wood shake roof, making it reminiscent of an English thatched cottage. *(fig. 170)*

After much discussion regarding the location, the new clubhouse was to be built on the site of the old clubhouse, on the crest of a knoll, to afford views of the stunning golf course to the west. That the location was ever in question is hard to fathom. The clubhouse was to be long and rambling with verandas on three sides. The veranda on the west side would overlook the golf course and the valley beyond. And by the summer of 1924, it was nearly done.

One entered the clubhouse from the driveway via a hooded entrance, which led directly into a hall where the club offices, cigar counter, telephone booths, the men's coat room, and main stairs were located. Directly ahead was the main lounge with its massive fireplace of brick and Cleveland sandstone, designed to resemble a typical English great hall. High-beamed ceilings and broad bays of leaded glass windows completed the room. The lounge opened into the dining room, and doors in the main lounge led out to the enclosed dining porches beyond.

171. Newspaper image of the Electric Home at 110 N. Broadmoor Blvd.

The kitchen occupied a level half way between the first floor and basement and was outfitted with the most modern culinary equipment. Off the kitchen were the servants' dining room, the locker rooms, restrooms for servants of both sexes, storerooms, and refrigerator rooms. On the lower level, which was half below and half above ground, were the men's locker rooms, showers, restrooms, the porters' room, drying rooms, a soft drink bar, grillroom and grill serving room. The grillroom and men's locker room could be reached either directly from the golf course, or by means of the main stair from the entry hall, or from the driveway by means of a private door.

The men's locker room was equipped with 250 lockers and benches, eight showers and separate restrooms. Locker areas were equipped with forced ventilation and the porters' room had a clothes dryer to take care of members' wet clothes. Women's lockers were above the kitchen, a half story above the main lounge level and reached by means of the main stairs, or from a private stairway leading directly to the ground near the first tee of the golf course. The women's locker room was equipped with 100 lockers, a rest room, dressing rooms, and shower rooms. The club manager's living quarters, containing a living room, two bedrooms, and a bath, were on the second floor, a half story above the women's locker room.

After two years of making do with their cozy quarters in the Manor House, club members were excited to inaugurate their new clubhouse. It was dedicated in late May of 1924 with a weekend of activities, which kicked off on Friday, May 30, 1924, with golf matches and a luncheon for members, followed the next day by a formal dance. The newspaper ran a large article on the following Sunday, complete with interior and exterior photos of the club and offered the following thoughts: "Although this will not compare in size with some of the larger country clubhouses in the larger cities, it will in completeness, efficiency, and beauty, take its place as one of the finer and most beautiful clubs in the country."

Nearby, in the Broadmoor addition, the Electric Home was also close to completion and would be ready for public inspection the following month. Stucco was being applied over the cinder block exterior and the interior was being plastered. All that was left was the installation of the woodwork and then the furniture could be placed. The Edward Wren Company, The People's Outfitting Company, and The Cappel Home Furnishing Company were providing the furniture. All of the interior decoration of the home was under the supervision of the artistic Mrs. Frank Dock, who lived on Dover Road in Ridgewood. *(fig. 171)*

While The Kissell Improvement Company and the James-Bauer Realty Company were obligated to try to differentiate their respective subdivisions in order to compete for customers, the residents of Broadmoor and Ridgewood were largely oblivious to any boundaries or distinctions between one neighborhood and the other. The minor kerfuffle over the initial naming of the streets in Broadmoor represented the only real tension that ever existed between the two subdivisions. The same was true between the principals of the two competing real estate companies. While they were ardent competitors in business, they mixed amicably in social settings and shared a commitment to promoting causes that added to the life of the community they were creating north of McCreight Avenue. A case in point was that J.Warren James and Walter B. Bauer became two of the biggest supporters of Ridgewood School.

The formal opening for the Electric Home was set for Sunday, July 20, 1924, at 2 p.m. On that day, signs with the words "Electric Home," with arrows pointing out the direction to the site, were placed on light poles along the principal streets of the entire city. "'Follow the Electric Home Arrows' will be the slogan of motorists Sunday when all roads lead to the Electric Home," said the newspaper on opening day. A separate, special section devoted solely to the house was inserted into the newspaper that day.

To accommodate all the cars that were expected on opening day, parking was available on empty land at the western end of the boulevards. Streetcar patrons were advised to take the Ridgewood car and get off on Broadmoor Boulevard, then walk two minutes west to "The House of Your Dreams." A large, electrically lighted sign pointed out the home, and giant floodlights were at the ready to illuminate the exterior of the house at night.

Prior to the opening that Sunday afternoon, and in lieu of a ribbon cutting ceremony, C.I. Weaver, the general manager of the Ohio Edison Company, one of the local companies that participated in the construction, presented the key to the home to Miss Anna B. Johnson, president of the City Federation of Women's Clubs. Miss Johnson then ceremoniously opened the front door to visitors.

At the time, the use of electricity in a home was still largely considered a luxury. Only 35 percent of all homes in the United States were wired for electricity. However, one of the goals of the promoters of the home was to convince visitors that the marvels of electricity were within the reach of everyone. One did not need to have a palace to partake in them. It cost a mere fifty cents a day for electricity to operate a house the size of the Electric Home. Trained demonstrators were on hand to guide visitors through the house and explain all the modern equipment, its advantages, and how it would contribute to the health, economy, and comfort of the residents.

One of the stars of the home was the modern kitchen with its electric refrigerator that operated automatically and did away with the need to purchase ice. The gleaming white porcelain electric refrigerator made its own ice and kept a uniform temperature at all times. The kitchen also boasted an electric stove, an electric fireless cooker (an early version of the modern-day slow cooker), and an electric "disher." The newspaper expounded on the virtues of the innovative appliance: "The electric disher is the machine which every housewife has at many times in her life wished for. It removes the drudgery of leaning over a steaming dishpan in the sink. Dishes can be put in this washer and no more thought given them except to stop the motor at the right time and turn on the drain."

By modern standards, the device was quite laborious. The housewife had to pour in hot water for the wash cycle, then draw it off, and repeat the same actions for the rinse cycle. A revolving paddle wheel threw water in the form of a driving, fine rain against the dishes from various angles. At the conclusion of the wash and rinse cycles, the lid was opened and dishes were allowed to dry from their own heat, but silver and glassware had to be dried by hand with a tea towel. It did spare the hands of the housewife from thrice daily exposure to water and harsh detergent, but the early version of the dishwasher was more of a novelty than a true labor saving device. The kitchen also had a drop down ironing board hidden in a closet, which was also equipped with an outlet for an electric iron. An electric fan, courtesy of Robbins and Myers, who provided all the decorative fans in the house, kept the kitchen cool. However, as the demonstrator noted, the electric stove directed the heat directly to the pan, and the kitchen did not get as hot as it would have with an old-fashioned stove.

There were plenty of other electrical gadgets throughout the three-bedroom, one-and-a-half bath home. In the dining room, there was a waffle iron, a table grill for pancakes, a percolator, a chafing dish, and a toaster, all of which could be plugged into an outlet built into the buffet, making it a self-serving dining room when no servant was available. Abundant electric lights could be found throughout the house, including in the closets. Lights came on and went off automatically in the closets by means of a switch that was compressed or released when the door opened or closed. All of the electrical outlets were placed at a convenient height on walls, an improvement over the typical baseboard outlet. In the 1920s, corsets were going out of style among young women, but many mature women still wore them, so baseboard outlets were considered a nuisance because they required extreme stooping. In the main bathroom, there was a radiant heater to take the chill off when the heating system was not in use. The house also had a lightweight, portable, electric sewing machine that could be used in any room.

The bedrooms boasted reading lights installed on the wall at the heads of the beds, as well as electric bed warmers and fans. On the vanity was a curling iron, a hair dryer, and a peculiar novelty of the period—a violet ray. The violet ray wand was an electrical device that delivered a low current that was thought to stimulate the scalp. An under-bed light in each bedroom made it possible to see at night and was described as especially useful during sickness. In order to accommodate the crowds, prevent traffic backups, and facilitate movement, the connecting walls between closets in the bedrooms were not put in place. On each floor of the home, there was an electric sweeper that gathered dirt into a dust proof bag instead of spreading it all over the house and a portable space heater that could be carried from room to room.

The well-equipped laundry room had a water softener to provide good water for doing laundry, an improvement over the old rainwater-collecting cisterns that could be found in the basements of nineteenth-century homes. There was also an electric washer and ringer, a gas dryer, and a gas-electric ironing machine for large linen flatwork—sheets, pillowcases, hand towels, tablecloths, and napkins. Demonstrators boasted that these appliances cut in half the time required to do laundry. Special lights made of blue glass, known as daylight lamps, hung overhead in the basement and were designed to permit the judging of color, which, according to the demonstrator, was essential so one would know if laundry was done thoroughly. And, finally, despite its name, the Electric Home had a coal furnace in the basement. Gas furnaces were starting to come into use, but the true all-electric home with an electric furnace was still in the future.

172. Newspaper image of the Model Home at 124 S. Broadmoor Blvd.

Also open for inspection at the same time was the "Model Home," a house on 124 South Broadmoor Boulevard constructed by Graham Woodhouse, a local builder. Woodhouse had built many homes for Springfield clients, and, as he did so, the concept of an "ideal" home crystallized in his mind. For the home on South Broadmoor, Woodhouse utilized ideas that worked well in other homes and discarded those that did not in order to create a comfortable, well-appointed home for a middle-class family. Seeing it as good publicity for Broadmoor and a chance to get building activity under way, The James-Bauer Realty Company donated the lot. *(fig. 172)*

As they had done for the Electric Home, locals businesses provided the furnishings, appliances, and décor. The Model Home was open for the same run as the Electric Home. Each woman who visited the home was presented a rose, and little Billy McCuddy kept either the radio or the Victrola in the living room going throughout the afternoons and evenings. To further drum up publicity for the Model Home, Graham Woodhouse conceived a gimmick to give engaged couples the opportunity to enter a contest to be married in the home. The lucky couple received a $100 worth of free furniture from Salzer Brothers.

Both homes were wildly successful. By the time the two homes closed two weeks later on Sunday, August 3, 1924, several thousand people had visited the Model Home. The Electric Home had an astonishing attendance of over 10,000 visitors. One in every seven Springfield residents had visited it. At the end of its run, Loren E. Brown, the treasurer of the Springfield Cinder Block Company, purchased the Electric Home.

The following year, 1925, marked the beginning of the end of development work in Ridgewood. Already, more than a decade of work and over $1 million had gone into the project. As the 1925 building season got started, construction work on the last street in The Woods section, Walnut Terrace, was underway, and work on the remainder of Phase IV was starting. The first wave of construction in Phase IV, which came as a tactical response to the announcement in 1922 of the development of the Broadmoor addition, had been completed as far as Longview Drive. A number of houses were now going up along Longview, and the Kissell Company was starting the final stage of improvements on the remaining empty land to the west of it. *(fig's. 173-177)*

By the middle of September 1925, there was still much construction work left to finish the project, but lots in the final sections went on sale and the publicity campaign for the new offering was launched. The Kissell Company ran a series of advertisements designed to create a sense of urgency among potential customers: "Today Ridgewood is writing the final chapter of its sale, and today's buyers are getting the last lots at original prices." "This is decision time in Ridgewood," another ad announced.

In the autumn of 1925, one of the most unique houses ever constructed in Ridgewood, the Guy and Jane Bayley house at 1926 North Fountain Boulevard, was nearing completion. The Bayley house was designed to have

173. Aerial view of Ridgewood west of Fountain Blvd., looking north. "The Woods" section is visible near the center of the image. Phase IV can be seen under construction at the top of the image, 1925.

174. Aerial view of Ridgewood west of Fountain Blvd., looking south. Phase IV can be seen under construction in the image, 1925.

the appearance of a rustic French farmhouse, and it was the first French-inspired home constructed in Ridgewood. Several years earlier, the Bayleys were traveling in California when they spotted a house that would serve as the inspiration for the one they would ultimately build. The home was an exacting replica of an actual farmhouse that its owner had admired in the French countryside. Guy Bayley had always been something of an architectural buff, and he and his wife, Jane, were so smitten with the unique storybook quality of the house that he knocked on the door and enquired about it. The owner graciously offered copies of his blueprints, and the Bayleys left for home with plans to build their dream house as soon as possible. *(fig. 178)*

Back in Springfield, the Hall and Lethly architectural firm made minor modifications to the blueprints to suit the needs of the family, and Guy Bayley purchased a lot on North Fountain Boulevard. The Bayleys' lot had been the site of the old Kissell sales office, erected in 1915 and dismantled in 1920 when most of the lots in the original section of Ridgewood were sold. Another couple had initially purchased the lot from Kissell in 1920 and later sold it to the Bayleys.

175. Looking south down Longview Dr. towards the triangular parklet at Berkley Rd. and Longview Dr. 1815 Longview Dr. can be seen to the right, circa 1925.

176. View from Longview Dr., looking southeast towards Berkley Rd. The rear of the homes at 100 and 118 Ardmore Rd., and the front of 131 Berkley Rd., are visible from left to right, circa 1925.

177. Image taken from the southeast corner of Longview Dr. and Dover Rd., looking northwest towards the Phase IV extension of Dover Rd. Houses under construction in the Broadmoor addition are visible in the distance, circa 1925.

The Bayley house was underway by March 1925 and was largely completed by the end of the year. The features of the house were painstakingly authentic to a French farmhouse, down to the smallest detail. Everything from the shake roof to the rustic interior plaster technique was meticulously replicated. The authenticity of the reproduction sometimes meant grudging concessions on the part of its occupants. Guy and Jane Bayley's daughters often lamented the fact that they couldn't hang pictures on the walls of their bedrooms because it would make a hole in the plaster that couldn't be repaired. The unique casement windows in the home were created by the William Bayley Company, the Bayley family business. Guy's father started the successful company in 1881, and it manufactured and exported metal doors and windows all over the world. They provided windows for many of the homes constructed in Ridgewood. *(fig. 179)*

Guy Bayley was one of the more notable personalities in Ridgewood because of his interesting hobbies. He kept bees and even set up a honey production facility in his basement, outfitted with an extractor to remove the honey from the honeycombs. His daughters then bottled it and labeled the jars. Guy Bayley made numerous attempts to get stores to carry his honey—Sue's Honey—named for his youngest daughter, but the enterprise never got off the ground. But he was perhaps best known in the neighborhood for his penchant for the show horses that he kept in a stable behind the Bayley house. *(fig. 180)*

180 (top). Sue Bayley, daughter of Guy & Jane Bayley, displaying a gift box of "Sue's Honey," one of Guy Bayley's many unusual endeavors.
178 (above). The Guy & Jane Bayley house at 1926 N. Fountain Blvd.

When he acquired the lot for his house, he also bought about an acre of ground immediately behind it, where the Clark Memorial Home now sits. There, he had an exercise track and a stable constructed for his horses. In the evening after work, he liked to hitch one of his horses up to the sulky and drive it around the track. It was not unusual to see several neighborhood children hanging over the fence watching the spectacle. Bayley even imported an experienced trainer from Kentucky, a tiny little man and former jockey named John Rolfes, to care for his horses. John went by the nickname "Dutch," and he lived in the beautiful little stable behind the Bayley house. Guy Bayley's beehives and horses remained a popular neighborhood curiosity for many years. After his death in 1952, his wife, Jane, donated the land behind their home so that a new Clark Memorial Home for Aged Women, an endeavor that she had long championed, could be constructed there.

But back in November of 1925, as construction of the Bayley house was just being completed, the Kissell Company was rolling out a creative promotional contest to draw publicity for the final sections of Ridgewood. A large notice placed in the newspaper on Tuesday, November 3, 1925, invited Springfield residents to help name three of the landscape features located in the final section of The Woods and the final section of Phase IV.

Another landscape feature was already named—The Mall—a semicircular grass plot at Pembrook Road and Ridge Mall, intersected by Ardmore Road, was the largest grass parklet in Ridgewood. At 400 feet wide to the north and south and 300 feet wide to the east and west, it was larger than the Big Four Park in downtown Springfield. The construction of The Mall, on the site of the second incarnation of Ridgewood tennis courts, spelled the neighborhood demise of tennis, a popular pastime that dated back to 1916. But it created one of the most unique "beauty spots" in Ridgewood.

Among the three "beauty spots" that remained to be named was a circular grass plot in Phase IV at the intersection of Walnut Terrace, Ardmore Road, and Dover Road, upon which a flagpole was to be erected in order to fly the American flag each day. Another landscape feature in Phase IV was an elongated triangular parklet, the largest of all the triangular parklets in Ridgewood, located just north of Harding Road, where Walnut Terrace and Pembrook Road diverged. And the final feature was a sunken garden at the intersection of Walnut Terrace and Brighton Road in The Woods section. The sunken garden, which featured one of the largest ash trees in this area of the country, was being walled and capped with limestone from a local quarry and would be beautifully planted with ivy and shrubbery. *(fig. 181)*

179. The rear of the Bayley house, taken in October 1930 during a gathering of William Bayley Co. district managers. William Bayley is seated in the center. Guy Bayley is standing to his right. Note the rustic detailing of the shake roof and dormer on the house.

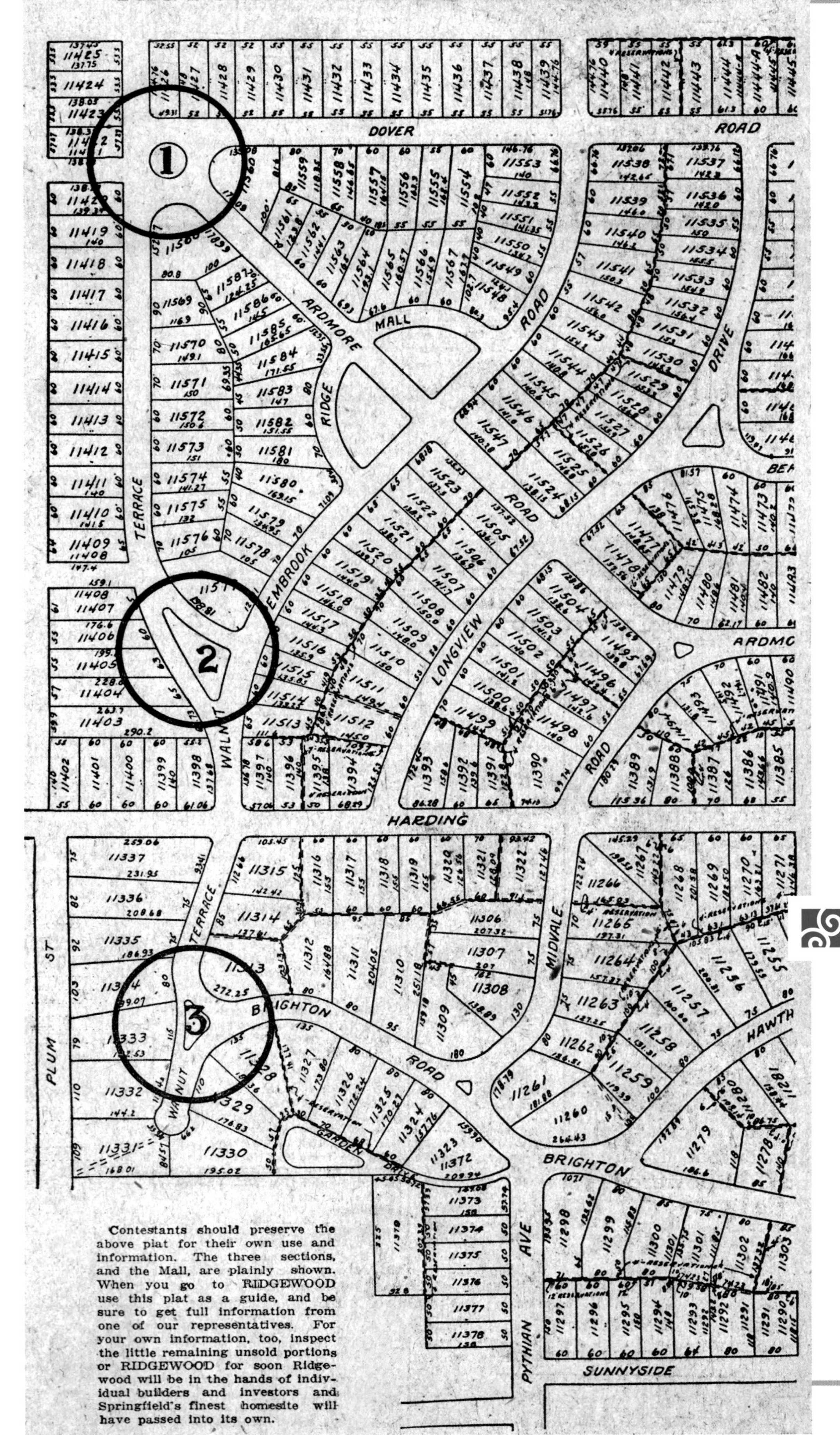

The Feature Sections to Be Named!

Contestants should preserve the above plat for their own use and information. The three sections, and the Mall, are plainly shown. When you go to RIDGEWOOD use this plat as a guide, and be sure to get full information from one of our representatives. For your own information, too, inspect the little remaining unsold portions or RIDGEWOOD for soon Ridgewood will be in the hands of individual builders and investors and Springfield's finest homesite will have passed into its own.

181. Map that appeared in the *Springfield Daily News* on November 3, 1925 for a promotional contest inviting citizens to name the new landscape features in the final phase of Ridgewood.

In the announcement for the contest on Tuesday, November 3, Springfield residents were invited to come out to the property either the next day, or on Saturday. Kissell representatives would be available both days to give information about each of the landscape features and provide blanks upon which people could submit their entries. The contest proved a great way to get people out to look at the newest sections of Ridgewood. Hundreds visited, and 375 people submitted entries.

Contest winners were announced in the newspaper on Sunday, December 6, 1925, and each winner received a $50 cash prize. Mrs. Maude Baker of 325 South Belmont Avenue chose the winning name—Ardmore Circle—for the circular grass plot at the intersection of Ardmore Road, Dover Road, and Walnut Terrace. Mr. Arthur Moore of 1621 North Limestone Street christened the triangular parklet at Walnut Terrace and Pembrook Road—Arrowhead Place. Home sites that fronted on this particular feature would henceforth be marketed as "in the Arrowhead District." Mrs. Margaret Sparrow of 126 West Euclid Avenue submitted the winning name—Forest Glen—for the sunken garden at Walnut Terrace and Brighton Road.

At the close of 1925, Harry Kissell predicted that Springfield, now at a population of 71,000, was at the threshold of the most prosperous times it had ever experienced. "We are backing our faith in Springfield with our dollars and we are going into the biggest program of expansion, both in the development of ground and in the building of our sales organization, which the company has ever undertaken," he stated. In November, national real estate activity exceeded all previous records, and the company's advertising, heady with optimism, invited Springfield residents to look ahead five or ten years to the city's eventual growth and development. "The picture of Springfield in 1935 is coming vividly into view—Springfield is SAFE—Ridgewood is SAFE." A December 30, 1925, Kissell advertisement predicted that "during 1926 real estate history in Springfield will be written in letters of gold," under the banner headline: "1926—We Are Ready!"

Harry Kissell was right about his prediction for 1926. It was a record-breaking year in building and real estate. All records for the volume of construction of buildings in the United States were shattered in July. In Springfield, there was more than $4 million in total building work that year. The largest project was the new power station of The Ohio Edison Company, which was under construction along Mad River, near the Masonic Home. And throughout the spring and early summer, teams of men had labored to finish The Woods section and Phase IV of Ridgewood. Curbing, guttering, and sidewalks were going in, and about fifty men were laying carloads of crushed stone in the roadways. By the middle of July, the final coating of Tarvia and pea gravel was going on.

And just as the final chapter of the development of Ridgewood was being written, it looked like the story of the Hills and Dales subdivision might finally have a happy ending as well. In the summer of 1926, Link and Link Real Estate Company acquired the beautiful wooded tract with lovely winding roads and century old trees overlooking the Mad River Valley. Constantine Link announced in the newspaper that the remaining improvements were to be started in the addition immediately. Eleven years after its start, much work was left to be done in Hills and Dales. The lighting system was not yet completed, nor were the sidewalks, curbs, gutters, water, sewer, and gas mains in some parts of the development. In addition, there were streets that still remained to be paved. *(fig. 182)*

Once the announcement of the acquisition was made, Harry Kissell took the opportunity to congratulate Link and Link. He took out a newspaper advertisement in which he stated that he was gratified to learn of it because "we are now assured that this development will be handled by a company which is financially strong and able to complete it in a proper manner. We feel that the taking over of Hills and Dales by Link and Link is not only very beneficial to Ridgewood, but to the entire north side where they have already done considerable building and some platting. It is always a pleasure to be able to work in cooperation with others in your own line of business providing their standards are high and their integrity unquestioned. That is why we are congratulating Link and Link this morning. The heartiest cooperation which has always existed between Link and Link and the Kissell Companies will continue in their operation and we wish them every success." News of the purchase by the Links was all that was required to revive interest in the subdivision. Lots were suddenly in demand and building activity was beginning again now that Hills and Dales was, at long last, in good hands.

182. Portrait of the five Link brothers. Constantine & Lewis Link, the principals of Link and Link Real Estate Co., are second and third from the left, respectively.

That summer in Ridgewood, a new house was under construction that marked the first appearance in the neighborhood of a home influenced architecturally by the Spanish Mission style. Gus and Sophia LeBolt were building their new house on the southeast corner of Brighton Road and Pythian Avenue. At the time their Ridgewood house was being constructed, the LeBolts were living at 918 North Fountain Avenue, a house that they had built about a decade earlier. Sophia LeBolt was the driving force behind the construction of both houses. Typically in this era, newspaper articles documenting the progress of new homes simply referred to the houses by the husband's name. For example, the LeBolt house would have ordinarily been referred to as the Gus LeBolt house. In this instance, however, that was not the case. Whenever a mention of the house appeared in the newspaper, it was usually called the "Mrs. LeBolt house," a practice unheard of at the time.

Her husband, Gus, ran a successful chain of cigar stores in Springfield, providing the means by which to indulge his wife's penchant for building new homes. In the 1920s, most gentlemen still routinely smoked cigars, so Gus LeBolt's business was thriving. He had five downtown stores, including one on the southeast corner of East High Street and South Limestone Street, one on the southwest corner of East Main Street and South Limestone Street, one in the Hotel Shawnee, one in the Hotel Bancroft, as well as his premier flagship store in the Fairbanks Building. He had entered the cigar business in 1904 when his brother died. Gus took over his brother's cigar store in the Arcade and expanded the business from there. Prolific Springfield architect Robert C. Gotwald designed the LeBolts' new house at 223 Brighton Road, and its Spanish Mission style was a fitting ode to the fact that the fortune that made it possible was built on selling fine Cuban cigars. *(fig. 183)*

183. The Gus & Sophia LeBolt house at 223 Brighton Rd.

Meanwhile, in Ridgewood as a whole, the task that had started nearly twelve years before was almost finished. To mark the occasion, the Kissell Company ran a large advertisement in the newspaper on Sunday, July 18, 1926, with the headline: "A Mountain of Materials Used in Ridgewood." The ad reported that in the development of 165 acres,

Follow the Arrows Through Ridgewood

WE HAVE erected in Ridgewood commencing at the corner of Fountain Boulevard and McCreight Avenue, black arrows on a yellow background. If you will start at this point and follow these arrows, they will lead you over 6.3 miles of the ten miles of Ridgewood roads. Turn to the left off Fountain Boulevard at the fountain and just as you get to the first triangle beyond the fountain, stop your car a minute and look at the delightful group of homes which are seen from this point. It is one of the most attractive views in Ridgewood and shows some of the most modern residences in Springfield, all of which have been built within the last five years.

After passing this point, you will see not only the delightful drives through the Wooded Section of Ridgewood, which includes Forest Glen, (still incompleted), but it will also take you through the Mall, on which there are no lots for sale but which is devoted entirely to park purposes; then on up to Ardmore Circle and down to Arrowhead Place. All of these sections will be beautifully landscaped this fall and in the course of a year or so will be most attractive. Facing these feature sections are some of the most pleasing home sites in the district.

Beyond this newer part of Ridgewood, the route leads by way of Dover Road and Crescent Drive through some of the original developments of Ridgewood, across Fountain Boulevard to Englewood Road, Hampton Place, Stratford Place, and then back on to Fountain Boulevard and up to Kensington Place.

These last streets, all east of Fountain Boulevard, are built solidly, there being hardly a vacant lot left. It will give you an opportunity to see a number of attractive homes with pleasing types of architecture all of which have been constructed during the last ten or twelve years. If you will then follow the arrows on out to the end of Fountain Boulevard at the entrance to the Country Club and back Fountain Boulevard to McCreight Avenue, you will find that your speedometer will register 6.3 miles if it is in correct working order.

"Follow the Arrows"

HOUSES OPEN FOR INSPECTION

In order that your tour of Ridgewood may be complete you are invited to stop at any of the new houses which have signs on them "Open For Inspection" and go through these houses and see how attractively they are built. A representative of the company will be at each house to give you any information you may wish.

REPRESENTATIVES OF THE COMPANY WILL HELP YOU

To render any possible service required or to answer any questions, representatives of the company will be at Ridgewood all day. You will find them either in automobiles with placards on the same, with the word "Ridgewood" in red letters or you will find them in some of the new houses which will be open for inspection.

Bring this plat with you. Watch for the arrows.

Follow the (Consecutively Numbered) Arrows

Special Instructions For the Trip

There are only three places where the route covers the same street twice and in each one of these cases it is but a short distance. There are several places, however, where you cross over the same street intersection. To avoid confusion, therefore, you will find numbers on arrows — number 1 beginning at Fountain Boulevard and McCreight Avenue. If from that point you will watch for number 2 then number 3, number 4, etc., you will be able to follow the entire route through the addition and will cover practically all of the interesting feature sections of Ridgewood and also see the many attractive types of the more than 200 homes which have been built in Ridgewood.

The Last Unit of Ridgewood Now Selling at $38.00 Per Front Foot

You have heard about Ridgewood so much during the past twelve years that you think you are going to continue to hear of it forever. You also think that we are going to continue developing more lots. Ridgewood was bought before the war and much of it was developed before the war at prices which would be unheard of at this time. For this reason we are able to sell our property cheaper than any other property, with similar improvements and in a similar location, can be sold in Springfield and we are able to sell Ridgewood at a lower price than we will ever be able to sell any other property which we may develop in the future. Many people have taken advantage of this fact and have already purchased. A few more can buy at the introductory offer of $38.00 per foot. As soon as the improvements are entirely completed, which will be sometime this fall, all unsold lots will be increased in price. Whether you believe it or not, a very short time will prove to you that you will never in the history of Springfield be able to purchase such lots at $38.00 per front foot as you can now buy in Ridgewood for this price. If you expect to purchase a lot within the next five years you had better select it now, save money and get a choice of location.

THE KISSELL COMPANIES
COMMUNITY BUILDERS · REALTORS
927-933 FAIRBANKS BLDG. · PHONES MAIN 650-651-652

FINISH — START — McCREIGHT AVE

fig. 184

$1.5 million had been expended. During the construction, over 100,000 cubic yards of dirt had been worked. Fifteen miles of storm and sanitary sewers, ten miles of gas lines, and ten miles of water lines had been laid, requiring 300 train carloads of pipe. Over ten miles of streets had been constructed using 575 carloads of stone, forty-one carloads of pea gravel, and twenty carloads of Tarvia.

Enough sidewalks, curbs, and gutters were laid that they could have extended all the way from Springfield to South Charleston, Ohio, and they had required 171,000 gallons, or 160 carloads of cement. Nineteen miles of electric cable had been run for the ornamental lighting system. Enough sewer had been built to reach from Springfield to Urbana, Ohio. If the roadway, curb and gutter, sidewalks, sewers, gas and water lines, and electric cable were laid end to end, it would have made a continuous piece of construction work ninety-three miles long, or long enough to reach from Springfield to Cincinnati. To haul it all would require the equivalent of twenty-one trains of fifty freight cars each. If one coupled the trains into one continuous train, it would have stretched from Springfield to Yellow Springs, Ohio.

With a rightful sense of accomplishment and great fanfare, the Kissell Company also announced in its July 18 advertisement that, "Over 12 years we have visualized these 165 acres of woods and fields converted into home sites . . . and worked persistently toward the realization of that vision. It is therefore with more satisfaction than probably anyone can realize that we now approach the completion of our task. We submit it to Springfield for its approval. We made many promises twelve years ago when this project was undertaken. We have kept every promise. Ridgewood is all that we said it would be."

The citizens of Springfield were invited to come out on the following Sunday—July 25, 1926—to inspect the completed Ridgewood. Consecutively numbered signs bearing black arrows on a yellow background would be erected that day throughout Ridgewood to guide motorists through the neighborhood in a manner in which they could see the entire development without retracing much of their course. On the appointed day, a map of the completed plat of Ridgewood was printed in the newspaper. Arrows on the map demonstrated the route through Ridgewood that Kissell associates had carefully devised. *(fig. 184)*

Motorists would start at McCreight Avenue and Fountain Boulevard and follow the arrows, making their first turn to the left at Sunnyside Place. A number of new speculative homes that were going up in Ridgewood were marked that day with signs that announced, "Open for Inspection." Kissell representatives, at the ready to assist prospective customers, were stationed in various places throughout the development in automobiles bearing placards that read, "Ridgewood."

Kissell sales associates were instructed to encourage visitors to envision what the new sections would look like in ten years when they were built up and the landscape had matured. This was a far easier task for potential buyers in 1926 than it had been for buyers who had taken the leap of faith in 1915. By 1926, 203 houses had been built in Ridgewood, and the landscape in the oldest sections was becoming quite lush. The spindly little elms trees, planted in 1915, were growing into fine shade trees. The terrible Dutch Elm Disease that would arrive in the United States a few years later and eventually require every single one of the 1,500 elms in Ridgewood to be cut down, shattering the spirits of residents, was still in the offing. *(fig's. 185 & 186)*

186 (top). 1930s image of the elm trees along S. Kensington Pl., before all the trees in Ridgewood had to be cut down in the wake of Dutch Elm Disease. 185 (above). View of the triangular parklet at Ardmore Rd. and Crescent Dr. In this 1927 view, landscaping in one of the oldest sections of Ridgewood had matured to the point that the Bauer house on Crescent Dr. was almost completely obscured by the plantings.

Life was good in Ridgewood. A new model home was being planned for 1927 at 1759 Walnut Terrace in the Arrowhead District. The home would have a two-car garage, which was starting to become more common in upscale neighborhoods as more women were driving thanks to the advent of the self-starting motor. As a result, many affluent families were motivated to get a second automobile. The model home would also have a side porch, an increasingly popular amenity on new homes of the era now that the front porch had passed to glory, and the backyard had not yet completed its rise as the family playground, a pinnacle it would reach in the 1950s. *(fig. 187)*

That fall, Ridgewood residents would have a pleasant new pastime—The Bulldogs—Springfield's own semi-professional football team, which was playing on its new field on part of the empty John Doyle land that lay east of Fountain Boulevard and north of North Kensington Place. The storm clouds were quietly gathering, however. An article ran in the local newspaper that fall on October 17, 1926, with the headline, "Speculators Shown to be Over Zealous." The article warned that "Over the last two weeks stock exchange prices have had one of the worst declines that have occurred in a similar short space in recent years." Washington officials, representative bankers, businessmen, and heavy traders, however, remained unqualifiably optimistic. Virtually everyone, it seemed, was blissfully unaware of what lay ahead. *(fig. 188)*

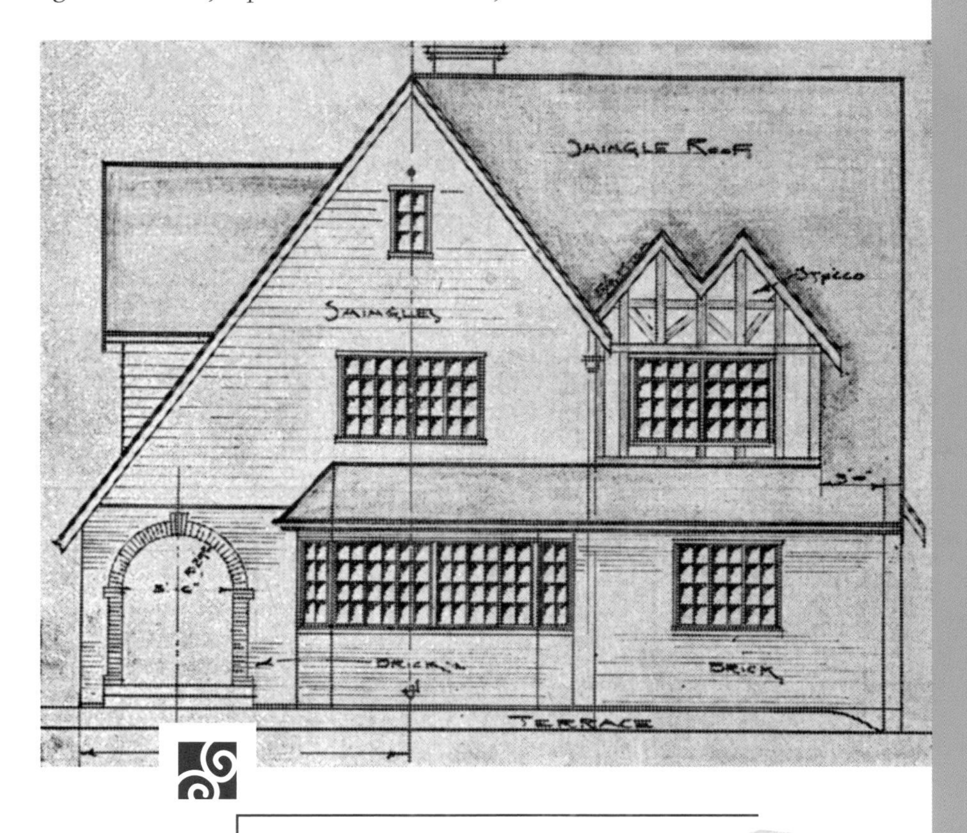

187. Artist rendering of the model home at 1759 Walnut Ter.
188 (screened image below). The Bulldogs, Springfield's semi-professional football team.

189. The original Jefferson School, destroyed by fire February 19, 1929.

TRYING TIMES

CHAPTER 7

TRYING TIMES

THE YEAR 1926 MARKED THE PEAK OF NEW CONSTRUCTION IN SPRINGFIELD DURING THE POSTWAR BOOM OF THE 1920s.

Then over the course of the next several years, new construction declined slightly each year. The same pattern was true for the rest of the country. A large part of the decline could be attributed to the fact that builders were finally catching up with the pent-up demand caused by the growth in population and the shutdown of building during the war. A more worrisome problem, however, was also contributing to the decline. The increasing diversion of capital to speculative purposes was causing a continued shortage of mortgage money, making interest rates skyrocket. Another factor in the decline in construction was that more and more Americans, especially young adults, were diverting much of their income to the purchase of consumer goods like automobiles, radios, appliances, fur coats, and jewelry instead of saving it towards the purchase of a home. When given the choice of having a home of their own, or living with their parents and having their own automobile, most opted for the automobile because it meant freedom.

Auto sales in the United States had skyrocketed in the latter half of the 1920s, making the automobile industry a driving engine of the economy that spurred many related industries. In 1926, a Model T Ford rolled off the assembly line every ten seconds. By 1929, total U.S. automobile production reached 5.2 million cars. However, in that same year, $1 billion less was spent on home building than had been expended in 1928. All real estate values had been slumping since 1927, but most people seemed oblivious to it. When it came to the economy, their attention was focused squarely on the bull market.

Virtually everyone, it seemed, was seduced by the intoxicating lure of the rising stock market and the possibility of getting rich quick. Tantalizing stories abounded about ordinary people making a fortune overnight. This had become such a problem in Springfield that, since 1920, the city had observed an annual Thrift Week, initiated by the YMCA, to call attention to reckless spending and unwise investments. The organizers of Thrift Week tried to convince residents to put their savings into local financial institutions instead of risking it in the stock market.

Even the Kissell Company made concessions to the growing trend. In the early days of Ridgewood, Kissell and Brown Burleigh had refrained from promoting Ridgewood lots as an investment. However, as the 1920s wore on, it became apparent that they were competing directly with the stock market as much as with fellow real estate developers. Near the end of the decade, they could no longer beat the investment craze and they were forced to join it, in essence by adopting the language of the stock market and marketing Ridgewood to would-be investors. By this time, however, Ridgewood was established and built up to the point that it seemed there was no longer any reason to fear speculative buyers.

A 1927 advertisement promoted Ridgewood as a "A Profitable Association " and read, "Just through a small investment in one of the attractive home sites in Ridgewood [buyers] indirectly become stockholders in a proposition with some of Springfield's most aggressive businessmen who have bought and built their homes in this desirable section. This indirect association creates a powerful advantage to those who someday will pilot Springfield toward the greatness which is inevitable. When investing in Ridgewood you not only help to build a better and bigger city but immediately lay a stone in the foundation of your own future. Ridgewood home sites are a good investment."

By 1927, however, the postwar building boom was already behind Springfield and the nation, and the decline was accelerating. By 1929, the total value of building permits nationally was down 43 percent from the previous year. The golden age of prosperity in Ridgewood and elsewhere had passed without anyone really realizing it.

The year 1929 had gotten off to an ominous start in Springfield. In mid-February, the Jefferson School on McCreight Avenue at the entrance to

Ridgewood went up in flames. Residents of Ridgewood were awakened around 2 a.m. on Tuesday, February 19, by the sounds of fire trucks responding to the blaze that appeared to be the work of arsonists. Firemen were handicapped in their efforts by a snowstorm of near blizzard proportions, accompanied by high winds and freezing temperatures. Flying embers threatened nearby homes, including the Eakins house to the rear of the school, requiring firefighters and frantic homeowners to wet them down. A new Jefferson School would be built on the same site and be ready for students by year's end, but the fire was just the first of a series of calamities to hit the town that in hindsight seemed like a foreshadowing of the bad times to come. *(fig. 189)*

A couple of weeks later, the temperatures in Springfield warmed and torrential rains caused serious flooding in the city. Several factories, including International Harvester, French and Hecht, O.S. Kelly, The Safety Grinding Wheel Company, and Buckeye Incubator were temporarily shut down due to flooding. Residents all over the city had basements full of water, and everyone in Springfield lost power for a day.

Several days later, on March 8, 1929, residents were awakened at 4 a.m. by an earthquake that shook western Ohio. In June came another flood. On Wednesday, June 19, a torrential rain dumped on the city for over an hour. Downtown, the Mill Run sewer burst, flooding businesses on South Fountain Avenue between High and Main Streets. Businessmen and their workers swept frantically but futilely, trying to try to keep water away from their buildings. Water filled the cellar of the Myers Market Building. Farther north, Buck Creek reached flood conditions. Autos were stalled everywhere and marooned by the high water that brought traffic to a standstill. City officials were deluged by calls from all parts of the city by citizens reporting that their homes were surrounded by water and their cellars filled. It was becoming apparent that the growing city's aging sewer system was simply no longer adequate to cope with the excessive rain. *(fig's. 190-192)*

In Ridgewood, the bane of Harry Kissell's existence from the early days of the development had reared its ugly head again. As more and more houses were being built in Ridgewood, it was suffering the same fate as the rest of the city: the storm sewer was simply not adequate when there was a huge downpour. Residents reported washing machines floating in basements and donned hip boots to rescue whatever they could. The two recent floods convinced city officials that the capacity of the sewers had to be increased. Harry Kissell came to the same conclusion about the Ridgewood sewer and resolved to fix it once and for all.

FAMILY
The
SELLY STO
BUTLERS
FOX'S
PICCADILLY
FEE SHOPPE
W.A. Biddle
PHOTOGRAPHER
STANTON STUDIO
TUTTLE
NAKED FACTS
BUTLER'S
COLUMBIA
387-315

190. Aftermath of the June 19, 1929 flood. Looking south down Fountain Ave. towards the esplanade in downtown Springfield.

High water maroons the city

191 (above). Looking west down a flooded High St. from Fountain Ave. Myers Market is to the left. The Tecumseh Building and the Arcue Building can be seen to the right.

192 (left). View looking north down Fountain Ave. after the flood waters receded and repair work began. The corner of the Fairbanks Building is visible in the distance to the left.

Construction work on the Ridgewood sewer improvement started by mid-September of 1929 and would be one of the largest sewer projects in the city. Trenching began immediately and the enormous sewer pipes were delivered to the site to the delight of the neighborhood children who loved to play in them after workers left for the day. The cost of the improvements, which the Kissell Company bore in its entirety, was over $150,000. The Ridgewood sewer problem was now permanently fixed. But there were bigger problems on the horizon.

Throughout the autumn of 1929, the stock market fluctuated wildly. Americans had built a house of cards and it was wobbling terribly. Since the end of World War I, the seemingly unstoppable craze for investing in the stock market had been fueled by credit. Many stocks were bought with credit, or "on margin," typically with 25 to 50 percent down, but some were purchased with as little as ten cents on the dollar down. Frenzied buyers were betting that they could cover their margins when their stocks rose rapidly in value. The wild stock market swings that fall were an indication that a day of reckoning was near, but only a few people were paying attention. The rest were still confident that permanent prosperity had arrived in America. *(fig. 193)*

The first warning sign that the party was truly over came on October 24, 1929, when the market was seized by a wild selling spree. Five days later, on October 29, forever after known as "Black Tuesday," the bottom fell out of the market. The headline in the *Springfield Daily News* that day read: "Stock Market Scene of Wild Selling." Brokers were demanding that buyers cover their margin loans on now worthless stocks and many investors faced complete financial ruin. Albert H. Wiggin, head of Chase Bank, the second largest bank in the country, commented, "We are reaping the natural fruit of the orgy of speculation millions of people have indulged in."

The market, however, rallied the next day and investors held their breath and waited to see what would happen next. On November 4, they got their answer. The headline of the local newspaper that day read, "Stock Prices Swing Downward." But it would be some time before Americans came to grips with the magnitude of the repercussions of the crash. The market continued to stage small gains for a while, perpetuating hope that the worst was behind them. Right after Black Tuesday, a rash of suicides had ensued among the banking and investment class. Sadly, two Ridgewood residents were among them. But for those who had no ties to those lines of work, or hadn't been caught up in the speculation frenzy, it would be a while before they felt the full impact of the crash.

On November 4, 1929, the same day that the newspaper reported that the stock market was once again retreating, a photo ran that was curiously placed on the Daily Market and Financial Review page of the newspaper. The image, taken in Ridgewood, showed a truck that had gone into one of the ditches being dug for the new Ridgewood sewer—an ironic occurrence given that Ridgewood itself, like so many other things in American life at the time, was about to go into the proverbial ditch. Harry Kissell did not have long to contemplate on the turning of his personal fortunes, though. Soon he would heed the call to address a problem facing the entire nation.

In 1929, Kissell was serving as first vice president of the National Association of Real Estate Boards (NAREB). On December 5, 1929, just a little over five weeks after the crash, Kissell and Herbert Nelson, the executive secretary of NAREB, represented their organization at a conference in Washington, D.C., called by the Chamber of Commerce of the United States at the request of President Hoover. Attending the conference were sixty key men representing thirty-two of America's leading industries and financial organizations. The purpose of the conference was to encourage cooperation between all lines of business and between business and the government in the aftermath of the crash in an effort to get building going again. New construction had virtually ground to a halt. Since one fourth of all labor in the United States was employed in construction and maintenance, jump-starting the industry was key to keeping the economy going.

193. This cartoon, which warned that Americans had built a house of cards by speculating heavily in the stock market, appeared in the *Springfield Daily News* on April 14, 1928, nearly a year and a half before the market collapsed.

At the conference, financial groups agreed to cooperate in trying to free up the credit market and make funds available for home builders and buyers "as far and as fast as good banking practice will permit." Credit was tight and interest rates were rising before the crash, but now the problem was becoming especially critical. Not only were people not building, but the ones who already owned a home were starting to face foreclosure as their jobs disappeared. At the close of this summit, Kissell was named by Secretary of Commerce Robert P. Lamont as one of fourteen of the nation's business leaders to compose the executive committee of the National Conference on Construction, which would continue the work started at this initial meeting. Kissell returned home hopeful and told the local newspaper, "American business is organized for the first time, and with American business organized nothing can stop it."

He was not alone in his optimism. Day after day, local and national leaders were quoted in the country's newspapers as to their confidence that everything would soon return to normal. On January 1, 1930, the headline in the Springfield newspaper read, "Prosperity Forecast for New Year." Even the Hoover administration was predicting that the prosperity and progress that Americans had enjoyed up until the crash would continue. Local leaders asserted that Springfield would escape any depression because it had been on such sound footing when the crash hit. The president of the Springfield Real Estate Board announced at the annual meeting in January of 1930, "Optimism tempered with judgment is the keynote of our activities during the coming year."

On March 16, 1930, an article ran in the local newspaper with the headline "Return to Normal is Indicated in Real Estate Field." But it soon became apparent that, despite wishful thinking, conditions were far from normal in the real estate field, or any other field for that matter. Developer and realtor Stanley S. Petticrew had offered words of encouragement at the beginning of the year to his staff when he told them that the stock break was now behind them and that 1930 was a new year with new conditions. Residential construction, however, would plunge 95 percent in the United States between 1928 and 1933.

Real estate agents and developers were facing the worst drought they had ever experienced and many of their projects would simply die on the vine. Unfortunately, one of Stanley Petticrew's ventures was among those casualties. Back in 1928, Petticrew had platted The Cedars, an upscale subdivision located at the junction of East McCreight Avenue and Mitchell Boulevard, east of the I.O.O.F Home. (At the time, The Cedars was considered to be located in the Mitchell Boulevard section of the road. However, homes west of Cedar View Drive were later given East McCreight Avenue addresses). The Cedars was to be a modern subdivision with all the desirable improvements. It featured the wide building lots that were now par for the course in new upscale neighborhoods, doing away with the need for back alleys. The Cedars would

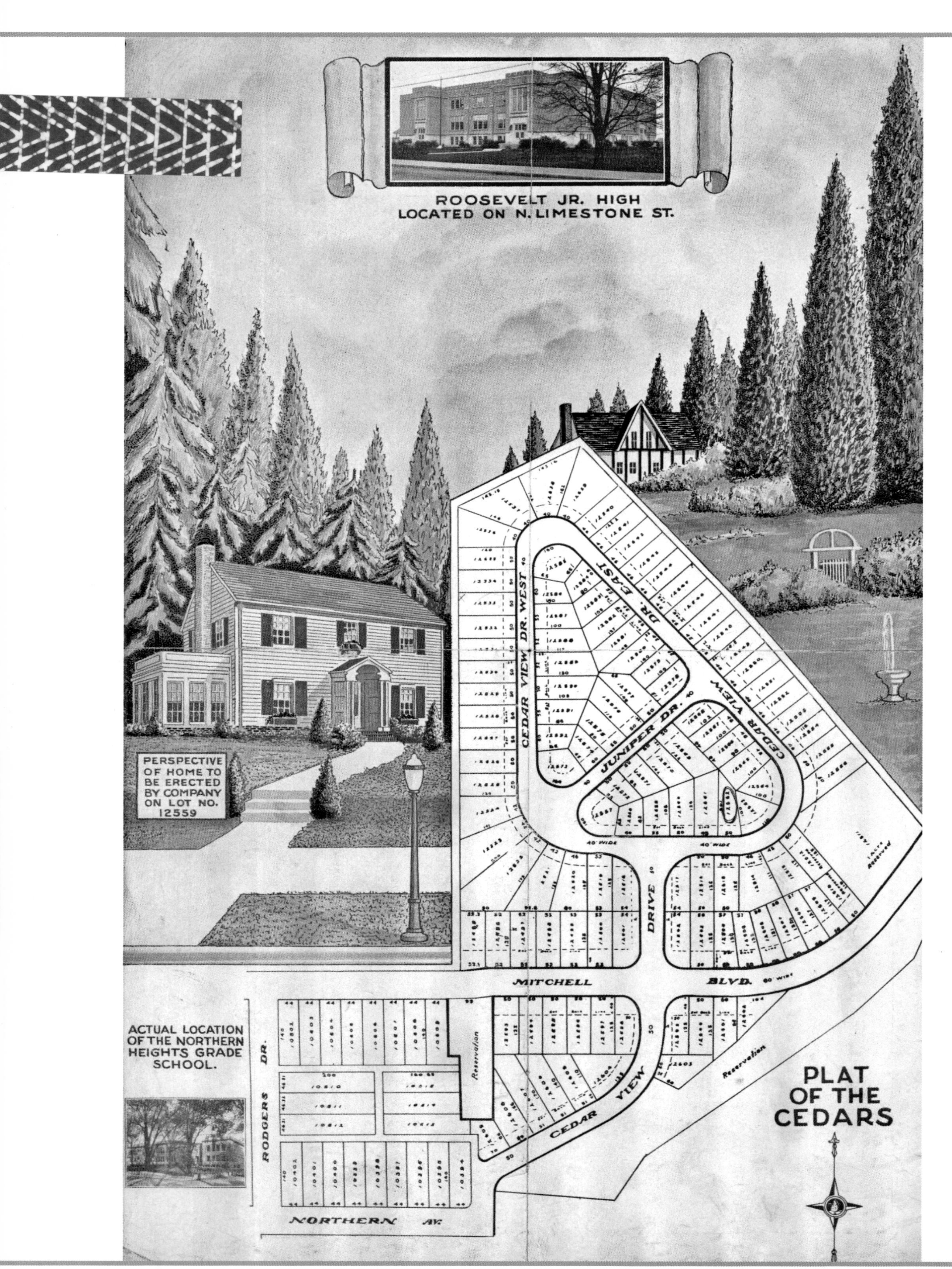
ROOSEVELT JR. HIGH
LOCATED ON N. LIMESTONE ST.
PERSPECTIVE OF HOME TO BE ERECTED BY COMPANY ON LOT NO. 12559
ACTUAL LOCATION OF THE NORTHERN HEIGHTS GRADE SCHOOL.
PLAT OF THE CEDARS
CEDAR VIEW DR. WEST
DR. EAST
CEDAR VIEW
JUNIPER DR.
DRIVE
MITCHELL BLVD. 60' WIDE
CEDAR VIEW
RODGERS DR.
NORTHERN AV.
Reservation
Reservation
40' WIDE
40' WIDE

offer 112 home sites and was within walking distance of the International Harvester shops on Lagonda Avenue. Petticrew hoped to attract the managers and supervisors from International to his new subdivision. He named the development "The Cedars" as part of an interesting gimmick in which no deciduous trees would be used in the development. Instead, it would be planted heavily with cedars and evergreens, making it green year round. *(fig's. 194 & 195)*

By the spring of 1929, construction forces were finishing sidewalks, curbs and gutters, and the sewer and water system in The Cedars. Mitchell Boulevard was being graded and readied for its Tarvia coat. One home was finished and eleven more were already under construction. Petticrew was constructing his own 4,000-square-foot home at 825 East McCreight Avenue (formerly 825 Mitchell Boulevard). His well-appointed home had a three-car garage with servants' quarters, and boasted a 22-by-36-foot living room with a 13 1/2-foot high arched ceiling. A special lighting system hidden in the cove that ran around the top of the living room walls was generating a buzz among those following the home's progress. The system reflected constantly changing colors on the ceiling, which would make for dramatic light effects when the Petticrews hosted parties and dances.

In September of 1929, Petticrew opened up his home and several speculative houses—"The Dudley," an English style home at 880 East McCreight Avenue (originally 880 Mitchell Boulevard), and "The Chantilly," a French style home at 902 Mitchell Boulevard—for public inspection. The two speculative homes flanked the entrance to Cedar View Drive on the north side of Mitchell Boulevard. Petticrew offered a free Chevrolet automobile for the wife of whomever purchased either The Dudley or The Chantilly. The Cedars was off to a good start, but a month later came the crash. Only about a dozen homes were underway in The Cedars at the time, and for many years they would stand there in the midst

194 (above). Cover of a promotional booklet for The Cedars.
195 (left). Promotional map of The Cedars.

of a hundred empty lots. During World War II, The Malowney Real Estate Company would acquire the remaining lots and build double apartment houses on them. *(fig's. 196-198)*

J. Warren James would also suffer a similar reversal of fortunes. In 1928, the first section of the Broadmoor development, Beautiful Broadmoor, was a success. The majority of lots on North Broadmoor and South Broadmoor Boulevards had sold, and thirty-five houses had been built. The land that the James-Bauer Realty Company owned to the west of the boulevards, Broadmoor Estates, and another tract they had acquired just to its south, Broadmoor Woods, had yet to be developed. *(fig. 199)* But the James-Bauer Realty Company was still expanding its endeavors. That year the company purchased a three-and-a-half-acre tract of land on the northwest corner of North Limestone Street and Floral Avenue, a small tract that abutted Ridgewood and the land where Guy Bayley had a stable and exercise track for his horses (the future site of the Clark Memorial Home). J. Warren James dubbed the new plat "English Village." Lots were platted along part of the north side of Floral Avenue, and a new street, Kewbury Road, was constructed off North Limestone Street and ran right up the center of the remainder of the plat. Several speculative homes were being erected on Kewbury and were designed to look like English cottages. To give the English Village an old country feel, low stone walls and pillars were erected at the entrance of Kewbury.

196 (top). Artist rendering of the Stanley Petticrew house at 825 E. McCreight Ave.
197 (above). "The Chantilly," a speculative house built at 902 Mitchell Blvd in The Cedars addition.

That same year the company also platted Sunnyland, a large development offering five hundred lots and fifty-six small farms, located south of town on the Yellow Springs Pike. Like the other James-Bauer development,

Garden Acres, Sunnyland was not contiguous to the city and was outside of its limits. It was two miles from the city by bus or car. Buses, by this point, were starting to replace the very troubled streetcar. The streetcar franchises had been in financial crisis for years and, by 1928, were fighting for their lives. For this new development, James and Bauer adopted the slogan, "Sunnyland is the Money-Land— The Place Where Money Will Grow." They actively encouraged would-be investors to buy in Sunnyland. In fact, they told them, "You should buy one for every member of the family. It is up to you to share in the great profits to be made in Springfield real estate." Lots in Sunnyland were economically priced at $395. Despite being somewhat remote, this new subdivision was proving quite successful. Over three hundred lots were sold in the first year.

J. Warren James was not only doing subdivisions in Springfield at the time—he was getting in on the action of the Florida land rush. He had just built a luxurious Spanish-style home, the second Florida home he had erected for himself and his wife, in a subdivision he had developed eight miles north of Miami. Florida had experienced a land boom after the First World War and Miami had become a hot tourist destination for an increasingly prosperous and mobile population. The land boom in Florida had been absolutely ripe for shysters who took advantage of "suckers" and sold them, literally, swamp land in Florida. Among these scam artists was Charles A. Ponzi, the namesake of the Ponzi scheme. However, many reputable businessmen like James, who made honest Florida land sales, capitalized on the boom as well. The popular Springfield architectural firm of Hall and Lethly even opened a branch in Florida to take advantage of the building boom.

After the crash, J. Warren James and Walter B. Bauer dissolved their partnership, and James took over all their interests and did business under the name, The Homesite Realty Company. He would later do business again as The James Real Estate Company, and then as Sunnyland, Inc. However, the effects of the Depression took its toll

198. Newspaper advertisement for "The Dudley," another speculative house in The Cedars, built at 880 E. McCreight Ave.

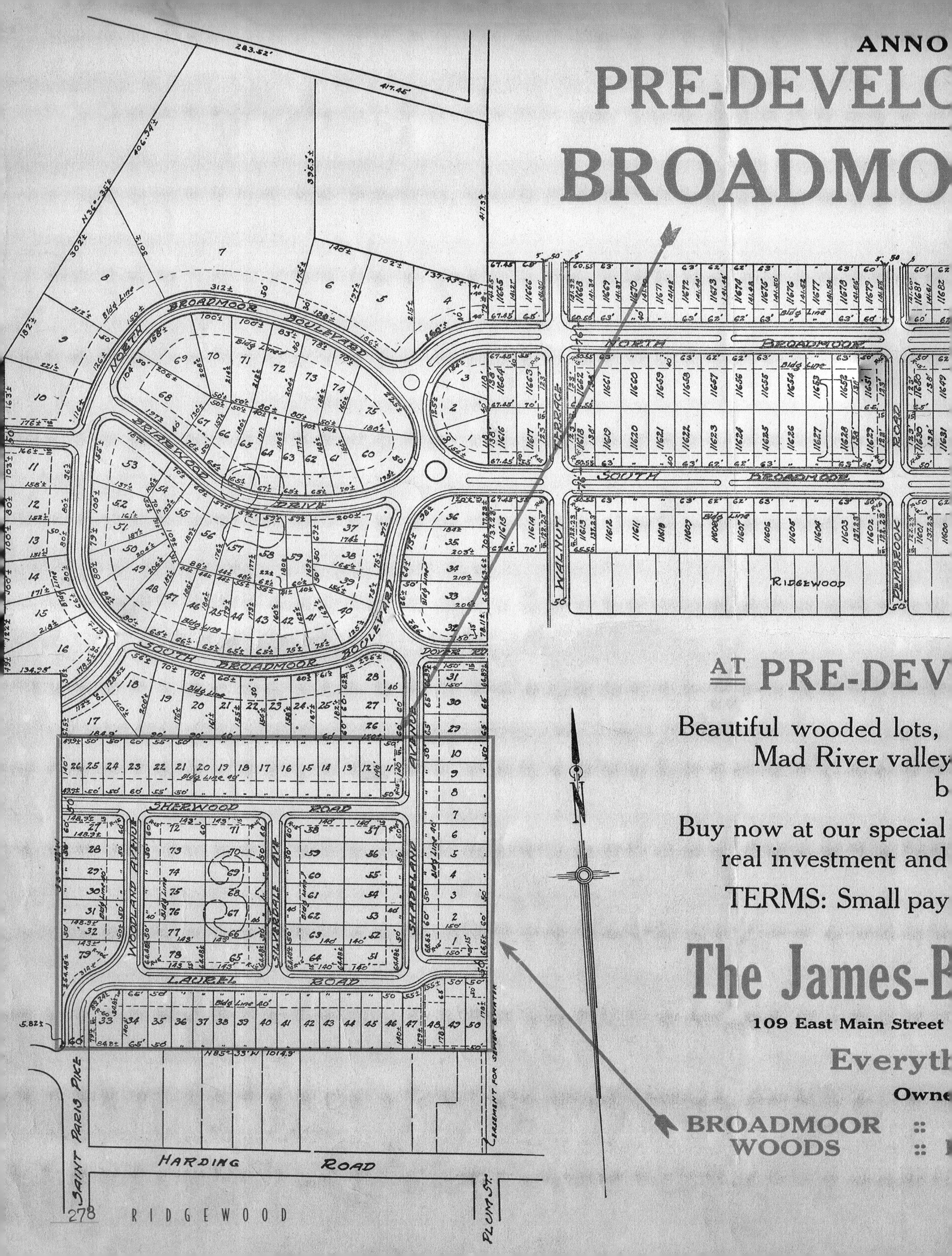
ANNO
PRE-DEVELO
BROADMO
AT PRE-DEV
Beautiful wooded lots,
Mad River valley
b
Buy now at our special
real investment and
TERMS: Small pay
The James-B
109 East Main Street
Everyth
Owne
BROADMOOR ::
WOODS ::
NORTH BROADMOOR BOULEVARD
BRIARWOOD DRIVE
SOUTH BROADMOOR BOULEVARD
NORTH BROADMOOR
SOUTH BROADMOOR
WALNUT TERRACE
DEMBROOK ROAD
RIDGEWOOD
DOVER RD
SHERWOOD ROAD
WOODLAND AVENUE
SILVERDALE AVE
SHADELAND AVENUE
LAUREL ROAD
SAINT PARIS PIKE
HARDING ROAD
PLUM ST.
EASEMENT FOR SEWER & WATER
N

CING

MENT SALE

R WOODS

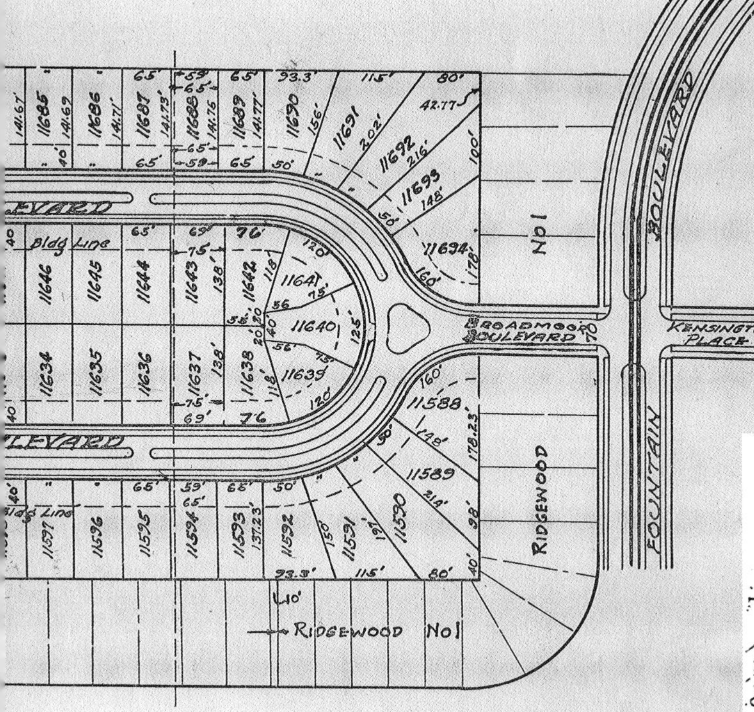

LOPMENT PRICES

that charming view overlooking
ust the home-site you have
looking for.

ount as these lots are priced for a
make you a handsome profit.

t down and balance monthly.

ner Real Estate Co.

Telephone: Center 402-403

g in Real Estate

nd Developers of

AUTIFUL :: BROADMOOR
ADMOOR :: ESTATES

199 (left). Advertisement showing all three sections of the Broadmoor addition—Beautiful Broadmoor, Broadmoor Estates, and Broadmoor Woods.
200 (above). Map of Audubon Park, developed by Link and Link in 1939 on land acquired from J. Warren James. James had originally intended to develop the land as "Broadmoor Woods."

on him, just as it did on his fellow real estate men. He was spread quite thin when the market crashed, but he continued to limp along, selling some of his subdivisions and holding on to others.

Eventually, in the 1940s, James would develop the Broadmoor Estates land, west of the boulevards, but the size of the building lots was downsized drastically from the original three to five acres that had been planned initially in the prosperous 1920s. Link and Link purchased the land to the south, Broadmoor Woods, from James and platted Audubon Park in 1939. The Links utilized James's original layout for the plat, but all of the streets were renamed. *(fig. 200, Compare to fig. 199)* The Malowney Real Estate Company, the same company that acquired The Cedars from Stanley Petticrew, would also acquire James's English Village and build houses there.

Link and Link weathered the Great Depression as well as any real estate company in Springfield, but no one escaped the grip of the shattered economy entirely. When it took over the Hills and Dales development in 1926, it turned around immediately. Improvements were finished, and building activity started up again. A number of exquisite upscale homes had been built in the northern section of the subdivision. By 1929, the Links were busy constructing their own old country village in Hills and Dales—Lormont. Lormont was a grouping of six homes on Tanglewood Drive, designed by Lawrence Hall of the popular Hall and Lethly architectural firm.

Our "Norman Village"

IN HILLS AND DALES - - Tanglewood Drive

Faith in Springfield

has been shown by Governor James M. Cox in erecting the handsomest business edifice in the city . . Keeping step with his example, we are building something as unusual, unique and artistic in residential construction.

Full announcements will be made when the above pictured project is completed

LINK and LINK, Inc.

Realtors **Insurers**

201. October 20, 1929 advertisement for the Norman Village in Hills and Dales.

Lormont was designed along the lines of the architectural and gardening tradition of the Normandy region of France. Aesthetically, Lormont would keep true to the fundamental characteristics of an old country village but be adapted for present-day living. The homes were grouped around a private thoroughfare that would serve only the families living there, eliminating traffic noise and providing a safe place for children. It had, according to a Lormont advertisement, the "quiet dignity of an old world rural lane." Homes fronted on the private drive, and the front yards, garages, and home structures were enclosed with brick and stone walls. An abundance of shrubs and climbing vines were planted, and grass terraces at the rear of the homes were screened from public eyes by shrubbery, trees, and tall hedgerows. Link and Link had planned to offer the homes at $12,000 each, but when the economy collapsed, they were forced to rent them for a time for a mere $75 a month. Eventually the homes sold for about $7,000 each, and the Links suffered a substantial loss on the properties. *(fig. 201)*

These were trying times for Harry Kissell, as well. In 1929, Kissell had just entered into a new business venture, the R.T.K. Corporation, with friends H.G. Root, the president of an automotive supply company, and Dr. Rees Edgar Tulloss, the president of Wittenberg College. They had purchased the last corner lot in downtown Springfield still occupied by a residential building, with plans to erect a modern commercial

202 (top). The old Munz residence on the northwest corner of Fountain Ave. and Columbia St.—the future site of the Columbia Building.
203 (above). The Columbia Building.

building in its place. Brown Burleigh had handled the negotiations for the land on the northwest corner of Fountain Avenue and Columbia Street. In January 1930, the new Columbia Building opened with one tenant on the ground floor —The Springfield Gas Company. Now the investors were anxiously hoping that they could fill the rest of the building. *(fig's. 202 & 203)*

The situation in Ridgewood was dire as well. In 1930, there were 263 houses in Ridgewood, meaning over half of all the lots in the development had yet to be built upon. Many of the vacant lots had been purchased on payment plans, and by late 1930, a number of buyers were starting to give them back because they could no longer afford to make the payments. The Kissell Company was resorting to trying to sell the returned lots for the balance owed by the original purchaser. During the course of the Depression, lot prices bottomed out in Ridgewood at $15 to $25 per front foot, about half of their initial offerings. Property values were also plummeting on existing homes in the neighborhood. In 1928, the Arthur Jones house at 1821 North Fountain Boulevard sold for $35,000, the second-largest residential real estate deal that

204. The Arthur Jones house at 1821 N. Fountain Blvd.

anyone could remember at the time. Two years later, in 1930, the home's value had plunged to $20,000. *(fig. 204)*

In 1930, one of the crown jewels of the neighborhood, and Harry Kissell's pride and joy—Ridgewood School—was also in trouble. Enrollment had been declining over the past several years, and had dropped precipitously after the crash. The school's board of directors faced the very real possibility of defaulting on the mortgage. To try to save the school, the board approached Wittenberg College about the possibility of taking it over. Wittenberg administrators agreed, and the head of teacher training activities at Wittenberg, Franklin H. McNutt, was put in charge of the school.

Ridgewood School would now offer grades one through six. The kindergarten would be combined with Wittenberg's own kindergarten and held in Blair Hall on the Wittenberg campus. In order to save the school, Harry Kissell executed a quitclaim deed freeing the college from the provision in the deed, made at the school's inception, that the Ridgewood School property would revert to him in the case that it was no longer used for school purposes. Wittenberg would operate the school for the next eighteen years. In 1948, a group of interested parties formed the Ridgewood School Association and raised enough capital to buy the property back from Wittenberg. The school would continue on there until a new Ridgewood School was built in 1961 on St. Paris Pike.

Springfield's travails during the Depression were, of course, just a microcosm of what was going on in the rest of the country. Real estate sales and new construction had fallen off the cliff everywhere. However, a more troubling problem on an individual level was brewing. By the middle of 1930, thousands of American homeowners were facing foreclosure. Six percent of all homes would be foreclosed on that year, and the foreclosure rate would peak at 10 percent in 1932-33. However, during the course of the Depression fully half of all homeowners would fall behind on their mortgages, so foreclosure was a constant source of worry.

Economic hardship, of course, was largely to blame, but tight credit, soaring interest rates, and the nature of mortgages exacerbated the problem. Even homeowners who were in relatively good economic shape could lose their homes if they had the terrible luck of having their five-year, interest-only mortgage come due during the Depression. Homeowners of the period typically

205. Caricature of Harry Kissell, drawn by fellow realtor W.P. Hunnicutt, at the 1931 meeting of the National Assoc. of Real Estate Boards at which Kissell was elected president of the organization.

refinanced several times when their short-term mortgages came due while they saved assiduously to amass enough cash to eventually pay off the principal. During the Depression, however, refinancing became difficult and it was not unusual at all to see someone with 50 or 60 percent equity in their home lose it because they could not obtain refinancing. Help was on the way, though, and Harry Kissell would lead the charge.

In July 1930, at the Twenty-Third Annual Convention of the National Association of Real Estate Boards (NAREB), held that year in Toronto, Canada, Harry Kissell received the singular honor of being elected to the association's presidency. In 1930, NAREB was the country's largest national business organization, with 562 boards and 42,000 members, and the announcement of Kissell's election made the *New York Times*. His selection, during one of the most trying times the real estate field would ever face, reflected the esteem in which his colleagues held him. *(fig. 205)*

After the Toronto convention, Kissell returned home and was feted at the Springfield Country Club by 125 leading Springfield citizens, as well as a number of prominent realtors and bankers from Columbus, Cincinnati, and Dayton. The governor of Ohio was among the many notables who sent telegrams congratulating Kissell. A tribute was offered that evening by fellow Springfield resident, William Bayley, who spoke on behalf of Kissell's friends and associates gathered that night, the people who knew Kissell and his talents best: "We all rejoice in seeing one of our neighbors and friends so outstanding amongst men of his own business, and so prominent before the people at large. We all know the ability and energy of Harry S. Kissell. We know the honor is highly merited."

In his own remarks at the dinner, quite characteristically, Harry Kissell chose not to reflect on his own accomplishment. Instead, he took the opportunity to encourage the guests, a cross section of the city's varied interests, to continue to boost Springfield: "There is a real opportunity in Springfield for a getting together on the common ground of civic advancement, and I urge all citizens of the city who are here tonight to give thought to the things that will make of Springfield an even better community than it is in which to live. There are two things I pledge myself to do during the next year and a half. First, I never expect to make a speech during my travels about the country without bringing in the name of Springfield, Ohio, and telling my audiences some of the advantages this city possesses. Second, I pledge myself to work with anybody or any organization at any time on any practical plan for the advancement of Springfield."

Kissell was inducted as president at NAREB's mid-winter meeting in St. Petersburg, Florida, on January 16, 1931. At his inaugural banquet, he gave a rousing speech. He reflected back over the growing pains and struggles he had seen while he and men like him had worked to transform the profession over the past thirty years. That they had been successful in that challenging endeavor gave him courage for what they were now facing.

He stated, "I recognize that over the past several years we have been confronted with many discouragements, but I also recognize that every business in the long sweep of time must experience similar periods of discouragement. Are we men of less courage than those in other lines of business who meet their problems and conquer them? I am afraid that over the years of prosperity, when business came to us with little effort, when many of our prospects sought our offices, when little initiative on our part was required—I am afraid during that time, because of the lack of necessity for effort, that our sales sinews became pliant, our muscles became flabby, we have lost some of our aggressiveness.

"Now is the time when we need men with nerves, hearts and backbones of steel. I would say to you that now is the time to gird yourselves for a real fight, that as surely as night follows the day clouds will fade, that another harvest time is ahead of us. We may not reap the harvest this year. We may have to sow and seed again. We may have to strengthen our muscles again by hard work, but if we are made of the same fiber of which our predecessors were made, who built this country into a great nation and who built our organization into a great institution, then we will assume the task without fear and without hesitation."

As president of NAREB, Kissell traveled the country in 1931 visiting state and local real estate boards, confident in the knowledge that, back home, the business was in the good hands of his dear friend and associate of that last twenty-three years, Brown Burleigh. Burleigh had his work cut out for him. A number of local real estate companies had gone under, and several more were on the brink, but the Kissell Company managed to stay afloat. However, sales were lean. That year, with great reluctance, Harry Kissell had to tell his daughter, Mary Lu, by now a college freshman, that she could no longer continue at Sarah Lawrence College in New York. She would have to come home and finish her remaining three years at Wittenberg. But Mary Lu was very much her father's daughter. She took the news in stride, and returned home to her family and her city, both of which she adored.

The defining moment of Harry Kissell's presidency of NAREB came when he and the executive secretary of NAREB, Herbert U. Nelson, wrote an article

for the *Magazine of Wall Street* in which they floated an idea to help solve the financial crisis and get real estate and building going again. Their idea was to establish a system of regional Federal Home Loan Banks to serve the needs of existing home financing agencies, somewhat similar to the way the Federal Reserve System served its member banks. The creation of such a mortgage discount bank system would provide a ready pool of credit for lenders and facilitate their ability to offer fully amortized, long-term, installment-type mortgages. Kissell and Nelson believed that their idea would rescue homeowners who could not refinance their short-term loans in the prevailing credit market. They also believed that it would stimulate building and aid unemployment. Perhaps most consequential, though, they felt that it would have the long-term effect of opening up the possibility of home ownership to more Americans.

Kissell and Nelson's idea caught the attention of President Hoover, and, on October 7, 1931, Hoover invited Kissell and nine other leading real estate men, builders, and bankers to the White House to discuss this new plan for better home financing. The plan would be taken up at the President's Home Building and Ownership Conference to be held by Hoover in Washington in first week of December that year. Kissell would return to Washington to take part in the conference and to meet one on one with the President. *(fig. 206)*

In his State of Union address, a few days after the Home Building and Ownership Conference adjourned, President Hoover called for the creation of the Home Loan Discount Bank, promising that it would revolutionize mortgages.

Congressional hearings were held on the creation of the Federal Home Loan Banking System in January and February of 1932, at which Kissell, now the retiring president of NAREB,

PATRONS ARE REQUESTED TO FAVOR THE COMPANY BY CRITICISM AND SUGGESTION CONCERNING ITS SERVICE 1201-S

CLASS OF SERVICE
This is a full-rate Telegram or Cablegram unless its deferred character is indicated by a suitable sign above or preceding the address.

WESTERN UNION

NEWCOMB CARLTON, PRESIDENT J. C. WILLEVER, FIRST VICE-PRESIDENT

SIGNS
DL = Day Letter
NM = Night Message
NL = Night Letter
LCO = Deferred Cable
NLT = Cable Night Letter
WLT = Week-End Letter

The filing time as shown in the date line on full-rate telegrams and day letters, and the time of receipt at destination as shown on all messages, is STANDARD TIME.

Received at 110 South Limestone Street, Springfield, Ohio Telephone Main 3500 Always Open

B4CZ R 44 NL

GH WASHINGTON DC DEC 2 1931

MRS H S KISSELL

DO NOT PHONE 1801 N FOUNTAIN AVE SPRINGFIELD OHIO

BEAUTIFUL WEATHER WONDERFUL CROWD HAD LONG PERSONAL AND PRIVATE TALK WITH PRESIDENT TODAY STOP FRIDAY IS GOING TO BE THE TEST AND IT SEEMS TO BE UP TO US TO LEAD THE FIGHT STOP IF WE WIN WILL WIRE YOU FRIDAY NIGHT WELL LOVE

H S KISSELL

513A3

WESTERN UNION GIFT ORDERS ARE APPROPRIATE GIFTS FOR ALL OCCASIONS

206. Telegram from Harry Kissell to Olive Kissell, December 2, 1931.

testified. Kissell told Congress, "[I am] not appearing for any financial organization or for banks or for the building and loan associations, but I want to speak for the people all over this country, who are having their homes foreclosed . . . There is no reason why a man who has saved for five or ten years to buy a home and put every dime he and his wife could scrape together into the home, and then when we get into a period like this, when this man is out of employment, cannot pay his interest or his mortgage falling due during this period of stress, and he cannot refinance it, should not be given a certain amount of time to get together enough to save that home . . .Those are the people that I would like to speak for, because there are thousands and tens of thousands and hundreds of thousands of people like that all over this country."

Kissell told Congress that the lending institutions were not to blame for the prevailing tight credit. Their depositors were in a state of hysteria and demanding their cash. Lending institutions had no choice but to maintain liquidity and foreclose on delinquent properties instead of refinancing them, and, in many cases, limit refinancing for those in good standing whose short-term mortgages were coming due. However, if the system of regional Federal Home Loan Banks could be created, it would provide financially stressed lending institutions with a reserve source of credit, freeing up the credit market, and, for the first time, allow for the amortization of the principal of a mortgage.

This would make obsolete the interest-only loans that required a lump sum payment when they came due. It would also make mortgages a less risky investment for lenders and assure a steady supply of money for home mortgages. This revolutionary idea would also open up more widely the possibility of home

207. The Kissell's first visit to the White House in 1924.

208. Harry Kissell presents President Franklin D. Roosevelt with the first dividend check from the Federal Home Loan Bank, October 1933.

ownership to the middle third of the country—the middle class. The Federal Home Loan Bank Act was signed into law by the President on July 22, 1932, and represented a major legislative achievement for the real estate field. During his tenure as President of NAREB, Harry Kissell had done his organization and his profession proud during its darkest hour.

The regional Federal Home Loan Banks got underway six months after the passage of the bill, and President Hoover appointed Kissell as chairman of the board of the Fifth District Federal Home Loan Bank, which was located in Cincinnati and served Ohio, Tennessee, and Kentucky lending institutions.

The respect that President Hoover had developed for Harry Kissell during the process of initiating and passing The Federal Home Loan Banking Act was evident when he invited the Kissell family to the final White House reception of his administration in January 1933. This was not the first time that the Kissells had been invited to the White House. They had paid a visit to the Oval Office at the invitation of President Coolidge nearly a decade earlier and had made a memorable entrance. Unbeknownst to them, oranges they had brought for the trip had gotten loose on the floorboard of their automobile and rolled out on to the driveway of the White House as Harry, Olive, and a young Mary Lu alighted from their vehicle. *(fig. 207, page 287)* This time they were back for the Army–Navy reception and Mary Lu, now 18 years old, had grown into a lovely debutante and was dancing with her proud father in the East Room of the White House.

Harry Kissell would return to the White House in October of 1933. The Fifth District Federal Home Loan Bank in Cincinnati was the first regional bank in the system to declare a dividend. And Harry Kissell was back at the White House to hand the new president, Franklin Delano Roosevelt, a dividend check for $95,000, evidence that the system was a success. The Federal Home Loan Bank Act would be the opening salvo in an effort to make home financing easier and to open up home ownership to a wider group. It paved the way for legislation that would soon

209. Fred & Edna Miller, 1927.
210. The Miller's first Ridgewood home at 1502 N. Fountain Blvd.

follow. In 1934, Congress passed the National Housing Act, which created the Federal Housing Administration (FHA). The act provided mortgage lenders with insurance against losses on any extended, FHA-approved mortgage. This had the effect of further broadening home ownership by making mortgage lending a less risky proposition. *(fig. 208)*

Back in Ridgewood, as the Great Depression wore on, families coped with the new economic realities in various ways. One couple, Fred and Edna Miller, started a business in the basement of their home after Mr. Miller's job disappeared when the Central Brass and Fixture Company went belly up. The Millers had built their first Ridgewood home at 1502 North Fountain Boulevard in 1922. But their growing prosperity had allowed them, just four years later, to erect the home of their dreams just a block north and on the opposite side of the street from their previous home. They were happily ensconced in their new home at 1601 North Fountain Boulevard in 1927 when their daughter, Sue, was born. *(fig's. 209-212)*

When Fred lost his job, the enterprising Millers founded Miller Frocks, a clothing company that made hand-smocked dresses for little girls. The Millers utilized piece workers, who worked out of their homes, to make their garments. The fabric was delivered first to the smockers, then to the seamstresses, and finally on to an embroider and finisher. At night, the Millers made the rounds in their auto with little Sue in tow, picking up finished products and handing out raw materials to the piece workers. Their charming little dresses were a hit from the start, and eventually they moved their business out of their basement and into a new Spanish Mission-style commercial building they had constructed nearby at 137 Roosevelt Drive, a building later occupied by the Springfield Engraving Company. *(fig's. 213 & 214)*

Little Sue Miller and her very best friend, Peggy Kent, who lived at 20 Brighton Road, served as the perfect advertisements for Miller Frocks. The girls would arrive on the first day of school each year at the Ridgewood School wearing matching smocked dresses. While Sue's

212 (top). A two-year-old Sue Miller in front of the Miller's second home at 1601 N. Fountain Blvd.
211 (above). Baby Sue Miller, 1927. The Bretney home at 1602 N. Fountain Blvd. can be seen in the background.

213. Sue Miller modeling a Miller Frocks creation.

parents worked day and night to keep their business going, the little girls contented themselves by hunting wild strawberries that grew on the many vacant lots that remained on North Fountain Boulevard. Horse-drawn mowers came each year in late June or early July to mow the empty lots. Until then, they were the favorite spring playground of neighborhood children. Sue and Peggy would roll in the high grass to mat it down and create "rooms" where they wiled away many an hour playing house. *(fig's. 215 & 216)*

Other favorite childhood activities included playing in the fountain on the triangular parklet where Brighton Road and Sunnyside Place left Fountain Boulevard, or listening in on the party line telephones that were then standard. The playground of the Ridgewood School was also a favorite haunt for its swings and slide. The entire playground was covered in fine gravel and oftentimes Sue and Peggy could be found sitting in it and sifting it through their fingers looking for pretty stones.

Unlike the adults in Ridgewood, the littlest residents were able to remain largely insulated from the worst effects of the Depression. Brown and May Burleigh's children had childhoods typical of those growing up in Ridgewood during the late 1920s and 1930s. Daughter Sybil was born in 1921, and her little brother, James, followed in 1924. Both were aware of the Depression when it came, but there were no televisions to bring images of bread lines into their homes. Communication in the era was limited and fragile, which helped preserve childhood innocence. Men selling apples on the street in downtown Springfield and a constant stream of men coming to

214 (top). Sue Miller at age 4 ½, playing with the dollhouse that her father built to resemble their home at 1601 N. Fountain Blvd.
215 (above). Best friends—Sue Miller and Peggy Kent.

216.. The Miller's third Ridgewood home at 1607 N. Fountain Blvd., built in 1941.

the back door of their house at 30 South Kensington Place looking for work were the most visible signs of a nation in distress. *(fig's. 217-221)*

May Burleigh did whatever she could in those trying times to help those who were less fortunate. Whether it was putting them to work sweeping out the garage or trimming bushes in the yard, she would always find something for the hungry, out of work fellows who knocked on her back door. Then she would provide them with a warm meal served on the back porch. May was active in the Young Woman's Mission, a charitable organization in Springfield, and would often load Sybil into the Model A Ford that Brown had given her one year for her birthday, to deliver baskets to the needy in the parts of town most acutely affected by the Depression. And May cautioned her daughter that if she saw any girls at church wearing dresses that looked like ones Sybil had previously owned, not to mention it to them so as not to embarrass them.

The Burleighs, like most everyone else in neighborhood, were feeling squeezed by the Depression and had to make concessions to the new economic realities. However, they were supremely grateful to be spared from the suffering that so many of their fellow Americans were facing. They had been lucky to ride the wave of rising prosperity in the 1920s, but now, like everyone else, they had to tighten their belts in both big and small ways. The downturn in the real estate business had caused them to permanently set aside their plans to construct a larger home on a lot they owned in The Woods.

May Burleigh, like most women in Springfield, made a weekly Saturday morning pilgrimage to the city market in downtown Springfield, where little boys clamored to carry the ladies' market baskets in exchange for a quarter. But as the Depression went on, the duty of carrying the basket was given to Sybil in order to save the quarter, a subtle indication to the little girl that times had changed. There was

217 (top). The Burleigh family's domestic servant holding baby Sybil, April 21, 1921.
218 (above). Sybil learning to walk in the driveway of the Burleigh home at 30 S. Kensington Pl., April 3, 1922.

only one family vacation for the Burleighs during those years, a trip to Niagara Falls. Instead, picnics in the countryside with neighbors served as a popular Depression-era pastime for Ridgewood residents. The women made the food, and everyone piled into automobiles and headed into the country. There, they climbed over someone's fence and spread out the contents of their picnic baskets on a blanket.

Ridgewood was, from its inception, a social neighborhood filled with bridge parties and dinner parties among neighbors and social events at the country club. Even during the lean years of the Depression, it remained a children's paradise. Sybil and Jim Burleigh filled their free time with diversions like watching the Bulldogs play football on the field just north of where they lived or watching the foundations of new Ridgewood houses being dug with a team of horses pulling a scoop. When they got a little older, a favorite activity was going downtown by themselves on the streetcar for lunch at Mattie Guthrie's lunch counter, followed by a movie at one of the many downtown theaters, and capped by a trip to Woolworth's to peruse the five-and-dime store's offerings. In the winter, a favorite pastime of the Burleigh children was sledding, and they delighted when their father would hitch up the sled to his automobile and pull them behind it.
(fig. 222)

In the summertime, all of the children in their section of Ridgewood played basketball in the backyard of Mary Jean Moores's house at 108 South Kensington Place, two doors down from the Burleigh's house. Mary Jean was the only daughter of W. Huston Moores and his wife, Helen. Huston Moores operated the Moores Lime Company out on Lower Valley Pike, a business started by his father in 1845 and sold products all over the world. Moores had married his wife, Helen, the daughter of a professor in the ancient languages department at Wittenberg, in 1922. That year, the newlyweds bought a house on South Kensington Place that had been constructed by a builder on speculation. The Moores welcomed their only child, Mary Jean, one year later. *(fig's. 223-226)*

Mary Jean grew into something of a tomboy. She

219 (top). Sybil and Bunny the dog, 1923.
220 (above). Nursemaid holding the infant Jim Burleigh, 1924. Big sister Sybil is to the left.

221. The Burleigh family, at home on South Kensington Place.

could often be found swimming at the pool at the country club, playing in the woods of Signal Hill or the orchard behind the Linn house just east of the club's entrance, taking nature walks in the grove of oak trees west of Walnut Terrace, or running her dog, Jerry, on the golf course of the club. Jerry, who had been purchased from the pet store in the Arcade, was a constant companion. She walked with Mary Jean to Ridgewood School each day, then returned home by herself, sometimes after first stopping to climb the steps of the big slide on the playground and taking a slide down it. Jerry also loved to accompany Mary Jean to get a pound of hamburger at the little neighborhood grocery store, Woody's, which was on North Limestone Street, directly across from the east end of North Kensington Place. It wasn't unusual for neighbors to observe the dog carrying the hamburger home in a paper sack in her teeth. *(fig. 227)*

Mary Jean's other constant companion and best friend was Jim Burleigh to whom she affectionately referred, much to his chagrin, as "Fait." Fait was his mother's maiden name, which he had been given as a middle name. Fait and Mary Jean were inseparable and could often be found playing baseball in the street next to the grassy triangle of Kensington Place with another neighbor boy, Ross Miller, whose father was the pastor of Covenant Presbyterian Church. Riding bikes or roller skating was another favored activity during the warm months. One of the daring feats of childhood in Ridgewood was the ability of one neighbor boy to jump both streetcar tracks in Fountain Boulevard at one time on his roller skates. At the time, everything north of Ridgewood was still countryside, so North Fountain Boulevard had yet to

222 (top). May & Sybil Burleigh being pulled on a sled, January 30, 1924.
223 (above). The W. Huston and Helen Moores home at 108 S. Kensington Pl., shortly after the couple purchased it in 1922.

226. Sybil Burleigh and Mary Jean Moores, 1925.

224 (far left). Helen Moores holding her infant daughter, Mary Jean, 1923.
225 (left). W. Huston Moores, in front of his home on S. Kensington Place.

become a busy thoroughfare. Traffic in the neighborhood was limited to residents and their visitors, and the curving roads deterred excessive speeds, making it a relatively safe haven for children to play. *(fig's. 228-231)*

Like the Burleigh children, Mary Jean was aware of the Depression. Her father talked about people he knew who were in such dire straits that they had to divide and share an egg, and she knew there were WPA workers in town employed on various work relief projects. But, thankfully, she never felt any real sense of deprivation. The Moores had always been conservative with their finances, never lived extravagantly, and were better prepared to weather the economic downturn than some of their neighbors.

The residents on South Kensington Place could set their watches by the comings and goings of Mary Jean's father. He left for work promptly each workday at 7:15 a.m. and returned at 4:45 p.m. However, it was by virtue of his hobby that he was best known to his neighbors in Ridgewood and to the residents of Springfield as a whole. Huston Moores had suffered a serious hearing impairment since childhood when an ear infection was not properly treated, but he never let his disability stand in the way of engaging in life. He read lips and had an ear phone (hearing aid) and a specially adapted telephone. And he had a hobby that helped him participate in social activities and events in which he might otherwise have felt isolated. During the Depression, in 1936, he had taken up photography, an interest that grew to the point that soon he had his own darkroom in the basement

227 (top). The Moores' dog—Jerry.
228 (following). Photo taken on one of the many Burleigh and Moores' family picnics in the country—a favorite pastime among Ridgewood residents in the 1920s and 1930s.
229 (middle). Inseparable friends—Mary Jean Moores and Jim "Fait" Burleigh, with Jerry the dog.
231 (right). Jim Burleigh, Sybil Burleigh, & Mary Jean Moores in the spring of 1930.

230. Jim Burleigh out and about in the neighborhood with Frosty, Bunny's replacement.

Dora Cage

232. Dora Cage, the Burleigh family's beloved domestic servant.

of his home. Through his photography, Huston Moores became a fixture at events in Springfield. He shot everything from social events at the club, to sporting events at Wittenberg, Christmas parties held for crippled children by the Rotary, and weddings of his friends' children. He also captured slices of life in the neighborhood and the city at large.

Helen Moores's daily life in the neighborhood was characteristic of most women living in Ridgewood during the era. She volunteered for the Young Woman's Mission, she read and gardened, but her focus was on making a home for her family. She took great pride in her home and kept it running with the assistance of a lady who came regularly to help with the cleaning, washing, and cooking. The Moores shared their domestic servant, Geneva Brown, with the Cookes across the street, and, as was typical of domestics of this era, Geneva worked for both families for many years. The Burleigh's domestic, Dora Cage, came to work for the family at age 14. It was not unusual at the time for girls to enter service at such a young age. Dora also remained with the Burleigh family for years. *(fig. 232)*

Most women in Ridgewood had daily help. Live-in servants were typically found only in the larger homes on North Fountain Boulevard, Crescent Drive, and The Woods section. In some of the homes that did have live-in help, a couple might be employed and the wife would take care of the interior of the home and the husband would be responsible for taking care of the automobile, the exterior of the home, and any jobs on the interior that required additional strength. Many Ridgewood families also employed a yardman, who often worked for several families in the neighborhood. Additional temporary help was usually hired for routine maintenance work and seasonal work, such as putting screens in windows each spring. When a new baby was born to a Ridgewood family, the mother usually had the help of a live-in nursemaid for the first few weeks of the baby's life. Some affluent families had live-in nannies when their children were small.

Ridgewood was a stable neighborhood with little turnover, and children often regarded neighbors as extended family. Mary Jean Moores referred to her parents' friends, Lewis and Nina Cooke, who lived directly across the street at 107 South Kensington Place, as Aunt Nina and Uncle Lewie. Neighbors visited regularly, and Mary Jean's father would go over to Uncle Lewie's in the evening and help him with his crystal radio set. Even the neighborhood dogs made the rounds. The Burleighs' dog, Bunny, was a favorite visitor of the Cookes, who had no children of their own. Bunny appreciated their hospitality so much that eventually she just stayed with the Cookes. *(fig. 233)*

The downside of living in such an interconnected neighborhood was that everyone knew everyone else's business. In the era before air conditioning, open windows made it easy for any "nosey parker" to eavesdrop, and the daily arrival of domestic servants helped facilitate the spread of gossip. Maids exchanged news of what their employers were up to as they made their way to Ridgewood via the streetcar and were, therefore, the go-to source if the lady of the house wanted to know the latest tittle-tattle about her neighbors.

Sundays in Ridgewood, like everywhere else at the time, were relatively quiet. Families went to church and then had a big Sunday dinner at home or at the country club. Then they would take an automobile ride in the country. One never dreamed of playing cards or any other such frivolous entertainment on Sunday. During the weekdays, the daily routine of life in Ridgewood was punctuated by the arrival of various service people. On South Kensington Place, the milkman, Mr. Augustus, or "Gus" for short, arrived early each day in a horse-drawn wagon filled with ice to cool the milk. Milk was placed in little boxes on the backs of houses. The boxes opened and were accessible from both the outside and inside of the house, making it unnecessary to go outside to retrieve the milk.

Gus was a popular figure with the neighborhood children during hot weather because he passed out ice chips. Sometimes Mary Jean Moores would ride with the milkman. Her dog, Jerry, perched on the back step of wagon and rode along too from house to house. The horse, which was equipped with rubber shoes to cut down on noise, knew the routine and just went to the next house and stopped. Another regular was the mailman, a short, cheerful fellow, affectionately nicknamed "Goofus" by the neighbor children. Goofus delivered mail twice a day. Mr. Strader, a rather seedy-looking character, collected the garbage. And the bread man delivered White's Bread regularly, also using a horse and wagon. *(fig's. 234 & 235)*

233. The Lewis & Nina Cooke residence at 107 S. Kensington Pl.

Among the highlights of each weekday for children in the neighborhood were the fifteen-minute serial radio programs, a passion they shared with children all over the country. Favorites were *Lum and Abner*, *Amos 'n' Andy*, and *Little Orphan Annie*. And many a neighborhood child sent away for his or her own Orphan Annie secret decoder pin and waited with eager anticipation for Goofus to deliver it. After dinner, their parents would listen to the news, delivered by popular radio broadcaster Lowell Thomas, while the children went outside to chase fireflies or play hide-and-go-seek in the dark until their parents summoned them in. "Mary Jean," Helen Moores would call out to her daughter. And to the abiding humor of the neighbors, Mrs. Baker down the street mimicked her back with an exaggerated "Maaary Jeeean!"

As the trying decade of the 1930s came to a close, the first generation of Ridgewood babies were growing up. Some were off to high school and were filling their free time taking lessons downtown at Mrs. Shearer's dance studio, in preparation for the cotillions that their mothers arranged for them at the country club. While the girls tried to fill their dance cards at the cotillions, a young Jonathan Winters held court in the corner doing the imitations that would make him famous, distracting the boys until eventually the parents had to break it up. Parties at friends' houses filled with dancing and eating were another popular pastime for the Ridgewood teenagers. And any boy in the neighborhood who happened to be in possession of an old jalopy enjoyed great popularity because he could facilitate the socializing between teenagers in the north end and those who lived out East High Street, because the once important streetcar was now a thing of the past.

After years of financial crises, the streetcar franchises had ceased activity in Springfield in 1933. Two years later, in April of 1935, the tracks in the center parkway of North Fountain Boulevard were removed using a work relief program, the Federal Emergency Relief Administration, instituted by President Roosevelt under the New Deal legislation. In addition to removing the tracks, all the trolley poles were taken out except those bearing streetlights. The parkway was sodded and shrubs were set out down through the middle. The scrap metal was sold to Japan and became part of the neighborhood

234 (top). Mr. Strader, the neighborhood trash man, with an unidentified child.
235 (above). 1930s era image of a bread wagon in Ridgewood.

lore during World War II, when residents complained that the metal was coming back to them, but this time overhead in the form of ammunition.

At the end of the 1930s, the oldest of the children who had grown up entirely in Ridgewood were getting married and starting families of their own. Mary Lu Noonan had met her future husband, Howard B. Noonan, when her father called her back to Springfield from Sarah Lawrence. Howard had graduated from Northwestern University in 1930 and was back home in Lima living with his family and struggling to find a job when the two met. Harry Kissell took a liking to the bright young man who would soon be his son-in-law. Kissell had no one to carry on the family business. His son, Roger, possessed a brilliant mind, but his physical challenges made it impossible for him to take over. So Harry Kissell invited Howard B. Noonan to come to Springfield and learn the business. It would prove to be a judicious move.

The real estate business was starting to show subtle signs of a recovery by 1939, but Harry Kissell had begun to contemplate retirement. His dear friend and the vice president of the Kissell Company, Brown Burleigh, had retired the year before after thirty years with the firm, only to later come out of retirement and begin a completely new career as the president and manager of the Springfield Security System Company. But Kissell had now run his family's business for forty years. In his hands, The Kissell Real Estate Company had weathered a world war and the Great Depression to which many other real estate businesses had succumbed, and now he was ready to place the company in the capable hands of his talented son-in-law. But another great war was about to hinder his plans.

Mary Lu Kissell and Howard B. Noonan had married in 1936, and the couple built a lovely home at 286

236 (top). Howard B. & Mary Lu Noonan's first home at 286 Ridge Mall.
237 (above). Howard & Mary Lu Noonan's second home at 1630 Midvale Rd.

Ridge Mall in Ridgewood. Four years later, they built a second Ridgewood home at 1630 Midvale Road. Mary Lu gave birth to their first child, Peter Kissell Noonan, on January 13, 1942, just a month after the Japanese bombed Pearl Harbor on December 7, 1941, drawing the United States into World War II. Howard soon heeded the call to duty and entered the Navy as an ensign. Harry Kissell put his retirement plans on hold and told his son-in-law, "I won't promise to get any new business, but I promise to keep it alive until you get back." Mary Lu rented out their house on Midvale Road and with little Pete, she moved back to her parents' home at 1801 North Fountain Boulevard. *(fig's 236–238)*

238. Harry Kissell with his grandson, Peter Kissell Noonan, on the front walk of the Kissell home at 1801 N. Fountain Blvd.

On the eve of the war, lot sales in Ridgewood had started to pick up again, but the Kissell Company was still holding one hundred unsold lots and was planning an aggressive campaign to move the remaining home sites. A promotional booklet was being prepared that contained testimonials from Ridgewood residents, and a new slogan was about to be unveiled, "Ridgewood— The Place to Build for a Lifetime," reflecting the permanency and stability of the neighborhood. The new marketing campaign promoted the idea that one didn't just build a house in Ridgewood, they were building a family home that children would delight in returning to once they were grown, a home that would be passed on to the next generation. *(fig. 239)*

Building activity had been picking up again, too, encouraging some local developers to move ahead with new plats. Link and Link had started its Audubon Park development in 1939 and was actively promoting it in 1941. It was confident enough that the economy was slowly but surely recovering that it started a new plat, The Country Club District, on the last undeveloped land on North Fountain Boulevard. Several years before, the old Doyle greenhouse on the southwest corner of Home Road and Fountain Boulevard, across from the country club, had shut down. The greenhouse had been demolished, to the relief of everyone in the area except the neighborhood boys who took great pleasure in throwing rocks through its panes of glass. John Doyle had also owned the land

Beautiful
RIDGEWOOD
A careful study of this aerial photograph will help you locate your new homesite!
THE PLACE TO

239. Aerial map from the promotional booklet, Ridgewood, The Place to Build for a Lifetime, distributed 1942.

BUILD FOR A LIFETIME

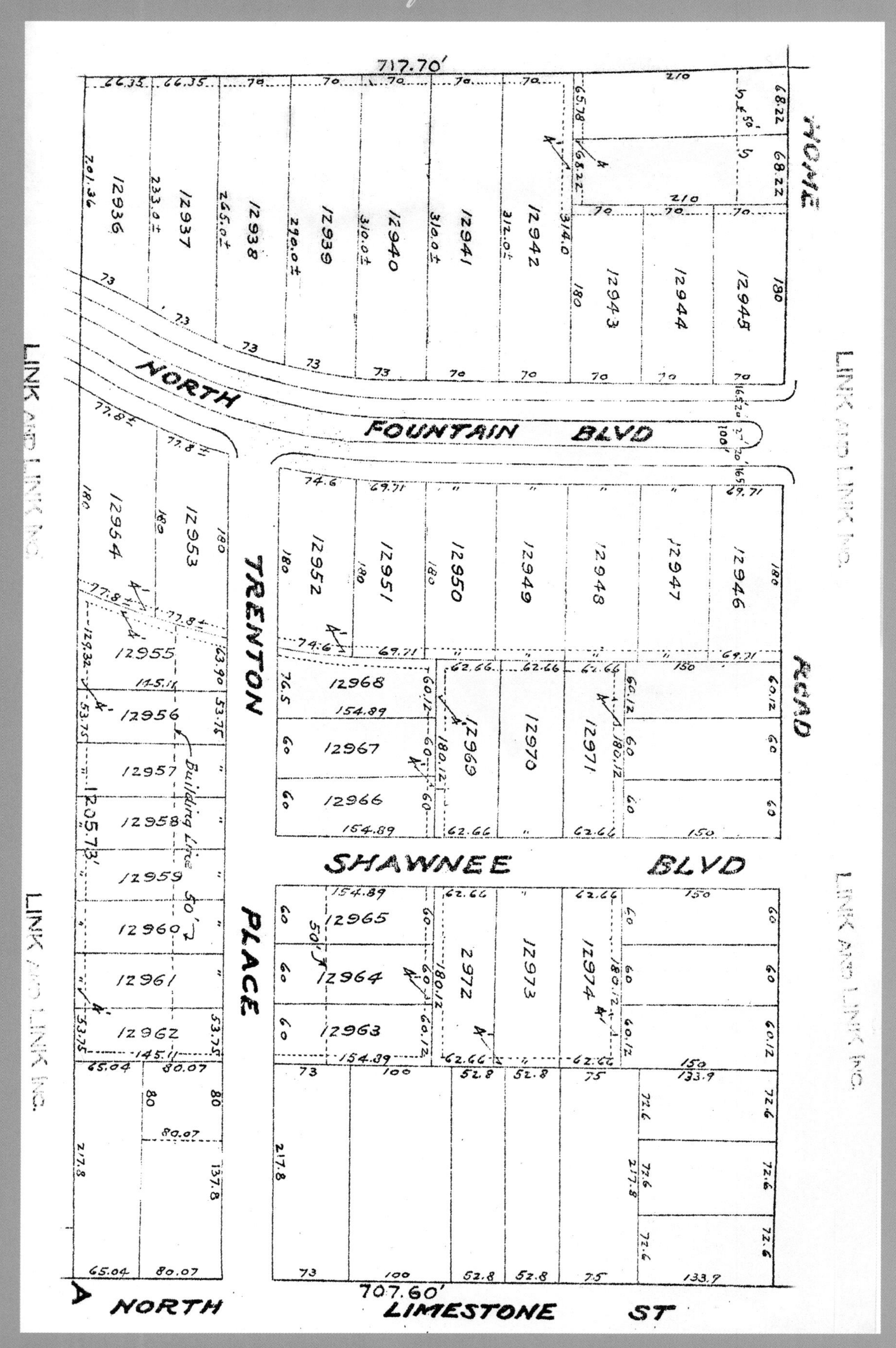

717.70'
HOME
NORTH FOUNTAIN BLVD
TRENTON PLACE
SHAWNEE BLVD
ROAD
LINK AND LINK INC.
Building Line 50'
1205.73'
707.60'
NORTH LIMESTONE ST

fig. 240

directly across the street on the east side of North Fountain Boulevard, the old playing field of the now-defunct Springfield Bulldogs football team. The Links acquired both sections of the Doyle land and platted thirty-nine new home sites on both sides of the boulevard and along the new streets of Trenton Place and Shawnee Boulevard, east of Fountain Boulevard. *(fig. 240)*

The old Signal Hill land, east of the country club, had been opened up for development in the late 1930s as well. Back around the time that Harry Kissell platted Ridgewood, Signal Hill was offered for sale by the heirs of William S. Thompson, and Harry Kissell purchased the property. It is unclear whether his intent was to develop the land, or if he simply bought it as an investment, but in 1918 he sold it to Wilbur J. Myers. Myers was the president of the Robbins and Myers Company, a highly successful local manufacturing company that made electric fans and exported them all over the world. Myers and his wife moved into a large, attractive house on the beautiful country estate that had been built by William S. Thompson in 1879 when the Signal Hill land was still part of his vast estate north of Home Road. *(fig. 241)*

In 1921, Myers sold a large tract of his land to the country club so that the existing nine-hole golf course could be expanded to eighteen holes. Two years later, the Myers sold their home and remaining acres to J.B. Cartmell, a local banker, and bought the home of George and Odessa Metcalf at 1828 Crescent Drive in Ridgewood. The Kissell Real Estate Company had negotiated the deals. By 1937, J.B. Cartmell, who just about everyone in Springfield referred to as "Uncle Joe Cartmell," began selling lots in Signal Hill for upscale homes. Among the earliest residents of Signal Hill Road were the Constantine Link family, the Samuel Nolte family, and the Merlin Robertson family.

But on Signal Hill and everywhere else construction came to a complete halt when the war started. Once again, building materials had to be diverted to a war effort. In Ridgewood, for example, there were 357 houses built by the end of 1941. Between 1941 and 1947, only twenty-three more homes were built due to scarcity of materials.

Because of the draft, World War II affected virtually every Ridgewood family. Everyone had either family members or dear friends going off to serve. The windows of Ridgewood homes were dotted with stars indicating households with a member in the service. And the neighborhood shared in a collective grief when one of the stars was changed to gold, indicating that the serviceman it represented had been killed in action. Constant worry for the ones that were "over there" pervaded life. Young Carol Robertson rode her bike home from Ridgewood School each day to Signal Hill and stopped with trepidation at the line of mailboxes next to the utility house at the entrance of

241. The William S. Thompson house on Signal Hill Rd., later occupied by Wilbur Myers, then J.B. Cartmell.

Missing in action

242. Jim & Brown Burleigh in March 1944, several months before Jim Burleigh was declared missing in action in WWII.

the country club. The little girl, unaware that bad news came via a telegram or a knock on the door, worried that the mail might contain some terrible word about the fate of her brother, Dave, who was serving in the war.

Brown and May Burleigh, unfortunately, were the recipients of one of those dreaded telegrams. Jim "Fait" Burleigh had spent one year in college at DePauw in Indiana when he was drafted in 1943. He had hardly gotten to England and then on to France when he was captured and taken to a prison camp in Germany. The Burleighs received the terrible news that their son was missing in action via a telegram from the War Department on August 20, 1944. They had last heard from him in a letter dated July 2, 1944. It would be seven tortuous weeks more before they received the news on October 7, 1944— he was alive and a prisoner of war held in Germany's largest prison camp, Stalag 7A in Moosburg, Germany. Thirty-seven thousand prisoners, including nearly fifteen thousand Americans, were being held in Stalag 7A. Following the telegram, the Burleighs lived for news from their son. By then, the mailman on South Kensington Place was Mr. Miller. During the course of the war, whenever there was a letter from a serviceman to be delivered to a home on his route, Mr. Miller called the family at 7 a.m. to let them know, so they could come immediately to the post office to pick it up. *(fig. 242)*

Everyone in the neighborhood supported the war effort and the men serving. Huston Moores made a regular habit of bringing his camera to Covenant Presbyterian Church on Sunday mornings. As the families with a family member fighting in the war left the church, where they had offered prayers for their son, father, or brother's safe return, Moores photographed them on the steps in their Sunday finery, so that the pictures could be sent as a memento to the serviceman who longed for family and home. Fred and Edna Miller spent fourteen to sixteen hours a day during the war churning out parachutes for the military. The business they had started out of desperation during the Depression, Miller Frocks, had done so well that the Millers were able to build a third home at 1607 North Fountain Boulevard in 1941. After the December attack on Pearl Harbor, they joined thousands of other American businesses and converted to war production.

Even the children of the neighborhood did what they could to help the war effort. They contributed to the metal drives by collecting tin cans and smoothing out tin gum wrappers, and they collected cooking grease that was used to make glycerin, an essential ingredient in various explosives such as dynamite. Tuesdays at Ridgewood School was War Savings Stamp Day. Each student had a savings stamp booklet and would bring either a quarter or a dime to their teacher, who acted as the banker and dispensed the savings stamps to be pasted in the booklets. When the student had filled a booklet with $18.75 worth of savings stamps, the booklets could be redeemed for a $25 war bond.

During the war, the threat of attack was not just limited to those serving oversees. Since Pearl Harbor, Americans had lived in fear of another attack on American soil in the form of an air raid. At Ridgewood School, during the course of the war, the windows were taped with criss-crossing brown paper tape to keep shattering glass from flying and injuring the children in the event that an air raid did come. Regular air raid drills were held at the school. All the students were directed to go to the stage in the little auditorium and sit with their backs along the interior wall with their feet sticking out in front of them.

Life was war-oriented for this generation of Ridgewood Children. The war was what families talked about each night at dinner. Children knew all the songs of the different branches of service. They had flash cards with images of the various warplanes, and they could identify them. Even the annual spring pageant at Ridgewood School took on patriotic themes.

Many movies were war-oriented and the newsreels were full of news from the frontlines. Families gathered in their living rooms after dinner at 6:30 p.m. each evening, and, as mother patched overalls or darned socks, the family listened to famous radio broadcasters Lowell Thomas, H.V. Kaltenborn, and Edward R. Murrow report on the events in Europe and the Pacific. *Life* magazine came out each Friday, and children ran home from school to try and be the first to get the latest news of war.

Every American, no matter his or her economic status, faced deprivations. Rationing stamps were required for everything from sugar, clothes, and shoes to tires and gas. Every child, whether from an affluent family or not, wore hand-me-down clothes and made do with two pairs of shoes a year. The motto was "Use it up, wear it out, make it do, or do without." But everyone was of the same mind, and the war united the country in a way that only the most horrific events can.

Finally, after nearly three and half years of war, came the glorious news of victory in Europe. President Truman declared May 8, 1945, as V-E Day, marking the end of World War II in Europe. A few days earlier, on May 1, 1945, Brown and May Burleigh had received the joyous news that their son had escaped from captivity while on a forced march and had made his way to friendly forces. V-J Day, victory in Japan followed on September 2, 1945, and slowly, fear and deprivation subsided, and life began to return to normal. America emerged from World War II as an economic superpower, and, although they didn't know it yet, Americans were about to experience the greatest economic boom they had ever known.

POSTSCRIPT

"Leave something behind to show that you have lived here."
—Harry S. Kissell, in an address to the
Springfield Kiwanis Club, 1923

Throughout the war, Harry Kissell had fulfilled his promise to his son-in-law and kept the Kissell Real Estate Company going. He also continued his involvement in the Federal Home Loan Banking system. When the war ended in 1945, he was serving on the national board of the Federal Home Loan Bank. That November, he traveled by train to Washington, D.C., to attend the national board meeting. While he was there, he took ill suddenly and had to return home by train. He had suffered a heart attack and was not well for several months afterwards, but his son-in-law was back from the war and handling the daily affairs of the Kissell Real Estate Company.

The official announcements that Howard B. Noonan would be taking over as the president of the company were printed and ready to be sent out on February 14, 1946.

Harry Kissell and his wife were scheduled to be in Cincinnati when the announcement was made so that Harry could attend the meeting of the executive committee of the Federal Home Loan Bank of Cincinnati. He had been the chairman of the board of directors off and on since the bank's inception and was holding the position again in 1946. The Kissells had planned to go down a few days early so that Harry could have a physical at a hospital in Cincinnati. His Springfield physician wanted him to see a specialist, but many of them weren't yet back from serving in the war, so arrangements were made to have Kissell's physical done by one in Cincinnati.

Kissell had turned 70 the previous September and had frequently told his family over the years, "Give me my four score and thirty," meaning that he would be satisfied to make it to 70, a ripe old age at the time when the average life expectancy for a man was less than 65 years. On February 13, 1946, Harry Kissell called his daughter from Cincinnati to report that the doctor had given him the bill of health of a man of 60. On the morning of February 14, Valentine's Day, Kissell had breakfast with his wife at their hotel, and then

went across the street to the bank building. He took the elevator up to the floor where the meeting was being held, went into the office of the president of the Federal Home Loan Bank of Cincinnati, Walter D. Shultz, and suffered a massive, fatal coronary.

Kissell's sudden death came as a shock to all who knew him. Upon hearing the tragic news, the board of directors of both the Federal Home Loan Bank and the National Association of Real Estate Boards sent resolutions of condolences and expressions of gratitude for his devoted service. But the loss was felt most keenly in the city that he loved. A grieving Springfield community joined the Kissell family in their sorrow. One of Springfield's finest citizens and greatest boosters was gone.

Friends and associates in his many business, social, fraternal, church, and civic endeavors offered eulogies that filled the *Springfield Daily News* on the day of his death. One particularly poignant one came from Dr. Rees Edgar Tulloss, the president of Wittenberg College: "Among those who mourn his passing, none will be more sincere in their sorrow than the hundreds of young people who in past years as crippled children found in him a helping and guiding friend, through whose service better health and straightened limbs and useful occupations later in life were made possible. For generations to come, what Harry Kissell has done will make Springfield a better, happier, more progressive city."

Harry Kissell had chaired the Rotary's Crippled Children's Committee from its inception in 1919 until his death in 1946. Given the disabilities of his own son, Roger, it was a cause close to his heart.

Time and time again, he had demonstrated his concern for his fellow citizens, whether it was helping establish a physiotherapy department at the Springfield City Hospital, spearheading the sale of Easter Seals, serving as the director of the local Red Cross, or organizing the Community Fund Campaign, the precursor of the United Way.

His involvement and leadership in the city's varied institutions was widespread. Whether serving as a church elder, or on the board of his beloved alma mater, Wittenberg, or helping found the local chamber of commerce, Harry Kissell was always ready to lend a helping hand. He heeded the call to leadership even in his fraternal associations. He was a 33rd degree Mason, and, for his efforts as the Worshipful Master of the local Anthony Lodge, No. 455 and as Grand Master of the Grand Lodge of Ohio, a new Masonic lodge was chartered in Springfield in 1921 and named the H.S. Kissell Lodge, No. 674. This represented one of the few times in Masonic history that a lodge was named for a living Mason, and it represented a rare instance of public acknowledgement of his contributions to the community.

And that is the way Harry Kissell wanted it. In 1917, he told his fellow real estate developers that he always tried to keep his civic and charitable work out of the newspapers unless the publicity was required for the cause. Instead, he preferred to appear in the newspaper only in relation to his business activities. He was quite successful at this, but his business represented just a fraction of his life's work. When his obituary appeared in the newspaper, even those who knew him well were likely surprised with the breadth and depth of his civic activities.

Throughout his life, Harry Kissell had operated on a motto that he claimed as his personal manifesto—"He profits most who serves best." And serve he did. A resolution issued upon his death from the board of directors of The First National Bank perhaps best summed up Kissell's philosophy: "For him the successful administration of his business was but a foundation upon which to build a finer structure of citizenship."

He was, proudly, a community builder. As he helped give millions of Americans the opportunity to participate in the American dream of home ownership, his efforts played out on the national stage, and yet he never failed to keep his beloved Springfield first in his heart. Whether it meant building the institutions of the city or building Ridgewood, the neighborhood he proudly called home, Harry S. Kissell created an enduring legacy. When he died, George H. Tehan, vice president of the Clark County Bar Association eulogized him with the following observation: "The best interests of the community were at all times foremost in his public vision. His death is a great civic loss—but the ripe fruits of his labors will long remain."

And so they do.

EPILOGUE

At the writing of this book, the Ridgewood neighborhood in Springfield, Ohio, is fast approaching the 100th anniversary of its development. Back in April 1916, at the dawn of the first full building season in Ridgewood, an article in the *Springfield Daily News* predicted that the neighborhood, one hundred years hence, would still be impervious to deterioration and remain *the* residence section of Springfield.

Thanks to the innovative "planning for permanence" approach that Harry Kissell and his fellow developers of early twentieth century suburbs took in creating their residential developments, these neighborhoods fared far better than their Victorian era counterparts. In the twenty-first century, Ridgewood is still a desirable upscale neighborhood in Springfield. The city's older, affluent neighborhoods of East High Street and South Fountain Avenue have had somewhat less illustrious fates.

By the time of the Great Depression, South Fountain Avenue had fallen out of favor with the city's elites, and the neighborhood and its once grand mansions began to decay precipitously. Toward the end of the twentieth century, a renewed appreciation for Victorian architecture revived interest in the neighborhood. A number of dedicated preservationists have settled there and work diligently to reverse the decline of the neighborhood and restore some of Springfield's greatest architectural treasures.

East High Street remained popular with affluent Springfield residents a little longer than South Fountain Avenue but fell victim to commercial intrusions after World War II. Today, East High Street is one of the busiest thoroughfares of the city. Many of its fine mansions, however, are beautifully preserved, well cared for by business owners who have converted them to various commercial uses.

By comparison, Ridgewood remains almost entirely residential in character save a lone doctor's office located in the old Ridgewood School Building. Kissell hoped that Ridgewood would be a neighborhood that multiple generations of Springfield families would call home. He got his wish. It is not hard at all to find current residents who are third or even fourth generation Ridgewood residents.

It is, however, no longer an isolated residential oasis at the edge of the countryside. North Fountain Boulevard became a well-traveled thoroughfare as the "northward trend" persisted throughout the second half of the twentieth century and new residential neighborhoods and commercial strips were developed north of Home Road. Harding Road, once a road to the countryside is also a well-beaten path to the city's nearby, current commercial mecca—Bechtle Avenue. But Ridgewood remains one of Springfield's most desirable and highly regarded neighborhoods.

The Kissell Company, however, is no more. Just prior to World War II, the company expanded into the mortgage loan origination business. After Kissell's death, his son-in-law Howard B. Noonan capitalized on the post-war housing boom and took the business to new heights, opening loan origination branch offices in a number of states. By 1964, the Kissell Company was one of the top ten mortgage banking firms in the United States. The successful business attracted the attention of the Pittsburg National Corporation, and it acquired the Kissell Company in 1969. The Kissell Company name was retained until Norwest Corporation acquired the company in 1993.

The Kissell legacy of real estate development carries on in Springfield, however, through Kissell's grandson—Peter Kissell Noonan. In 1981, Noonan and his partner, Tom Loftis, founded Midland Properties, Inc., which is active in commercial real estate brokerage, property management, and development. At about the same time, Peter Noonan developed Sean's Woods, a residential development commonly referred to locally as Roscommon for the name of the boulevard that runs through the heart of the development. Today, Roscommon reigns as one of Springfield's premier upscale neighborhoods.

AN ARCHITECTURAL

HOMES THAT WERE CONSTRUCTED IN RIDGEWOOD DURING THE NEIGHBORHOOD'S PERIOD

of greatest historical significance—1915 to 1946—are typical examples of the architectural styles found is most affluent neighborhoods developed in the United States during that period. At the beginning of the twentieth century, the ornate Victorian home had fallen out of favor, and fashionable architects of the era were embracing and popularizing Colonial American precedents in architecture. These simpler, classically detailed residences seemed the perfect antidote to the excesses of Victorian architecture.

At the same time, a number of American architects were being trained in Europe, and they brought back a penchant for replicas of historically-correct copies of European architectural styles. As a result, the American craze for English Tudor, Spanish Mission, Mediterranean, and French Norman-style homes was born.

After World War II, however, tastes in domestic architecture in American suburbs changed dramatically. The prevailing trends gave way to simple Cape Cod bungalows, Split Level homes, and one-story Ranch homes. Most of the homes constructed in Ridgewood after World War II are of these types. Before the war, a two-story home was considered a symbol of affluence, and a one-story home was equated with a working class cottage. In fact, the deed restrictions in most pre-World War II suburbs prohibited the construction of one-story homes. After the war, however, many of the restrictions in early twentieth-century suburbs had expired and the one-story Ranch home was all the rage. It became the most popular house style in America in the 1950s and 1960s.

Harry Kissell's widow, Olive Kissell, even built a one-story home in Ridgewood in the 1950s. At the time, her son, Roger, was finding it increasingly difficult to navigate the stairs in their home at 1801 North Fountain Boulevard due to his physical infirmities. Mrs. Kissell investigated the idea of installing an elevator in the home, but upon learning that its installation would cause considerable destruction to the interior fabric of the home—something she was not willing to consider—she changed her mind. Instead, she built a Ranch home at 1720 North Fountain Boulevard, and joined millions of other American home builders in embracing modern style homes. The era of residential architecture based on historical precedents was officially over.

The Edwin E. & Alice Kramp home at 320 Ardmore Road is an example of the "Garrison" version of the Colonial Revival Style.

COLONIAL REVIVAL

Colonial Revival architecture was the most popular style of residential architecture in the United States in the first half of the twentieth century. The numerous examples that can be found in Ridgewood provide evidence of its appeal. Colonial Revival homes are typically two-to-three stories and are essentially rectangular blocks with side-gabled roofs. The homes are usually symmetrically arranged. A variation of the style—the Dutch Colonial—features a gambrel style roof.

Colonial Revival homes can be either of wood frame with clapboard finish, or of masonry or masonry veneer finish. In another variation of the style—the Garrison Colonial—the top story slightly overhangs the first story, and the first story may be finished with brick or stone. The Garrison version of the Colonial Revival style was extremely popular in the Audubon Park subdivision, which is now colloquially regarded as part of Ridgewood.

The stylistic features of Colonial Revival homes include emphasis on the front door, which is typically centered on the front of the house and topped with a decorative pediment. Windows are generally symmetrically arranged, and fan lights and Palladian windows are a favorite decorative element. Classical detailing is a hallmark of the style.

The Cliff C. & Margaret Corry house at 215 Brighton Rd.

The George F. & Odessa Metcalf house at 1828 Crescent Dr., designed in the Dutch Colonial version of the Colonial Revival style.

The Edwin A. & Laura Carlisle home at 1905 N. Fountain Blvd.

The Gardner Hazen home at 1850 Crescent Dr.

The Harry E. & Sarah Hebrank home at 37 S. Kensington Pl.

The Daniel W. & Alice Clauer house at 33 S. Kensington Pl., another Dutch Colonial version of the style. Note the "his and hers" sleeping porches.

The Ralph W. & Marie Patterson home at 140 Brighton Rd.

The Walter V. & Gertrude Edwards home at 1748 Walnut Ter. is a more simplified version of the Colonial Revival, which became popular in the 1930s.

The Robert W. and Nellie Snyder house at 128 Ardmore Rd.

TUDOR/ENGLISH REVIVAL

In early twentieth-century suburbs, Tudor/English Revival style was second only in popularity to the Colonial Revival style. Tudor/English Revival style was first popularized at the end of the nineteenth century in England by influential British architect Richard Norman Shaw. It made its way across the Atlantic, becoming very popular before WWI and gradually waning in favor by WWII. The grand example of this style in Ridgewood is the Harry S. and Olive Kissell house at 1801 North Fountain Boulevard. The Kissell house features most of the identifying characteristics of the Tudor Revival style, the hallmark of which is a decorative wood half-timbering effect on the gables. However, there are many examples in the neighborhood of more modest homes that show English influences but lack the half-timbering detailing, and, therefore, would be more accurately characterized as simply English Revival.

The Tudor/English Revival style draws its inspiration from a variety of English homes—everything from the humble, medieval English cottage to the grand English manor house.

Stylistic features may include steeply pitched roofs; steep front or side gables; tall, prominent chimneys; tall, narrow windows, which are often grouped together and may feature multi-paned leaded glass, oftentimes in the shape of diamonds. Exterior finishes may include stucco, stone, or brick. On some of the simpler versions of the style, wood cladding or shingles may be used on the exterior. Decorative half-timbering may be used on the gables. Occasionally one might see a house in this style where the roofing materials are rolled around the eaves to imitate a thatched roof. Doorways may be simple rounded arches or feature the distinctive Tudor arch.

The Dr. A. Richard and Elizabeth Kent house at 20 Brighton Rd.

The George H. & Anna Happer house at 1840 Crescent Dr.

The Lee L. & Edna Woodhouse home at 1821 Walnut Ter.

The James S. & Lucy Webb house at 1802 N. Fountain Blvd. Note the way that the roofing materials are rolled around the eaves to emulate a thatched roof.

The Harold L. & Claribel Binning house at 124 S. Kensington Pl.

The Peter J. & Cleo Dennerlein house at 1616 Midvale Rd.

The Morris M. & Jane Gold house at 115 Brighton Rd.

The C. Warren & Ruth Mapes house at 141 Hawthorne Rd.

The Joseph R. & Elsa Misel house at 1719 Midvale Rd.

The Karl F. & Millie Eipper house at 120 Brighton Rd.

The Harry S. & Olive Kissell house at 1801 N. Fountain Blvd.

The Edwin F. & Isabella Rober house at 204 Ardmore Rd.

SPANISH MISSION REVIVAL

The Spanish Mission Revival style first gained popularity in California during the late nineteenth and early twentieth centuries. While the eastern portion of the United States was celebrating its English colonial past with the Colonial Revival home, California architects were drawing inspiration from their region's Hispanic colonial heritage and propagating the Spanish Mission style. The Mission style spread eastward, but it remained most popular in the Southwest and Florida. However, most early twentieth-century American suburbs had one or two examples of the style. The stylistic features of a Spanish Mission house may include low-pitched roofs with clay tile roofing and wide, overhanging eaves. Scalloped parapets that rise above the roof line and arched entrances are also popular. The exterior finish is usually stucco, but brick or stone was used as well. Landmark examples of the style sometimes include a Mission-like bell tower. The Gus and Sophia LeBolt house at 223 Brighton Road is a magnificent example of the style. A few other Ridgewood homes display some Spanish Mission influences. Of particular note is the Edwin F. and Isabella Rober house at 204 Ardmore Road.

The Gus and Sophia LeBolt house at 223 Brighton Rd.

FRENCH NORMAN REVIVAL

The Edward S. & Mary Montanus house at 1620 Woodedge Ave.

The French Norman Revival style became extremely popular after WWI. Soldiers returning home after service in France brought with them a newly acquired taste for French domestic architecture. By WWII, the style had waned in favor. Tall, steeply pitched roofs are the hallmark of the style. Homes that fall into the French Norman Revival style can range from copies of formal French manor houses to those of picturesque rambling French farmhouses. Formal houses in this style may have round towers with conical roofs. Generally, the main door is housed in this tower. Overhanging upper stories and massive chimneys are other key features. French Norman Revival houses may also have decorative half-timbering. The exterior of homes in this style may be brick, stone, or stucco. In some of the rustic farmhouse versions of the style, roofing materials were often utilized to emulate a thatched roof. Leaded glass casement windows are often seen on both the formal and informal versions of the style. The Guy D. and Jane Bayley house at 1926 North Fountain Boulevard is an outstanding example of a French Norman Revival farmhouse, and the Edward S. and Mary Montanus house at 1620 Woodedge Avenue is an exceptional example of a French Norman Revival formal house.

The Guy D. & Jane Bayley house at 1926 N. Fountain Blvd.

The Arthur E. & Mabel Jones house at 1821 N. Fountain Blvd.

MEDITERRANEAN REVIVAL

The Mediterranean Revival style was first popularized in the early twentieth century by American architects who had traveled to Italy and were inspired by Italian country villas. The style became widely disseminated in the United States for several reasons. Its aesthetic characteristics and informal layouts made it well-suited for tropical climates and laid-back lifestyles, making it a natural choice for the mansions that the wealthy were building in Florida. The rise of Florida as a major tourist destination in the early twentieth century exposed many people to the style.

A concurrent rise in public interest in Hollywood and the film industry had the same effect. Mediterranean style architecture was a favorite choice of Hollywood celebrities and film industry executives, and when images of their homes appeared in popular magazines it gave cachet to the style. The popularity of the style reached its zenith between 1920 and 1940, and it is not unusual to find examples of it in many American suburbs. The style was most typically used for large landmark houses, but Mediterranean influences may be seen in more modest homes. The Charles I. and Elizabeth Shawver house at 101 Brighton Road and the Arthur E. and Mabel Jones house at 1821 North Fountain Boulevard are excellent examples of the style.

The style shares some characteristics with the Spanish Mission style, particularly the low-pitched tile roof. Typically, however, one would see more rectangular doorways and windows utilized on the Mediterranean style house, as opposed to the arched forms that are ubiquitous in Spanish Mission style. The Mediterranean house usually has a long, low horizontal orientation and is devoid of excessive exterior ornamentation. Side porches are common and may include Palladian windows or doorways. The exterior is usually stucco or a smooth stone finish.

The Charles I. & Elizabeth Shawver house at 101 Brighton Rd.

SWISS CHALET

One particular home in Ridgewood, the Emanuel and Anna Thomsen home at 1440 North Fountain Boulevard is especially worth noting, due to its unusual style. The design of the Thomsen home was heavily influenced by the Swiss Chalet style. Swiss Chalet homes are rare because the style enjoyed only a fairly brief period of popularity. The style first became fashionable in the late nineteenth century as part of a wave of revivals of other exotic styles, including Egyptian, Moorish, Oriental, and Byzantine, that Victorian era architects were experimenting with. Its popularity waned by 1920, however, and few houses were built in the Swiss Chalet style after that. The Thomsen house was built at the very end of the style's heyday, in 1921, and features the decorative stick work that is typical to the style. The roofs of Swiss Chalet style houses often have broad overhanging eaves with decorative brackets. Second-story porches or balconies with patterned cutout balustrades are also typical.

The Emanuel & Anna Thomsen home at 1440 N. Fountain Blvd.

The Gus Sun, Jr. house at 1 South Broadmoor Blvd.

INTERNATIONAL

When the Gus Sun, Jr., house was built in 1939 at the southwest corner of North Fountain Boulevard and Broadmoor Boulevard, it was probably as alarming to the residents of Ridgewood—given their penchant for picturesque European revival styles—as the Burton J. Westcott house was when it was built in 1908. The Prairie style Westcott house, designed by famed American architect Frank Lloyd Wright, was constructed on East High Street in Springfield, right in the midst of a neighborhood of ornate Victorian mansions. Both the Burton J. Westcott house and the Gus Sun, Jr., house were radical departures from prevailing tastes in residential architecture during the periods in which they were constructed.

The Gus Sun, Jr., house was designed in the International style by Yellow Springs, Ohio, architect Max Mercer. (Several years later, Mercer would collaborate with one of the most renowned modern architects of the period, Eero Saarinen, to design Birch Hall at Antioch College in Yellow Springs.) The very modern International style was first introduced in the United States in the mid-1920s. At the time, American architects were taking their inspiration for domestic architecture mostly from historic precedents. But a group of European architects, including Le Corbusier in France, and Walter Gropius and Mies van der Rohe in Germany, were experimenting with a new style of architecture that looked to the present and took its inspiration from modern technology and machinery. Le Corbusier, for example, famously called a home designed in the International style "a machine for living." Function and efficiency were the focus of home designs in this style. All excess ornamentation was stripped away, and kitchens and bathrooms were outfitted with the most modern equipment.

International style homes typically have flat roofs, asymmetrical facades with smooth wall surfaces completely devoid of ornamentation, and metal casement windows set flush with the outside walls. Windows and doors lack any decorative details. Most International style homes date from the 1930s, but the style never gained widespread acceptance. The Gun Sun, Jr., house, however, was not only considered eccentric by the residents of Ridgewood because of its nonconformist architecture, but because of the profession and habits of its occupant. Gus Sun, Jr., was part of a Springfield show business dynasty. His father was the famed Vaudeville impresario Gus Sun. Like his father before him, Sun, Jr., enjoyed hosting his many celebrity friends when they traveled through Springfield. Curious neighbors were always on the lookout to spot which famous house guests the Suns were entertaining at any given time.

LUSTRON

One of the most unique houses in the Ridgewood area was constructed slightly after the neighborhood's period of greatest historical significance and is actually located in the adjacent Broadmoor addition. However, it bears chronicling because of its unusual appearance and intriguing history. The little metal house at 265 North Broadmoor Boulevard is one of only about 2,500 Lustron homes constructed in the United States between 1948 and 1950. Lustron homes were mass-produced, prefabricated houses made of porcelain-enameled steel.

The Lustron home was the brainchild of Columbus, Ohio, businessman, Carl Strandland. Strandland envisioned the pre-fab Lustron house as the answer to a severe housing shortage in the United States caused by an almost complete shutdown of building during the Depression and WWII years. The shortage was then exacerbated by the thousands of veterans returning to the home front eager to marry and establish their own homes. Strandland sought and received financial backing in the form of loans from the Federal government and established his factory in 1948 in a former airplane factory adjacent to the Port Columbus airport. The Lustron factory utilized assembly lines patterned after those found in General Motors and Ford factories, and Strandland's goal was to turn out a hundred Lustron homes a day to satisfy the housing demand.

Lustron homes received rave reviews in many of the popular national periodicals of the day. They were promoted as being fireproof, rodent proof and rustproof. The two-bedroom, one-bath homes had about a thousand square feet of living space and were designed to be efficient and require low maintenance. Every interior and exterior surface of the home was of a porcelain-enameled steel that never needed painting and could be cleaned with soap and water. The floor plan was efficiently laid out, and to maximize space the home boasted many built-ins including bookcases, china cabinets and vanities. The kitchen had an unusual combination sink-dishwasher-clotheswasher.

Despite the positive press, however, cost overruns quickly led to the demise of the operation after just two years of production. Lustron houses were initially supposed to cost approximately $7,000, but ended up being more in the $10,000 to $12,000 range, not including the price of land. In most cases, it was cheaper for home seekers to buy a traditionally built house from a large-scale homebuilder who could offer lower prices because of the economies of scale.

More than sixty years after its construction the little metal house on North Broadmoor Boulevard remains a curiosity because it stands in stark contrast to the homes that were built in the neighborhood before WWII. But it serves as an important cultural artifact that represents a transition in suburbia—a transition from the early twentieth-century picturesque suburbs populated with handcrafted homes to the post-WWII suburbs in which mass-produced homes in a limited choice of styles became the standard.

The Lustron home at 265 N. Broadmoor Blvd.

LUSTRON

ABOUT the AUTHOR

Tamara Dallenbach, *née* Nesselrotte, is a lifelong resident of Springfield, Ohio. She graduated from Shawnee High School and received her bachelor's degree in History and master's degree in Public History from Wright State University. Before joining The Turner Foundation in 2004 as Public Historian, she held the same position with the Clark County Historical Society.

Passionate about her community's history and its historic architecture, she has served on the Springfield Historic Landmarks Commission and the board of the Springfield Preservation Alliance and is active in many other preservation and public history initiatives.

She resides in the city with her husband, Nathan Dallenbach, and her two children—Richard and Jacob Wait.

BIBLIOGRAPHY

Berkhofer, George H. *No Place Like Home: A History of Domestic Architecture in Springfield & Clark County, Ohio*. Wilmington, Ohio: Orange Frazer Press, 2007.

Beers and Company, W.H. *History of Clark County Illustrated*. Chicago, 1881.

Boehme, Sybil Burleigh. Interview by Tamara K. Dallenbach. March 25, 2009, Cincinnati, Ohio. Digital audio recording.

Burleigh, Brown. "Ridgewood Development at Springfield." *National Real Estate Journal*, March 1, 1920, 15-18.

Christiansen, Harry. *Ride the Red Devils Along Ohio's Trolley Trails*. Euclid, Ohio: Transit House, Inc., 1971.

Clark County, Ohio Plat Books, Clark County Recorder's Office, A.B. Graham Building, Springfield, Ohio.

The County of Clark, Ohio: an Imperial Atlas and Art Folio. 1894. Reprint, Milford, Ohio: Little Miami Publishing Company, 2002.

Davis, Charles Henry. "How National Highways Are Necessary to the Automobile." Paper presented at the Washington Automobile Show, Washington, D.C., January 19, 1914.

Directory of the City of Springfield, Ohio. Cincinnati, Ohio: The Williams Directory Co., 1914 – 1946.

Drais, Sue Bayley. Interview by Tamara K. Dallenbach. July 3, 2009, Springfield, Ohio. Digital audio recording.

Fogelson, Robert M. *Bourgeois Nightmares: Suburbia, 1870-1930*. New Haven; London: Yale University Press, 2005

Foy, Jessica H., and Thomas J. Schlereth, eds. *American Home Life, 1880-1930: A Social History of Spaces and Services*. Knoxville: University of Tennessee Press, 1992.

Gordon, Stephen C. *How to Complete the Ohio Historic Inventory*. Columbus, Ohio: Ohio Historic Preservation Office, 1992.

Gray, Caroline Robertson. Interview by Tamara K. Dallenbach. July 3, 2009, Springfield, Ohio. Digital audio recording.

Handlin, David P. *American Architecture*. 2nd ed. London: Thames & Hudson Ltd, 2004.

"Harry S. Kissell Elected National President." *National Real Estate Journal*. (July 23, 1930): 57.

Harwood, John. Interview by Tamara K. Dallenbach. June 4, 2009, Springfield, Ohio. Digital audio recording.

Hayden, Dolores. *Building Suburbia: Green Fields and Urban Growth, 1820-2000*. New York: Vintage Books, 2003.

Huddleston, Dorothy Anderson. Interview by Tamara K. Dallenbach. July 3, 2009, Springfield, Ohio. Digital audio recording.

Jackson, Kenneth T. *Crabgrass Frontier: The Suburbanization of the United States*. Oxford: Oxford University Press, 1985.

Jackson, Sue Miller. Interview by Tamara K. Dallenbach. February 10, 2009, Springfield, Ohio.

Kinnison, William A. *Springfield & Clark County*. Windsor Publications: Northridge, California, 1985.

The Kissell Company – 1884-1984: A Century of Service. (self-published booklet), 1984.

Kissell Company Records, Clark County Historical Society, Springfield, Ohio.

Kissell, H.S. "Community Features for Subdivisions." *Annals of Real Estate Practice*, 124-37. Chicago: National Association of Real Estate Boards, 1925.

Kissell, Harry S. "Fighters are Winning!" *National Real Estate Journal.* (January 19, 1931): 9-10.

Kissell, Harry S. "The Outlook for 1930." *National Real Estate Journal.* (February 17, 1930): 23-26.

Kissell, Harry S. "Realty Has Not Failed!" *National Real Estate Journal.* (June 8, 1931): 30-31.

"Kissell Inaugurated 1931 National President." *National Real Estate Journal.* (February 2, 1931): 20-22.

"Kissell to Serve on National Committee." *National Real Estate Journal.* (November 10, 1930): 48.

Link, Richard. Interview by Tamara K. Dallenbach. November 2, 2009, Springfield, Ohio. Digital audio recording.

Lynd, Robert S., and Helen Merrel Lynd. *Middletown: A Study in American Culture.* San Diego; New York; London: Harcourt Brace & Company, 1957.

Matheny, Dorothy. "Announcement of the Ridgewood School." 1927-1928.

Mayo, James M. *The American Country Club: Its Origins and Development.* London; New Jersey: Rutgers University Press, 1998.

McAlester, Lee, and Virginia Savage. *A Field Guide to American Houses.* New York: Alfred A. Knopf Inc., 1984.

McCulloch, Mary Jean Moores. Interview by Tamara K. Dallenbach. January 30, 2009, Springfield, Ohio. DVD recording.

Nelson, Herbert U. "Real Estate Now Has a Federal Reserve System." *National Real Estate Journal.* (August 1932): 17-19.

"The New President." *National Real Estate Journal* (January 5, 1931): 16-17.

Noonan, Mary Lu Kissell. Interview by Tamara K. Dallenbach. September 26, 2005, Springfield, Ohio. DVD recording.

Noonan, Mary Lu Kissell. Interview by Tamara K. Dallenbach. January 10, 2006, Springfield, Ohio. DVD recording.

Noonan, Mary Lu Kissell. Interview by Tamara K. Dallenbach. September 24, 2008, Springfield, Ohio. Digital audio recording.

Noonan, Mary Lu Kissell. Interview by Tamara K. Dallenbach. June 1, 2009, Springfield, Ohio. Digital audio recording.

Noonan, Mary Lu Kissell. Interview by Tamara K. Dallenbach. October 27, 2009, Springfield, Ohio. Digital audio recording.

Prince, Benjamin F. *A Standard History of Springfield and Clark County.* 2 vols. New York, 1922.

Proceedings of the First Annual Conference of Developers of High Class Residence Property. Meeting at Kansas City, Missouri, May 10-12, 1917. Microfilm of transcript,

Manuscripts and Archives Section, Olin Research Library, Cornell University.

Proceedings of the Second Annual Conference of Developers of High Class Residence Property. Meeting at Baltimore, Maryland, 1918. Microfilm of transcript, Manuscripts and Archives Section, Olin Research Library, Cornell University.

Proceedings of the Third Annual Conference of Developers of High Class Residence Property. Meeting at Birmingham, Alabama, February 20-22, 1919. Microfilm of transcript, Manuscripts and Archives Section, Olin Research Library, Cornell University.

Rockel, William A. ed. *20th Century History of Springfield and Clark County, and Representative Citizens*. Chicago, 1908.

Springfield Daily News, The. January 1, 1914 – December 31, 1946.

U.S. Bureau of Census. Thirteenth Census of the United States: 1910. Population schedule, City of Springfield, Clark County Ohio.

U.S. Bureau of Census. Fourteenth Census of the United States: 1920. Population schedule, City of Springfield, Clark County Ohio.

U.S. Bureau of Census. Fifteenth Census of the United States: 1930. Population schedule, City of Springfield, Clark County Ohio.

U.S. Congress. Senate. Subcommittee of the Committee on Banking and Currency. *Creation of a System of Federal Home Loan Banks*. 72nd Cong., 1st sess., Part 1, January 14, 1932.

U.S. Congress. Senate. Subcommittee of the Committee on Banking and Currency. *Creation of a System of Federal Home Loan Banks*. 72nd Cong., 1st sess., Part 2, February 15, 1932.

U.S. Department of the Interior, National Park Service and National Register of Historic Places. *National Register Bulletin: Historic Residential Suburbs*. By David L. Ames and Linda Flint McClelland. September, 2002.

U.S. Department of the Interior, National Park Service, National Register of Historic Places Inventory Nomination Form, North Side Historic District, Clark County, Ohio. Prepared by Kathy Mast Kane & Nathalie Wright, 2009.

U.S. Department of the Interior, National Park Service, National Register of Historic Places Inventory Nomination Form for Roland Park, Baltimore City, Maryland. Prepared by Catharine F. Black, 1973.

Waln, Peggy Kent. Interview by Tamara K. Dallenbach. March 13, 2009, Springfield, Ohio. Digital audio recording.

Weaver, C.I. "Springfield Country Club" (self-published booklet), 1956.

Worley, William S. *J.C. Nichols and the Shaping of Kansas City: Innovation in Planned Residential Communities*. Columbia, Missouri: University of Missouri Press, 1990.

Winger, Marthena. "Announcement of the Ridgewood School." 1920-1921.

SOURCES of IMAGES

Art & Architecture Collection, Miriam and Ira D. Wallach Division of Art, Prints and Photographs, The New York Public Library, Astor, Lenox and Tilden Foundations: Figures 91, 143, 144 & 145.

Boehme, Sybil: Figures 31, 49, 69, 70, 71, 72, 109, 217, 218, 219, 220, 221, 222, 226, 230, 232 & 242.

Clark County Historical Society: Figures 1, 4, 5, 7, 12, 13, 27, 28, 29, 34, 36, 38, 40, 41, 42, 44, 45, 46, 47, 51, 54, 55, 56, 58, 59, 60, 61, 62, 63, 64, 68, 83, 90, 93, 94, 95, 98, 104, 105, 106, 107, 108, 113, 116, 117, 118, 124, 127, 128, 130, 131, 132, 134, 136, 137, 138, 141, 142, 146, 147, 148, 150, 151, 152, 153, 154, 157, 158, 159, 160, 161, 162, 163, 165, 167, 168, 169, 173, 174, 175, 176, 177, 186, 188, 190, 191, 192, 194, 195, 199, 202, 203, 204, 206, 233, 234, 235 and pages 186-187, 204-205, 228-229, 234-235, 333 (top image) & 334.

Clark County, Ohio Recorder's Office: Figures 32, 33, 65, 67 & 99.

Clark County, Ohio Public Library: Figures 35, 57, 66, 111, 120, 129, 135, 171, 172, 181, 184, 187, 193, 196, 197, 198, 200, & 201.

Dayton History: Figures 75, 78, 79 & 82.

Demana, Teresa: Figure 19.

Drais, Sue Bayley: Figures 179 & 180.

Faust, Cynthia Lamb: Figure 97.

Glessner House Museum: Figure 37.

Harris Brisbane Dick Fund, Metropolitan Museum of Art: Figure 14.

Jackson, Sue Miller: Figures 209, 210, 211, 212, 213, 214, 215 & 216.

John Turner Landess Collection: Figures 2, 8, 9, 10, 11, 16, 17, 22, 23, 24, 25, 26, 30, 39, 43, 50, 73, 74, 92, 96, 100, 101, 102, 103, 114, 115, 139, 140, 149, 155, 156, 166, 170, 178, 183, 185, 189, 239, 240, 241 and pages 324-332, 333 (bottom image) & 335.

Link, Richard: Figure 182.

Lutzenberger Collection, Dayton Metro Library: Figures 76 & 77.

National Association of Realtors: Figures 6, 85 & 205.

National Park Service, Frederick Law Olmsted National Historic Site: Figure 15.

McCulloch, Jean: Figures 223, 224, 225, 227, 228, 229 & 231.

Noonan, Mary Lu: Figures 3, 20, 21, 48, 84, 86, 87, 88, 89, 121, 122, 123, 125, 126, 133, 207, 208, 236, 237, 238 and page 320.

Oakwood Historical Society: Figure 81.

Roush, Elsa: Figure 112.

Springfield Country Club: Figures 52 & 53.

Springfield Polo Club, Gift of Mr. & Mrs. John Harwood: Figure 164.

Stafford, Tom: Figure 110.

Wait, Richard: Pages 336 & 338.

Western Historical Manuscript Collection-Kansas City: Figure 18.

Wittenberg University Library: Figure 119.

Wright State University Special Collections & Archives: Figure 80.

INDEX

A

B

C

D

E

F

G

H

I

J

K

L

M

N

O

P

Q

R

S

T